OXFORDSHIRE'S
BEST CHURCHES

OXFORDSHIRE'S BEST CHURCHES

Richard Wheeler

Fircone Books

for Su and Sam and Joe, with all my love

First published in 2013 by Fircone Books Ltd
44 Wales Street, King's Sutton, Banbury OX17 3RR
www.firconebooks.com

ISBN 978 1 907700 00 2

Cover design by Dot Little
Designed and typeset by Richard Wheeler
Printed and bound in China

Fircone Books is committed to a sustainable future for our business, our readers and our planet. The book in your hands is made from paper certified by the Forest Stewardship Council®

British Library Catalogue in Publishing Data
A CIP catalogue record for this book is available from the British Library

FRONTISPIECE: Burford St John the Baptist from the south-east

CONTENTS

LIST OF CHURCH PLANS

ACKNOWLEDGEMENTS

Without the kindness and support of a number of people and organisations this book would not have been possible. Heartfelt thanks are due to Charles Baker and Basil Eastwood of the Oxfordshire Historic Churches Trust for backing this project; to Peter Howell, Geoffrey Tyack, Andrew Saint, Geoff Brandwood and Lyn Roberts for reading the manuscript and providing a wealth of invaluable comments and observations; to Sara Long for her work on the layout design, and to Dot Little for the jacket design; to Mike Salter for the church plans; to Yale University Press for permission to use the images reproduced in the glossary; to Anthony Burrett for permission to use his photograph of the ceiling of the Lady Chapel at Abingdon; to Mr Bernard Taylor of Rycote Park for permission to photograph Rycote Chapel; to Andy and Karen Johnson of Logaston Press for their generous help and advice; to my parents, Julian and Pippa Wheeler for reading the manuscript and for igniting my interest in churches in the first place; and finally to my wife Su, for doing all of the things I cannot do and for always being there for me.

THE OXFORDSHIRE HISTORIC CHURCHES TRUST

The Oxfordshire Historic Churches Trust was established in 1964 to help with grants for the repair and restoration of the churches of Oxfordshire, to encourage wider interest in these churches, and to raise funds for both purposes.

There are some 550 churches of all denominations in Oxfordshire, 300 of which are of medieval origin. While their continuing primary purpose is to provide places of worship, they are treasured for their architectural beauty, their connections with national and local history, and as focal points within their communities. Without them our landscapes and towns would be much the poorer.

Places of worship built before 1945 (and in exceptional cases later) that are open for public worship may apply to the Trust for a grant for repairs to the fabric and for the installation of facilities. Deanery representatives will advise on the scope of grant support. In considering applications the Trust takes into account the applicant's own financial resources and its ability to raise additional funds. Detailed guidance notes and application forms – together with membership forms for those wishing to join the Trust and support its work – can be downloaded from the Oxfordshire Historic Churches Trust website (www.ohct.org.uk).

FOREWORD

Sitting in the pews in the Abbey at Dorchester-on-Thames, during the English Music Festival, is hard to beat as a cultural all-rounder – a feast for the eye and the ear, an invitation to reverie. And that is just one church and one occasion in a county that can also boast Rycote Chapel; paradigm Norman at Iffley; the medieval glories of Bloxham, Adderbury and Yarnton; sweet little Chislehampton, the sort of eighteenth-century export that was often at home in the colonies; Swinbrook, tucked into the Windrush Valley, the oasis of calm where Jessica, Unity and Pamela Mitford all chose to be buried; Kelmscott where Morris laid his head under a tomb designed by Philip Webb; Pearson's jewel box at Freeland and, as a more esoteric pursuit, John Newman's settlement church at Littlemore. And where else can equal the poetry of the grouping at Ewelme of church and almshouses? In the quadrangle itself it is possible to believe that an Oxford college has pupped whilst the church has the most poignant of all *memento mori* – the beauty of Alice, Duchess of Suffolk, grand-daughter to Geoffrey Chaucer, reduced to a worm-eaten cadaver. And it is a county where one need not be afraid of the modern – there is great power in Nicholas Mynheer's polyptych and elongated chairs in the Wilcote Chapel at magical North Leigh and the reordering at Charlbury shows how it can be done with grace.

The resource of record for churches has to be the volumes of Nikolaus Pevsner, but the most enticing of all combinations is authoritative, individual text interlaced with photography that saturates you in the colour and atmosphere of the given church. That is the Wheeler Way. A key model undoubtedly is (Sir) Simon Jenkins' guide, *England's Thousand Best Churches*. Richard Wheeler does for one county what Jenkins does for a nation.

Everybody who loves Oxfordshire is in his debt.

MATTHEW SAUNDERS
Director, The Friends of Friendless Churches
Secretary, Ancient Monuments Society

Oxfordshire

PREFACE

In the centre of Hereford, fabulously half-timbered and gabled, with big leaded windows and a chimney like the turret of a castle, stands the Old House. Built in around 1620 and miraculously well preserved, the building is all that remains of the historic Butcher's Row.

Hereford was my home for more than twenty years, and while living there I must have passed the Old House hundreds of times. And in all those years, how many times did I go in? Not once. And why was that? I couldn't have missed it. It stands right in the bustling heart, the block paviors of High Town lapping at its walls. Probably I didn't go in because it was always there, because I got used to seeing it there. It's on my doorstep. I can go in tomorrow, or tomorrow, or tomorrow.

We are sometimes guilty of taking wonderful old buildings for granted precisely because they are all around us. This is especially the case with parish churches. Here's the village and here's the church. It's more unusual to find a village without a church than one with, and even a small settlement may have more than one. And yet all churches are special. For in these places what we leave of ourselves as we pass through, both the visible and the invisible, is nowhere richer.

This book contains a selection of the finest churches in just one English county, Oxfordshire. Although just that, a selection, it is my hope that a majority of readers can acknowledge a case for the majority of entries. The selected churches are dealt with in two ways. Some are covered by detailed, fully illustrated entries in the main gazetteer. A further group is covered by shorter entries in a second gazetteer. I readily acknowledge that some of the churches covered only by shorter entries might have been covered at greater length, and vice versa.

In terms of the parameters of selection, I have attempted as fairly as possible to represent both the finest medieval and post-medieval churches in Oxfordshire, and to avoid any geographical bias that might favour certain parts of the county over others. The vast majority of the churches included in the book are Anglican parish churches.

I did eventually visit the Old House, twenty-odd years after leaving home. Through its uneven, bubble-flecked windows I saw Hereford four hundred years ago. Somewhere I'd never been.

INTRODUCTION

We are blessed with churches. There are more than sixteen thousand in England alone: a figure rivalled across the entire globe by only France and Italy. In size and ambition they range from plain little boxes to colossal treasure chests. The factors governing their creation are as many and complex as we are: the wealth and motives of benefactors; the choice of site, builder and material; the transmission of architectural influence; trends in ritual and liturgy. As a manifestation, not only of religious life in England but of its culture and society over more than a thousand years, they are collectively peerless. Few churches have nothing to say to those who trouble to step inside.

Oxfordshire, though perhaps not as celebrated for its churches as, say, Norfolk or Devon, remains one of the most rewarding counties in England for church visiting. As well as being numerous – there are more than five hundred in the county – its churches show tremendous variety and quality, both of architecture and of fixtures and fittings. The county was further enriched with churches in 1974, when a boundary change saw it gain a large chunk of Berkshire, including eighty-one parishes and the outstanding churches at Abingdon, Faringdon and Uffington.

As well as architectural wealth – indeed, crucially informing this wealth – is a diverse geology; variations below ground which find memorable expression in the churches above: rust-coloured ironstone in the folded landscapes of the far north, flint and chalk in the rolling downlands of the south, and mellow grey limestone in a swathe between.

The classic grey limestone so redolent of the Cotswolds in particular is one of the defining features of the county's churches. Its fine grain and relative ease of working made it not only a superb building stone, but also one well suited to carved detail. It was used not only as the main building material across most of the county, but for certain features (such as windows and doorways) both in the north, where the ironstone could prove friable, and in the south, where the chalk and flint were respectively too soft or too brittle for such work. Fine limestone was locally abundant, most famously from Taynton and Burford, whose quarries provided stone for Windsor Castle, St Paul's Cathedral and several Oxford colleges.

In terms of both architecture and building materials, it is important to recognise that the Oxfordshire border has never formed a meaningful line of demarcation, and that there is far more that relates the churches of Oxfordshire to those of surrounding counties than sets them apart. Furthermore, the principal developments traceable in Oxfordshire churches, from the Norman Conquest in the

Wheatfield: Georgian window in the south wall of the chancel

eleventh century until the Reformation in the sixteenth, and beyond, largely follow those traceable across England as a whole.

Since the early nineteenth century, four labels have been used to describe English church architecture during this period: 'Norman', 'Early English', 'Decorated' and 'Perpendicular' – the latter three being subdivisions of Gothic architecture – with a fifth, 'Saxon', used to describe the style current before the Conquest. Not only have the labels endured, but they have become so embedded in the vocabulary of medieval church architecture that explanations of what is meant by the labels – or more particularly what the sources and influences might be for each style or period – are rarely offered.

While such labels are useful as shorthand, flagging up characteristics which define each period, they imply firstly that each style exists as architecturally distinct from the others, and secondly that each finds expression only within a fixed timeframe. Of course, neither is the case. Each of the styles was a development and refinement of what had gone before, and each was built upon by successive generations. All defy precise containment by date. While Perpendicular may have become established in one district, in another Decorated may have lingered on for fifty years or more. Elsewhere, characteristics of both styles might be found in the architecture of a church of one build. Not only are junctions between the styles not sharply drawn, they do not exist. From the earliest churches the story is one of continuous transition.

ORIGINS

The most striking prototype for English church architecture is the Roman basilican church, a building whose origins lie as far back as the first century AD, and whose essential characteristics were firmly established during the reign of Constantine in the fourth: a rectangular building with a nave and side aisles, an apse (and sometimes transepts) at one end, and an atrium or narthex at the other; the nave separated from the aisles by arcades or by openings in the dividing walls, and lit by clerestory windows above (see FIG. A). Such churches took as their starting point the secular Roman basilica (used principally for the practice of law and the transaction of business) but adapted its variable plan to the distinct requirements of religious, and ultimately Christian, worship.

In Britain, basilican churches, such as the Roman church at Silchester, existed at least as far back as the fourth century. Such Romano-British architecture, or the remains thereof, provided sources both of inspiration and of reusable materials – or even complete features – for the builders of some later Saxon churches. Influence also emanated from abroad, and continued to arrive from Rome, as exemplified by church types imported into Kent by Augustine at the end of the sixth century, and into Northumbria by Bishop Biscop towards the end of the seventh. The Kentish type has an oblong nave with a rounded apse beyond, and the additional feature of a triple chancel arch; the Northumbrian type has a longer nave with a squared apse beyond, taller proportions and a single narrow chancel arch.

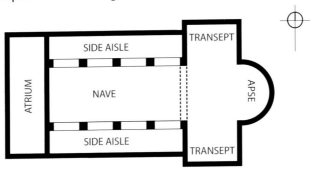

FIG. A **Basilican church plan**

Arguably the most significant feature of Roman architecture to find expression, both aesthetically and structurally, in western church architecture is the rounded arch. The feature is so ubiquitous that its defining contribution is often overlooked. It is in the reliance upon this feature that Roman architecture fundamentally differs from Greek architecture. For the latter depends almost solely upon horizontal lintels, rather than rounded arches, to span the voids between columns for the purposes of support.

ANGLO-SAXON (c.600–1066)

In Oxfordshire, although Christianity is unusually long established, Saxon remains are scant. In AD 634, less than forty years after the arrival of Augustine in Kent, Birinus arrived in Oxfordshire and founded an abbey at Dorchester. Soon after, in about AD 675, an abbey was founded at Abingdon. While magnificent churches remain at both, the survival of original Saxon fabric at either appears minimal.

The most important Saxon remains in the county are the church towers at Langford and Oxford St Michael, both of which belong to the eleventh century. Langford's tower has the greater finesse, combining monumental architecture with a deftness of carved detail. The north and south faces of the tower are divided vertically by pilaster strips: a distinctive characteristic of pre-Conquest work, deriving from Rhineland churches of the eighth century, and ultimately from late Roman decorative pilasters. The porch also has sculpture, including a headless Christ figure, possibly dating from before the Conquest.

The tower of St Michael's is rougher but equally impressive, standing implacably amid the helter-skelter of Oxford's busiest shopping street. It incorporates another characteristic late Saxon feature in its bell openings: the baluster shaft. This stumpy approximation of a column, complete with a cap and base, does not appear in Norman or subsequent work.

Elsewhere, when Saxon fabric is encountered, it is frequently in the towers of churches that have been otherwise largely rebuilt. The towers at Caversfield, Cholsey and North Leigh are among a handful in Oxfordshire to contain Saxon masonry. Other notable Saxon remnants include the chancel arch at Waterperry, and a pair of round-headed windows at Swalcliffe.

The later Saxon period saw the establishment of patterns of church building which were to be consolidated in the aftermath of the Norman Conquest. Whilst few records exist for who commissioned and paid for these churches, it seems clear that the building of churches at this time was the preserve of landowners, be they local lords or monasteries. Their churches might be little more than family chapels in the case of the former, or large minster churches in the case of the latter. In Oxfordshire, there is evidence that Bampton and Burford churches were both minsters, acting as regional hubs for a number of surrounding, and otherwise churchless, communities.

Also during this period, clear hierarchies were established in the administration and operation of churches. The parish developed as the basic unit of ecclesiastical administration (and territorial organisation) across England: 'an area large enough in population and resources to support a church and its priest, and yet small enough for its parishioners to gather at its focal church', as the historian Norman Pounds characterised it (*A History of the English Parish*). Although all churches were ultimately controlled by a bishop (the parishes later falling within dioceses or bishoprics) the right to appoint priests remained with the landowner. For the churches themselves, a clear legal distinction became established between the chancel and nave; the clergy or landowner being responsible for the chancel and the parishioners the nave.

NORMAN (c.1066–c.1180)

The Norman Conquest was followed in the late eleventh and twelfth centuries by a programme of church building rivalled only by that seen in the nineteenth century. Even now, hundreds of Norman or part-Norman churches survive across the

Iffley: the Norman south doorway

country, with several thousand later churches retaining a Norman font as the only tangible reminder of a Norman predecessor on the site.

The architectural style informing this building programme – specifically the Romanesque architecture of Normandy – was not entirely new to England. It shared the same Continental roots as Anglo-Saxon architecture, and had already arrived in England by the time of the Conquest, with the building of Westminster Abbey in c.1050 by the half-Norman Edward the Confessor. What the Norman Conquest did do was to initiate the abandonment of the native Saxon style for the Norman Romanesque style imported by the victors. 'Now you may see', wrote the contemporary historian, William of Malmesbury, 'in every village, town and city, churches and monasteries rising in a new style of architecture'.

For English parish churches, the defining characteristics of the imported Norman style are: the consistent use of the semi-circular arch, thick un-buttressed walls with windows that are relatively few and relatively small, and a resultant architecture that is robust and heavily planted, whose rhythms are deliberate and regular, and whose interiors – at least now, shorn of original colour and decoration – are dark and sober.

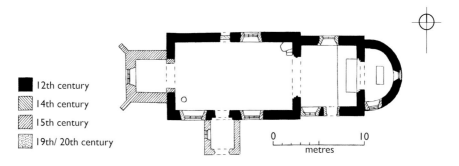

FIG. 1 Norman plan: Checkendon St Peter and St Paul, with distinct chancel and rounded apse

In plan form, the chancel of a Norman church is almost always architecturally distinct from the nave, forming a separate unit in the plan. It may have a rounded apse, as at Swyncombe and Checkendon, but more often is rectangular, as at Cassington and Iffley (reflecting the influence of the Cistercians, whose monastic churches had square east ends). In aisled churches, the piers are always cylindrical, with capitals that perform the function of adapting the circular cross-section of the pier to the square cross-section of the arch it supports.

Adding greatly to the visual interest and appeal of many Norman churches is their highly distinctive carved decoration. This tends to be concentrated in doorways and chancel arches, corbels and capitals. It also occurs, often most memorably (and accessibly) on fonts. The overriding aim of most Anglo-Norman architectural carving was decorative rather than narrative, with conspicuous delight taken in pattern making. Even when the objective was narrative, principles of anatomy and proportion were often sacrificed in order more pleasingly to fill a given space with carving.

This last quality is particularly evident in the tympana of Norman doorways, where figures or beasts were often elongated or compressed to better fit the semi-circular compartment. A number of fine examples survive in Oxfordshire, including at Church Hanborough (figure of St Peter), Kencot (Sagittarius killing a beast; a similar Sagittarius appears on the font at Hook Norton), Fritwell (two affronted beasts, a panther and lion), Great Rollright (beast and shrouded man), Newton Purcell (dove with serpents), Charney Bassett (a figure, possibly Alexander the Great, flanked by griffins), Brize Norton (Tree of Life) and Barford St Michael (knotwork).

Norman pattern-making is also seen to good effect in door surrounds, and in their arched heads in particular. The decorative use of radiating voussoirs originated in Aquitaine, and the most widely used and characteristic carved motif found in arches is the chevron or zigzag: a device used to spectacular effect at Iffley, one of the finest of all Norman churches. This simple device becomes strikingly effective when repeated, especially arrayed in diminishing arches. Even more striking is the beakhead: a mask-like grotesque whose long beak is perfectly adapted to the voussoirs of an arch, and the variety of whose possible forms was limited only by the imagination of the sculptor.

In arches, the distinctive Norman characteristic of treating each stone individually is especially well seen. Rather than setting the stones in place and then carving the arch *in situ* with a regular design, each voussoir was first carved with a complete chevron or beakhead, and only then set in place. In this way, variations in stone width and carved element give a happy, un-mechanical freedom to the arch as a whole.

The sources of this rich and often barbarous decoration are diverse. In an era of surprisingly widespread travel (including pilgrimages to the likes of Santiago and Jerusalem) ideas arrived from all quarters. A number of devices found in Norman stone carving, including the chevron, the billet and chip-carved geometric forms (such as triangles and stars), can be found in Anglo-Roman work, including stone altars, of the early centuries AD. Interlace (such as that covering the Norman font at Lewknor) is also found in some Roman work, including sarcophagi and mosaic pavements. However, it is also found in Celtic, Germanic, Byzantine and Viking ('Ringerike' and 'Urnes') work, and is evident in cross shafts, metalwork and illuminated books of the later Saxon period.

Sources for figurative carving include the Bible, the bestiary and contemporary secular subjects. Biblical representations include the primitive figures of Adam and

Eve on the font at Hook Norton, and the seated Apostles on the font at Dorchester (the latter is one of five Norman lead fonts to survive in the county). Bestiaries became particularly influential in the second half of the twelfth century, and must partly account for the diversity of creatures found in architectural sculpture of the period. The bestiary, or 'book of beasts', derived from the Greek *Physiologus*: a text written between the second and fourth centuries, which described and assigned moral meanings to animals both real and mythical. Secular subjects – perhaps unsurprisingly given the period in which they were carved – include knights or armed men, such as those found on the south doorway capitals at Iffley.

Although churches in the Norman style continued to be built far into the second half of the twelfth century, the stylistic transition to Gothic architecture was also taking place. Again, it cannot be emphasised too strongly that this was a transition rather than a new departure. As Francis Bond explains it, 'Our Romanesque and Gothic are not two styles but one style. Gothic is perfected Romanesque; Romanesque is Gothic not fully developed, not carried structurally to its logical conclusion' (*Gothic Architecture in England*).

While the phases between each period of English church architecture are, by definition, transitional, the label 'Transitional' primarily applies to the phase between Norman and the first (Early English) stage of Gothic architecture. Transitional architecture is characterised by the mixing of stylistic elements that are resolutely Norman with those that were to become characteristically Gothic. It is exemplified by nave arcades (such as those at Faringdon) in which the arches are rounded and thus Norman, but the capitals are carved with stiff-leaf decoration and thus Early English Gothic. Oxfordshire is especially rich in Transitional work. Indeed, the Oxford architect-writer F. E. Howard claimed that, 'in North Berkshire and West Oxfordshire it is perhaps commoner than pure Norman' (*Mediaeval Styles of the English Parish Church*).

EARLY ENGLISH GOTHIC (*c.*1180–*c.*1250)

The fundamental difference between Romanesque/ Norman and Gothic architecture is structural, and relates to the ways in which loads and thrusts are borne and distributed, as manifested in what are traditionally seen as the three defining features of Gothic architecture: the pointed arch, the buttress and the rib vault. In a Norman church, the outward thrusts of the roof are counteracted by walls of great and unvarying thickness. In a Gothic church, however, these forces are counteracted by means of buttresses, allowing the walls between to be thinner and to be pierced by much larger window openings. For parish churches, the pointed

Stanton Harcourt: the Early English Gothic chancel

arch and the buttress are especially relevant, the rib vault being a feature largely restricted to cathedrals or monastic churches.

The pointed arch – a feature as redolent of Gothic as the rounded arch is of Norman – was adopted by church builders for its constructional rather than aesthetic properties (though the latter was recognised and exploited as the form became established). Its advantages over the rounded arch are: its greater strength (particularly at the apex, where the arch is less flat and the joints between stones are less close to the vertical – a weak spot in rounded arches); its greater downward thrust (thereby reducing outward pressure on the adjoining fabric), and its elasticity (with the arch not semi-circular, its height is no longer wedded to its span but can be varied, making it more adaptable).

The origins of the pointed arch are vague, but it appears in the East (for example, in Egypt and Sicily) at least as far back as the ninth century. In France, it first appears in the second half of the eleventh century, and in England in the first half of the twelfth century. The pointed arch was imported into England by, amongst others, Cistercians from Burgundy in the middle of the twelfth century, and is well seen in their abbey churches at Fountains, Kirkstall and Furness. The form became widely adopted in English parish churches in the first half of the thirteenth century.

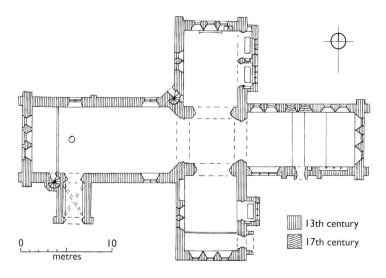

0   10
metres

13th century
17th century

FIG. 2 Cruciform plan: Uffington St Mary, with transepts and central tower

In England, this first phase of Gothic architecture – inappropriately named, given its origins, 'Early English' – is characterised by a number of significant developments. Partly owing to the huge supply of newly built Norman churches covering the land at this time, these developments most frequently find expression in additions and alterations to existing churches, rather than in entirely new churches (though Oxfordshire possesses a fine exception at Uffington).

Popular changes in the thirteenth century included the addition of side aisles (and thus nave arcades) to cater for growing congregations, the enlargement of chancels to cater for increasingly elaborate services and liturgy (including the High Mass and the singing of the Hours), and the raising of spires (most magnificently at Witney and Oxford St Mary). Also during this period, the small round-headed Norman window began to give way to the taller, pointed-arched lancet window. Lancets, being proportionately more slender than their Norman predecessors, were sometimes grouped together, typically in threes.

Some of the starkest differences between Norman and Early English Gothic churches lie in their architectural detailing and carved decoration. Doorways in particular became much plainer, the arch typically carved with nothing more than dogtooth, nailhead or chevron ornament. Attached or detached shafts were widely used in doorways and windows. Such shafts are particularly effective when used in windows to form an arcade flush with the inner face of the wall, as is the case in the chancels at Stonesfield, Stanton Harcourt and Uffington. Occasionally – and in a way more commonly found in cathedrals – the shafts might be of contrasting Purbeck marble, as at North Stoke and Ipsden (chancel windows) and Iffley (crossing arches). In the Prebendal chapel at Thame, the window shafts are clustered and stand clear of the wall.

Early English Gothic displays the sparest carved decoration of any of the main phases of English church architecture. However, it is from this period that some of the loveliest survives, most notably in the capitals of the numerous, newly built nave arcades. Most of this decoration is plant-based and sometimes classical in origin, with waterleaf and stiff-leaf predominant. Waterleaf decoration comprises broad, tapering leaf shapes that curl over at the top. Stiff-leaf is reminiscent of the volutes on Corinthian capitals, and is characterised by a variety of fleshy, curling leaf forms. There are fine examples at Faringdon, Little Faringdon, Langford and Kelmscott. Occasionally, human heads peer out from the foliage – most boldly in the capitals at Woodstock, but also at Stanton Harcourt, and the related churches of North Stoke and Ipsden.

All of this gives Early English Gothic architecture a different feel to that of its Norman predecessor. It is lighter and less massive, dynamic rather than static; the visual emphasis, due in part to the pointed arches and narrow lancets, vertical rather than horizontal. The overall character is more graceful and aloof, less earthly. While physically lighter, the churches of this era are still lit by comparatively small windows – certainly nothing like the expansive windows of the subsequent phases of Gothic architecture.

DECORATED GOTHIC (c.1250–c.1350)

In the middle of the thirteenth century, patterns of church patronage began to alter. The growth in monastic influence was checked, as was the acquisition of land by the Church (for example by the Statutes of Mortmain, enacted by Edward I in 1279 and 1290 to prohibit the donation of land to the Church). There was a shift in focus from the founding of new abbeys to the further enlargement and enrichment of parish churches (especially through the creation of chantries); from the aristocracy as patron to the smaller landowner – including the newly wealthy commoner made rich by the wool trade.

During the last quarter of the thirteenth century and the first half of the fourteenth century, a series of key developments saw Gothic architecture enter a new and distinctive phase, known as 'Decorated' Gothic. As with the preceding Early English phase, the period was generally characterised by alterations – albeit often major changes – to existing churches, rather than by the widespread construction of new churches.

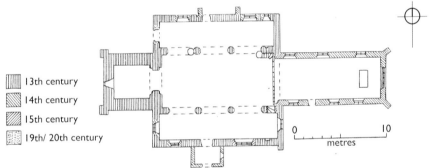

13th century
14th century
15th century
19th/ 20th century

0   10
metres

FIG. 3 Fourteenth-century plan: Charlton-on-Otmoor St Mary, with aisles and enlarged chancel

Changes during this period included comprehensive remodelling in the new style (Cropredy and Chinnor), the rebuilding or extending of chancels (Great Haseley and Lewknor), the widening or raising in height of side aisles, the erection of spires (Bloxham), and the addition of chantry chapels – and porches for those churches that did not already have one. In a typical development for the period, the nave of Adderbury was given a clerestory and a new arch-braced roof. Inside, rounded piers began to give way to octagonal or clustered piers, and chamfered and double chamfered arches were widely employed (the latter is a conspicuous feature of many Oxfordshire churches).

The most spectacular developments of the period were in windows and window tracery. Significant advances in structural know-how and glass technology (resulting in cheaper stained glass) led to the creation of expansive, traceried and

Dorchester: the Decorated Gothic choir and chancel

mullioned windows. The corresponding loss of walling was offset by larger but-tresses, whose increased prominence as architectural features saw them enriched with carved detail (including blind tracery and gargoyles at Merton College chapel in Oxford) and niches for statues (as at Ducklington, Bloxham, Dorchester and Great Rollright). The impact of larger windows was felt both inside and out; for not only was more daylight admitted, but the architectural character was radically altered by the shift in the proportion of wall area to window area – especially as windows and not doorways were now the focus for external decoration.

The evolution of window tracery followed a number of clearly discernible steps (*see page 248*). In the first, lancet windows were grouped together, sometimes in pairs (as at Oxford St Giles) and sometimes in groups of three or more. Initially, each lancet retained its own hood-mould, but later a single hood-mould was used to form an arched head over the group as a whole. With a two-light window this resulted in a blank space in the head of the arch. The logical next step was to make an opening in this space, and then to treat all three openings as part of a single composition contained within its framing arch. This earliest form of tracery is known as 'plate tracery', and is well represented by the unusual chancel windows at Langford, whose upper lights take the form of concave lozenges.

From plate tracery it is but a short step to the bar tracery that was to domi-nate subsequent window design. While plate tracery involved the cutting out of geometrical shapes from slabs of stone, bar tracery entailed the stone first being worked into curved or straight 'bars', then fitted together to form a lattice within the window opening. Bar tracery first appeared in France in c.1200, but was rarely seen in England before the middle of the thirteenth century. Early examples include the choir windows at Westminster Abbey (begun in 1245) and the presbytery east window at Lincoln Cathedral (begun after 1256). An even earlier contender is the largely bricked-in east window at Binham Priory in Norfolk, dating from the sec-ond quarter of the thirteenth century.

While bar tracery forms a logical evolution of plate tracery, there is another sense in which its development can be seen as inevitable. As it became understood that, with buttresses, ever more of the wall could be lost to openings, so it was also understood that the glazing needed to fill such openings required a suitable framework for its support – such as that provided by bar tracery.

At no point during the development of English church architecture does the richness and inventiveness of window tracery exceed that of the fourteenth cen-tury. Several highly distinctive forms of bar tracery were developed during this period. The simplest is 'intersecting' or 'Y-tracery' (of c.1300) in which curves of the same radius as the window arch intersect in the head of the window (the five-light east window at Horley is a good example).

More elaborate but appearing at a similar time (specifically in the second half of the thirteenth century and the first quarter of the fourteenth) is 'geometric', or 'geometrical', tracery. This evolved from the cut-out forms found in earlier plate tracery, and makes prominent use of circles and other geometrical forms, such as trefoils and quatrefoils, spherical triangles and squares.

'Curvilinear' tracery (also known as 'flowing' tracery) developed later (c. 1315–60) and is altogether freer and more animated. It employs curves and ogees, together with foiled shapes such as mouchettes and daggers, in compositions with a flowing or flame-like quality. The earliest form of curvilinear tracery, known as 'reticulated', comprises a net-like pattern of ogee-ended lozenges, and was widely used in the first half of the fourteenth century. Curvilinear is perhaps the defining tracery type of Decorated Gothic.

Oxfordshire has some of the finest window tracery in the country, most notably at Dorchester Abbey. A circuit of this large church takes in exquisite examples of the main types of tracery found during the last quarter of the thirteenth century and the first half of the fourteenth century: geometric in the north choir aisle; reticulated in the north wall of the nave; intersecting along the south wall; and reticulated and curvilinear in the east windows. The three east windows are striking for another reason. As a rule, tracery is restricted to the head of the window, the lower half generally being subdivided by straight mullions; and yet at Dorchester, in a wonderfully successful experiment surprisingly not taken up elsewhere, the tracery was carried the full height of the window, from bottom to top.

Beyond Dorchester, fine geometric traceried windows survive at Bloxham, Broughton, North Moreton, Hampton Poyle and Chipping Norton (the south aisle east window at Chipping Norton is especially fine). Reticulated tracery is widespread, with particularly good examples at Chalgrove, Charlbury, Great Milton, Cropredy, Brightwell Baldwin and Thame. Curvilinear tracery is less widespread, but when encountered is often of high quality, with fine examples at Taynton, Merton, Cogges, Witney and Ducklington (the windows in the last three are probably the work of the same group of brilliant local masons).

Aside from in windows, decorative stone carving is not a conspicuous feature of the exterior of churches during this period. Oxfordshire, however, has some notable exceptions. The west doorway, tower and eaves at Bloxham are all enriched with sculpture. The Twelve Apostles, each sheltering beneath a canopy, line the hood over the west door. Flanking the doorway on the left-hand side, the Blest clamber from their coffins, while to the right the Damned tumble into the jaws of Hell; all overseen by Christ in Judgement above. The cornices of the tower balcony and eaves also carry a startling array of sculpture, including human and animal figures drawn from life, popular fables and the bestiary.

The highly distinctive, richly sculpted cornices at Bloxham are closely related to those at Adderbury, Hanwell and Alkerton. They are probably the work of the same mason or masons working in north Oxfordshire in the first half of the fourteenth century, and are of unrivalled quality and interest for their date. The same workshop was also responsible for memorable nave capitals at Bloxham, Adderbury and Hanwell, all featuring outward-facing human figures with linked arms.

Inside churches, tomb recesses and sedilia in particular were also the subject of lavish stone carving. Spectacular Decorated tomb recesses survive at Asthall, North Leigh, Sparsholt and Witney. Richest of all is the double tomb recess in the north aisle at Ducklington, carved with a probable Tree of Jesse and with arches and spandrels crowded with heads and foliage. More elaborate still are the sedilia at Dorchester, whose canopies and pinnacles are a miniature forest of sculpture. Less refined but equally enjoyable are the chancel fittings at Lewknor and Piddington. At Lewknor, the priest's door, tomb recess, vaulted triple sedilia and piscina are all topped with big, popcorn-like crockets. The little chancel of the otherwise unremarkable church at Piddington is stuffed with good stonework, including a double sedilia and piscina that bristle with carving.

Two of the defining motifs of Decorated Gothic are the ogee arch and the ballflower, both of which enjoyed huge popularity in the first half of the fourteenth century in particular. Owing to its structural deficiencies, the ogee arch was not generally used for support, but rather for its aesthetic potential, most notably in window tracery, doorways and tomb recesses. Its origins remain vague. However, while certainly in use in the East (including in India), it is possible that its appearance in England at the end of the thirteenth century was as a consequence of developments in bar tracery here; for an ogee arch is naturally suggested when a circle is pressed into each side of a pointed arch. Interestingly, the form only came into use in France late in the fourteenth century.

The ballflower – a bud-like device with three petals enclosing a ball – was also widely used in the first half of the fourteenth century (though less abundantly in Oxfordshire than in Herefordshire and Gloucestershire to the west). In Oxfordshire, there are tiny ballflowers on the sedilia windows at Dorchester and the north aisle windows at Swinbrook; standard (fist-sized) examples on the west door at Broughton, the windows at Taynton and the font at Tadmarton, and cabbage-sized ones on the cornices at Hanwell, Adderbury and Bloxham. The origins of the ballflower motif are also uncertain. It appears in England in late Norman work, and in France in the twelfth and thirteenth centuries, and may ultimately derive from a horse- or hawk's bell, or perhaps a globe-flower (or trollius). Whatever its origins, its appeal for masons is clear, being a simple ornament which nonetheless gives a pleasing richness of pattern and texture to surfaces when repeated.

PERPENDICULAR GOTHIC (*c.*1350–*c.*1540)

The Perpendicular phase of English Gothic is aptly named. It marks a sometimes striking contrast to its predecessor, forsaking curves and fluidity for straight lines and the rigidity of the grid (except in vaulting), decorative freedom for restraint, the heart for the head (or so it can seem). In fact, the difference in character can be exaggerated. Francis Bond portrayed it as a shift, 'from poetic fancy to plain prose'; but the 'prose', if this is what it is, can be far from 'plain'. While Perpendicular architecture at its least inspired can be mechanical, repetitive and uninvolving, at its best it can be exquisitely refined, breathtaking in its spatial effects and capable of unparalleled compositional unity.

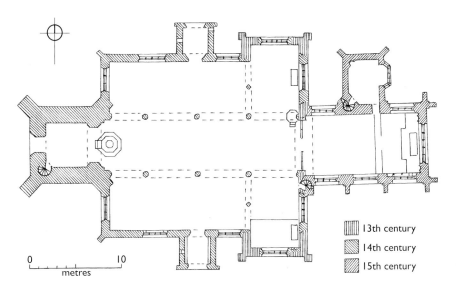

FIG. 4 Late medieval plan: Adderbury St Mary, variously enlarged and with a rebuilt chancel

During this period, common alterations to existing churches included rebuilding and enlargement, most notably of naves (Chipping Norton and Church Hanborough), but also through the addition of chapels (the Wilcote chapel at North Leigh, the Harcourt chapel at Stanton Harcourt and the Milcombe chapel at Bloxham). Side aisles were often added or enlarged where existing, and naves given clerestories. Towers and spires were raised or remodelled, and porches, sometimes vaulted and with an upper storey, became almost universal. Fine new roofs, often of a much shallower pitch, lay partly hidden behind parapets, which were often crenellated. Gargoyles threw the water carried by hidden gutters clear of the walls below.

The Gothic preoccupation with translating wall into window, while minimising the material needed (and *apparently* needed) to ensure the church's stability, was being carried to its logical conclusion. The buttress was exploited as never before, allowing windows to become increasingly expansive. Architectural components, such as piers, shafts, buttresses and pinnacles, were made thinner and given finer mouldings. The aim was to create churches that were physically light and un-massive, and for the spaces within to admit as much light as possible, be it through clear or stained glass.

One of the defining features of Perpendicular Gothic is the four-centred arch. The pitch of this much flatter arch could be made to correspond more happily with the shallower pitches of roofs in gable walls. This is especially well seen in the east window at Ewelme. Flatter arched windows of this type were also used in flanking walls, and enabled the church builder to fill more of the wall below the eaves with glazing.

Window tracery, too, was being carried to a resolution guided by logic and refinement. There are arguably two problems with the flowing curvilinear tracery of Decorated Gothic: firstly, there is a pronounced aesthetic disconnect between the lower half of the window, which almost always comprises a series of straight, vertical mullions, and the head of the window, in which the straight mullions break into a series of fluid curves. Secondly, the tracery patterns formed in the upper half of the window tend to leave individual apertures of awkward shape, especially at the edges of the window. At best, such apertures are fiddly, and at worst impractical, to infill with stained glass – and this during a period when stained glass was becoming more viable, more a part of the overall architectural concept.

Solutions to both problems were realised at Gloucester Cathedral, whose east end was radically remodelled in the second quarter of the fourteenth century. In the great east window (completed *c.*1350) straight mullions extend from the base of the window up to its arched top, and the window is further subdivided by horizontal transoms, creating what came to be known as 'panel tracery'. While the function of the mullions and transoms here is partly structural in what is a huge window, the master mason was clearly intent on a more integrated overall composition, and on creating a series of uniform frames for the stained glass figures inserted in *c.*1350–60. It is also clear that at Gloucester the intention was for an architectural experience in which detail is subordinated to overall effect: a characteristic fundamental to Perpendicular Gothic.

The developments at Gloucester, including panel tracery, began to be taken up elsewhere only towards the end of the fourteenth century, but had been widely assimilated by the middle of the fifteenth century. Early dated examples of Perpendicular Gothic in Oxfordshire include the former Canterbury College, of 1364–97, and New College chapel, of 1379–86.

Adderbury: the Perpendicular Gothic chancel

Also in Oxford itself, though later, is the University church of St Mary the Virgin, the body of which belongs to *c.*1462–1510. Ranks of large windows light the aisles, clerestory and chancel (the chancel windows being especially tall). Slender, stepped buttresses break clear of the parapet in spiky, crocketed pinnacles, and shallow pitched roofs lie concealed behind parapets (which are unusually elaborate along the nave and side aisles). The interior is washed with light, the mouldings are slender and fine-grained, and the overall effect is one of polish and finesse.

Perpendicular Gothic is also well represented beyond the city. The chancel of Adderbury, built in 1408–19 by Richard Winchcombe, is a supremely accomplished design, its interior a light-flooded space with a wealth of crisply carved detail. The nave of Chipping Norton (possibly by John Smyth of Canterbury, master mason of Eton College Chapel and Westminster Abbey) and the Milcombe chapel at Bloxham (also attributed to Richard Winchcombe) are fine examples of the lantern-like quality and overall compositional unity sought by church builders of the period. In both cases, large expanses of walling are given over to glazing, and in both, the tracery of the windows is carried down over the wall plane below in blind form, in an effort more fully to assimilate wall and window.

Other fine examples of Perpendicular Gothic in Oxfordshire include the Wilcote chapel at North Leigh (*c.*1440, again possibly by Richard Winchcombe), which boasts a surprising and exquisite fan vault; the richly carved south porch at Burford (second half of the fifteenth century), which remains insistently upward thrusting, despite being sandwiched between flanking chapels; Rycote chapel near Thame (*c.*1449), celebrated for its theatrical seventeenth-century fittings, but also as a rare and finely detailed example of an unaltered Perpendicular church of a single build; and Alice of Suffolk's church at Ewelme (*c.*1432), made unforgettable not only for being distinctly East Anglian in style, but also for its well-preserved interiors, and for the extraordinary monument to Alice herself.

During the fourteenth and fifteenth centuries, patterns of church patronage and building continued to evolve. Opportunities for those outside the aristocracy to commission – or at least to play a role in – the building of churches increased. By the fourteenth century, the wool trade had helped to establish a merchant class with both the inclination and the means to embellish churches through generous bequests. Its members, be they individuals or guilds, showed themselves eager to demonstrate their piety or attempt a degree of immortality through the building of chapels. This is especially striking in the churches at Burford and Chipping Norton, whose elaboration and quality owe much to the profits of the wool trade.

Seismic national and international events also led to shifts in church patronage. The Black Death saw wage rises due to labour shortages, while wars both internal and with France depleted the wealth of the aristocracy. Opportunities for commoners to become patrons began to increase – if only through collective action, such as paying for works to a church through subscription (as attested to by the churchwardens' accounts for Thame). In the aftermath of the Black Death, worship became more publicly inclusive, and the enlargement of naves and aisles may be due in part to a new emphasis on the nave becoming more of a focal point for worship, as an auditorium for preaching; and on both nave and side aisles being better able to accommodate processions and other forms of participatory ritual.

One of the side-effects of protracted war with France was a significant reduction in the transmission of architectural influence from across the Channel. It would be wrong to suggest that such influence was halted altogether; the French 'Rayonnant' style, which saw window area maximised and blind tracery applied to adjoining walls, evidently influenced the work at Gloucester. However, of all the iterations of English Gothic, Perpendicular was to become the most insular, the most truly English, and also the longest lived, being dominant up to and beyond the Reformation, two centuries after its birth.

DECORATION, FIXTURES AND FITTINGS

Today it is difficult for us, in a land of scrubbed and whitewashed churches, to imagine the teeming splendour of the late medieval church interior, alive with colour and gilding, imagery and carvings, stirred by the dance of candlelight. Colour in particular once abounded, and in ways we might now find inappropriate or even garish. Walls and ceilings, rood-screens and rood-lofts, statues and carved stonework, even fonts, were painted and gilded, and windows filled with coloured glass. Narrative cycles unspooled in cartoon-like strips along the walls of nave and chancel, and wallpaper-like patterns decorated arcades and window reveals. Rood-screens were populated by saints, and windows by the kneeling figures of donors. At the head of the nave stood the Rood itself: the carved figure of Christ on the Cross, generally flanked by the figures of Mary and John. Painted over the chancel arch behind was the 'Doom': the unflinching depiction of the Last Judgement and Resurrection.

While several Oxfordshire churches retain medieval wall paintings, most of these are fragmentary. Chalgrove is the most striking exception. The chancel walls of this otherwise unremarkable church are lined with a near-complete set of fourteenth-century paintings which depict, amongst other things, the Life of the Virgin. Less complete but of the highest quality (and depicting rare subject matter) are the north aisle paintings at South Newington, unusually in oil on plaster. Other notable wall paintings survive at Horley (a colossal St Christopher); North Stoke and Black Bourton (faded but extensive narrative cycles); Shorthampton (several

rare fragments); Combe, Hornton, North Leigh and South Leigh (all with Dooms over the chancel arch). The finest painted decoration of all survives on the wooden ceiling of the Lady Chapel at Abingdon – a unique and exquisite late fourteenth-century Tree of Jesse.

The same general point holds for stained glass as for wall paintings, many churches having fragments but few anything comprehensive. The finest complete window is the early fourteenth-century east window in the south aisle at North Moreton, depicting scenes from the lives of Christ, the Virgin Mary and a number of saints. An exceptional collection of mainly sixteenth-century royal heraldic glass, including a superb portrait possibly of Henry VII, survives at Radley. Examples of fine if fragmentary medieval stained glass are almost too numerous to mention, but include those found at Dorchester, Chinnor, Asthall, Brightwell Baldwin, Burford, Waterperry, Shiplake, Stanton Harcourt, Stanton St John, Kidlington, Great Milton and Heythrop. Yarnton contains a magical gallery of stained glass of various dates, deposited here early in the nineteenth century.

For much of the Middle Ages, the stonemason, rather than the carpenter, was the pre-eminent church craftsman. As well as being largely responsible for the construction and enrichment of the church itself, he was also responsible for certain of its fixtures and fittings. To the fine examples of stonemasonry found in Oxfordshire and listed above must be added the fonts at Lewknor (covered with interlace and decorated roundels), Westwell (of quatrefoil cross-section), Shilton and Burford (with carved figures, both Norman fonts re-cut in the fourteenth century), and Idbury (octagonal, similar to the example at Bloxham); the reredoses at Somerton (Last Supper) and Bampton (Christ and the Apostles); the pulpit and triple sedilia at Combe; the beautiful Shrine of St Edburg at Stanton Harcourt (removed from Bicester Priory and retaining some original colour); the rare Decorated chancel screen at Broughton, and the unique piscina-monument at Long Wittenham, with its tiny effigy of a knight.

The finest sculpture of all is found in monuments – much but not all of it in stone: the stunning knight effigy at Dorchester, frozen in the act of drawing his sword; Alice of Suffolk at Ewelme, amid a spectacular tomb; the comically stacked Fettiplaces at Swinbrook; and the exquisite oak figures of Joan and Agnes Achard at Sparsholt. Other fine tombs include those at Broughton, Minster Lovell, Burford, North Leigh, Thame, Cogges, Wroxton, Great Milton, Rotherfield Greys, Radley, Somerton and Little Rollright. Although several larger churches (most notably Burford and Dorchester) have been conspicuously stripped of their medieval brasses, others retain theirs. Chipping Norton, Ewelme, Thame and Chinnor all have good collections. Fine individual brasses survive at Broughton, Great Tew, Swinbrook, Checkendon, Rotherfield Greys, Mapledurham and Waterperry.

South Newington: fourteenth-century wall painting of St Margaret and the dragon

While some monuments were made elsewhere – the Fermor tomb at Somerton is by the Roileys of Burton-on-Trent; the Tanfield tomb at Burford, the Knollys tomb at Rotherfield Greys and possibly the Williams tomb at Thame are by the Southwark School – others came from local workshops. The best of these, including the wall monuments to the Harmans at Burford and the Trinders at Westwell, are hugely characterful and engaging works of sculpture. Also by local masons are the bale tombs found in West Oxfordshire, many to prominent wool families of the seventeenth century. Good examples remain at Burford, Fulbrook, Swinbrook, Letcombe Bassett and Shipton-under-Wychwood.

By the end of the fifteenth century the carpenter's status was approaching that of the stonemason, and woodworkers were increasingly being entrusted with the beautification of the church, rather than merely the construction of parts of the fabric. Many features and fittings were his alone, including finely carved roofs, benches and screens. Standing at the head of the nave, the rood-screen and rood-loft afforded the carpenter perhaps the ultimate opportunity to demonstrate his artistry, and the patron and parish their piety and generosity. Consequently, these were often the most sumptuous of all church fittings – particularly when painted and gilded – and were also the fittings most often updated and replaced, reflecting changes in taste and wider developments in architectural style.

Oxfordshire is one of the richest 'Midland' counties for medieval rood-screens, with at least forty churches retaining examples. The exceptional screen at Stanton Harcourt is almost certainly coeval with the church's chancel, and thus of c.1260. This makes it one of only a tiny handful of screens to survive from this date (and of these it is the most complete). Less complete but still notable are the rare fourteenth-century screens at Chinnor, Sparsholt and Cropredy. The rest date from the fifteenth or early sixteenth century, and include the fine rood-screens at Somerton (Perpendicular); Adderbury (with renewed coving and loft); Charlton-on-Otmoor and Thame (Renaissance); Church Hanborough and Bloxham (with some original colour). The Spencer chapel at Yarnton is fenced off by one of the finest of all surviving seventeenth-century screens.

Other woodwork of note includes the fantastical, steeple-like font cover at Ewelme; the exceptionally rare rood-loft door at Blewbury; the bench ends at Kidlington, Great Tew, Tadmarton, Woodeaton, Sparsholt and Idbury; the rustic pews at Cassington; the poppyheads at Stanton St John (carved with human heads and beasts) and Sunningwell (lining the nave); the handful of misericords at Swinbrook and Bampton; the choir stalls at Radley, Cassington, Dorchester, Oxford St Mary and Thame (the latter being an especially fine set); the pulpit at East Hagbourne and pulpit canopy at Radley (reputedly from the House of Commons); and the remarkable seventeenth-century canopied pews at Rycote.

REFORMATION

For churches, it was by riches such as those listed above, rather than by the church buildings themselves, that the impact of the Reformation in the sixteenth century was most acutely felt. In an atmosphere of growing European discontent towards the Catholic Church (aggravated by what were seen as abuses of its powers, such as the sale of Indulgences) crisis was precipitated in England by the failure of Henry VIII to secure a papal annulment for his marriage to Katherine of Aragon. A series of Acts of Parliament was passed severing administrative, financial and judicial links with Rome. The break was made explicit in 1534 with the Act of Supremacy, confirming Henry as, 'the only supreme head in earth of the Church of England'.

In the years that followed, further Acts struck at aspects and manifestations of the newly discredited Catholic faith. First to be targeted were revenues once owed to the Pope, but now appropriated by the Crown through the Annates Act of 1534. Next were the monasteries, through Acts authorising their dissolution in 1536 and 1539. And then the parish churches: their religious shrines and images in 1538, and their guilds and chantries in 1547 (the year of Henry's death).

For both religious institutions and their buildings, the consequences were catastrophic. Lands and property were forfeit, lead and other materials were stripped from churches, valuable items were packed off to London, and less valuable items were auctioned on site or simply given away or destroyed. Following Henry's death, a new Order of Council effectively erased the former distinction between images that were and were not in themselves objects of veneration, demanding that all images be totally 'extincted and destroyed'.

The Order encompassed wall paintings, statues, stained glass and Roods. Wall paintings were limewashed (ironically, an act which often preserved them), statues and panel paintings were literally defaced, and while there was some resistance to the destruction of stained glass (this still being hugely expensive at the time) this was more than made up for by the destruction of that most provocative of images, the Rood. Today, of the many thousands of Roods thought to have existed before the Reformation, just four mutilated Christ figures survive from the whole of England and Wales. The rood-loft's association with the Rood ensured that this once near-universal fitting was also pulled down in the majority of cases (today, only about thirty survive across Britain).

Religious upheaval brought with it notable additions to, and alterations of, church interiors. The first Book of Common Prayer (of 1549, revised in 1552) saw the replacement of the Mass in Latin with Holy Communion in English. For interiors, it saw the replacement of images with words, most notably over the chancel arch, where previous depictions of Christ in Majesty and the Doom were generally limewashed and replaced with the Creed, the Lord's Prayer and the Ten Commandments ('Decalogue'). The status of the Crown as the new head of the Church in England was emphatically asserted by the replacement of the Rood itself with the royal arms (sometimes painted, sometimes carved).

With the practice of worship becoming more inclusive and accessible, focus shifted from the chancel to the nave. The altar, in the form of a wooden altar table, became less remote, moving to the centre of the chancel or even into the nave itself (a change generally reversed in the seventeenth century). Naves were newly furnished with box pews, and from these the congregation would listen to readings from the scriptures delivered by the clergy from often elaborate new pulpits. While there was a general opening up of church interiors, an Order of Council in 1561 insisted that, 'there remain a comely partition betwixt the chancel and the church'. As a result, rood-screens (if not the rood-lofts above) were spared – at least for the time being.

SEVENTEENTH AND EIGHTEENTH CENTURIES

Further harm was visited upon churches by the Puritans in the seventeenth century, particularly during the Civil War in the 1640s, when religious imagery that had survived (or appeared after) the first flush of Reformist zeal was again targeted. Oxford and other towns (including Banbury and Abingdon) formed Royalist strongholds during the Civil War, and others were dragged into the conflict. Violence affected the fabric of churches as well as their contents. During the siege of Faringdon House in 1645, Parliamentary troops destroyed the tower of the nearby church together with its south aisle and south transept. At Radley, the north aisle and north transept were destroyed during an assault also made by Parliamentary forces; and at Burford, there was damage to, and loss of, brasses and monuments.

Far fewer new churches were built in the seventeenth and eighteenth centuries than in previous centuries. For existing churches, the eighteenth century in particular witnessed much neglect and deterioration in a period characterised by religious lethargy and conservatism. The pattern was followed in Oxfordshire, where just a handful of new churches appeared. The most notable of these are at Shrivenham (c.1660, part-Gothic, part-classical); Wheatfield (c.1740, small and chapel-like in a field); Chislehampton (1763, rustic with a fancy clock tower); Nuneham Courtenay (1764, a Greco-Roman oddity in a landscape setting) and Banbury St Mary (1797, the monolithic replacement for a magnificent medieval church on the site). Fine chapels were also built at Water Eaton (c.1610) and Burford Priory (1662).

Elsewhere during this period, churches were altered or added to. New towers were erected at Dorchester (1602), Warborough (1666), Deddington (completed 1683–85) and Woodstock (1785). New chapels were built at Rotherfield Greys (1605, housing a spectacular monument to the Knollys family), Yarnton (1611, part of a series of additions during the seventeenth century) and North Leigh (early in the eighteenth century by Christopher Kempster of Burford). Rare examples of seventeenth-century tracery can be found at Chipping Norton (north aisle) and Thame (west window of the nave).

NINETEENTH CENTURY

The nineteenth century brought with it a resurgence in church building, driven in part by huge population growth in urban areas (including a burgeoning, churchgoing middle class). Stylistically, these new churches might be classical or more often Gothic (particularly in the second half of the nineteenth century). While some of the latter were Gothic only in a vaguely decorative, rather than a properly constructional, sense (like Christ Church in Long Hanborough, whose Gothic pretensions are limited to its simple lancet windows), others were more thoroughly and authentically Gothic. The best, however, recognisably took Gothic as their source, but remain brilliantly and resolutely creations of their own age.

The catalyst for a revival in a proper understanding of, and appreciation for, Gothic architecture was Augustus Welby Pugin. Having collaborated with his father (himself an architectural draughtsman and writer) in the production of illustrated volumes on Gothic architecture in the 1820s and 1830s, the younger Pugin went on to become the nineteenth century's most passionate and influential advocate for a Gothic revival. For Pugin, the greatest achievements of Gothic architecture belonged to the Catholic Middle Ages, during a sumptuous time of architectural and artistic refinement. He railed against what he saw as the meanness and ignorance of much church building, arguing for a return not only to the style, but to the methods, of medieval workmanship.

Pugin's writings fostered a more learned approach to the study of medieval church architecture, and directly influenced a number of leading Victorian architects, including George Edmund Street, William Butterfield and George Gilbert Scott. Street, for one, travelled to the Continent, and made careful studies of the medieval architecture of northern Italy and Spain. Pugin's beliefs were disseminated and developed upon in turn by a number of newly-formed societies through their periodicals. These included the Cambridge Camden Society (later the Ecclesiological Society), and the Oxford Society for Promoting the Study of Gothic Architecture (later the Oxford Architectural Society), both set up in 1839.

Pugin's advocacy of a return to the architecture and spirit of a Catholic golden age coincided with that of churchman John Henry Newman and others for a recognition of the Catholic heritage of the Anglican Church. The so-called Oxford Movement, of which he was a part, espoused the revival of some of the old doctrines and practices through a series of theological publications, *Tracts for the Times* (thus another of the labels applied to the Movement: 'Tractarian') which appeared between 1833 and 1841. Developments both architectural and religious were thus drawn by the same currents.

The Cambridge Camden Society in particular became a tremendously potent arbiter of taste, most influentially with its pronouncements on which phase of medieval Gothic was the most 'correct'. Pamphlets published in the 1840s (casually entitled, *A Few Words to Church Builders*) first prescribed the use of either Early English or Decorated Gothic, but later exclusively Decorated. Meanwhile, the pages of the Society's hugely influential journal, *The Ecclesiologist*, were filled with advice on how church interiors should be organised, together with designs for fashionable fixtures and fittings. The journal was avidly read by the incumbents both of new churches, and of those existing churches that had been so neglected in the preceding centuries.

Pugin died in 1852, and his voice was replaced by those of John Ruskin and William Morris in the second half of the nineteenth century. Ruskin was not an architect, and claimed he owed little to Pugin (once stating, 'I have not felt the smallest possible interest in his opinions'). However, he too became a passionate and articulate advocate for the Gothic Revival, promoting Gothic as a secular – not simply a religious – style, and further widening its popularity. For church architecture, perhaps the most conspicuous legacy of his writings is the decorative use of polychrome brick or stonework: a defining feature of Victorian Gothic architecture whose champion was William Butterfield, and whose ultimate expression remains Keble College in Oxford.

Like Ruskin, William Morris had a powerful social conscience, and believed that social reform could be attained through the arts. Also like Ruskin, he was never an architect (though he trained as one, in the offices of the architect George Street). For new churches, Morris's influence was not so much architectural as decorative, through the fixtures and fittings – and most famously the stained glass – produced by the firm of Morris & Co. For medieval churches, his influence was also profound. In 1877, Morris and others set up the Society for the Protection of Ancient Buildings (SPAB) in response to what they saw as the destructive restoration of old churches. Legend has it that its formation was triggered by an incident at Burford church in 1876. On objecting to the removal of old plasterwork, Morris was told by the vicar, 'This church, sir, is mine, and if I choose to, I shall stand on my head in it.'

Oxford St Philip and St James by George Street (1860–66): the interior looking east

Morris's manifesto forms the wellspring for an approach to restoration that remains current; namely that the additions of all ages – rather than those of one age to the exclusion of all others – should be protected. In Morris's words, 'every change, whatever history it destroyed, left history in the gap, and was alive with the spirit of the deeds done midst its fashioning'; a belief that led to his plea, 'to put Protection in the place of Restoration'.

While it cannot be said that Oxfordshire is rich in fine Victorian churches, many of the leading architects of the day are represented in the county, and in a handful of cases outstandingly so. George Street, diocesan architect for Oxford for more than thirty years, is represented by six churches in the county. Of these, the best is the church of St Philip and St James on the Woodstock Road in Oxford. Subtle, imaginative and lifted by the understated richness of its materials, it is one of the finest of all Street's churches. Of his other Oxfordshire churches, the most successful are Wheatley and Milton-under-Wychwood. The former has a brilliantly resolved broach spire; the latter includes a school and teacher's house also by Street, and features an attractive and unusual mansard-roofed lychgate.

Two other leading architects are represented by outstanding churches: George Gilbert Scott at Leafield and John Loughborough Pearson at Freeland. The impressive Leafield (1860–74) shows Scott following Pugin, and carefully interpreting thirteenth-century Gothic as an approach to construction, not merely to decoration (which here is minimal). Scott was also responsible for the dramatic remodelling of Clifton Hampden (1843–67), and for the church plus school at Burcot (1869) – a homely little building in red brick, with a shingled spirelet that could have come from a Norwegian stave church. Pearson's church at Freeland (1866–71) forms part of an ensemble with a school and parsonage, and is one of his most effective smaller churches. Its greatest satisfaction lies in the completeness and coherence of an interior perfectly attuned to the sensibilities of the new Anglo-Catholicism, and particularly in its gorgeously decorated chancel with vaulted apse.

William Butterfield is represented in Oxford by the dazzling Keble College. Beyond the city he is represented by the neatly resolved Milton St Mary near Banbury (1856), and the softly coloured St Barnabas at Horton-cum-Studley (1867). Also in Oxford, Arthur Blomfield was responsible for the striking church of St Barnabas in Jericho, (1868–69); George Bodley for the powerful St John the Evangelist on Iffley Road (1894–1902), and Samuel Teulon for the characteristically individual St Frideswide on Botley Road (1870–72).

Of the Victorian additions to existing and new churches, stained glass often represents the most eye-catching. Many of the leading firms are represented, including John Hardman at Iffley, Henley, Dorchester and Cuddesdon; Charles Kempe at Burford and Watlington; Thomas Willement at Kirtlington and Littlemore; Clayton

& Bell at Witney, Freeland and Oxford St Philip and St James; and Morris & Co., of which arguably none is better than the Morris/ Burne-Jones/ Webb east window at Bloxham. The architects themselves were sometimes responsible for the design of windows (Street at Cuddesdon and Butterfield at Dorchester) – and sometimes the fixtures and fittings (Scott at Clifton Hampden, Street at Oxford St Philip and St James, and Butterfield at Horton-cum-Studley). Elsewhere decorative schemes were carried out by firms specialising in this work. The wall paintings and glass at Freeland are by Clayton & Bell; the mosaics in the south transept at Buckland are by Powell & Sons, to designs by the artist Henry Holland.

One of the most significant legacies of the Victorian period is the restoration work carried out to medieval churches. Many had been neglected in the seventeenth and eighteenth centuries, and were in need of renovation; others, it was felt, were in need of updating. While both are legitimate impulses, such work varied in its sympathy for existing fabric. For one thing, fabric surviving from different periods was not always equally esteemed. One unhappy consequence of the belief, propagated in *The Ecclesiologist*, that the ideal architecture was Decorated Gothic of the fourteenth century, was that the work of other periods was sometimes deemed less worthy of preservation. It is precisely this that Morris sought to counter when he set up the Society for the Protection of Ancient Buildings.

While a great deal of medieval fabric (especially carpentry) was lost during this period – some because it was seen as beyond repair and some as outmoded; some reasonably and some senselessly – there are notable examples of sympathetic and scholarly restoration, including by John Chessell Buckler and Scott at Adderbury, R. C. Hussey and Buckler (among others) at Iffley, and John Sedding and Henry Wilson at Somerton.

ABINGDON
ST HELEN
Broad town church with exquisite Lady Chapel ceiling

Abingdon is one of Britain's oldest towns, and possibly the home of Britain's first monastery, Abingdon Abbey, founded in AD 675. The two were inextricably linked, the latter providing employment for the former. The Abbey was ransacked in 1327 by townsfolk (bolstered by reinforcements from Oxford) angered at the power of the Abbot, and jealous of his hold over the town's market. Today, little of the Abbey survives.

Abingdon from the south-east

The church of St Helen stands close to the river, and offers one of the most peculiar architectural experiences of any Oxfordshire church. Due to the constricted nature of the site, extensions to the building could only be added widthways to the south. While the church possibly occupies the site of a Saxon predecessor, the earliest parts are the tower and some of the east wall of the two north aisles, which contain fabric belonging to the twelfth and thirteenth centuries. The two north aisles originally formed the nave with chancel and single north aisle of an earlier church. In the fifteenth century the current nave, chancel and inner south aisle were added (nave and chancel thus essentially jumping one bay to the south). The outer south aisle was added in the sixteenth century.

Arguably the most interesting external feature is the tower. Unusually, this stands at the north-east corner of the church, forming a memorable focal point in views south along West St Helen Street. The tower has an Early English north doorway with attached shafts and stiff-leaf capitals, but the spire belongs to the fifteenth century (it was rebuilt in the seventeenth century, and again in 1883). From the outside, efforts to make sense of the church's internal layout are hindered both by its sprawling footprint and the degree to which it is hemmed in by other buildings. Its plan only becomes fully intelligible once inside, and even then not immediately.

Early English tower doorway

The interior is memorably odd. The usual eastward dynamic is dissipated by a combination of the church's

Abingdon: detail of the fourteenth-century Lady Chapel ceiling

Nave arcade capital

Nave chandelier of 1710

immense breadth, and the fact that both the chancel and the Lady Chapel are contained within the almost-square body of the church, rather than extending to the east of it. Partly because of this, some of the most compelling views are across the church from north to south, through rank upon rank of columns and arches. The distinctive piers and capitals (octagonal and with hollow-moulded faces) are closely related to those found in several Perpendicular 'wool' churches in the region, including Church Hanborough, Chipping Campden and Northleach.

The nave and aisles are enlivened by several notable fittings that date, quite unusually, from the early eighteenth century. The magnificent organ case was made in 1726 by master organ builder, Abraham Jordan, and is similar to another of his in St George's church, Southall (close to where the firm was based). The organ once occupied a west gallery, and was moved to its current position in 1873. The brass chandeliers, each one a tangle of curls topped by a gleaming bird (including a dove bearing an olive branch), date from 1710.

The recent decision to bring the altar forward to a position roughly at the centre of the plan makes practical sense, but has further marginalised the chancel, which now feels rather a forgotten space. Efforts made by the Victorians to reinvigorate the chancel included the addition of Woodyer's bold rood-screen in 1873, and Bodley's ornate reredos in 1897. A further strategy might have been simply to plain-glaze the east window, thereby making the chancel lighter than the adjoining spaces.

Immediately to the north of the chancel is the Lady Chapel. This is home to one of the great treasures of English church art: a painted ceiling of c.1390, depicting a gallery of figures together forming a Tree of Jesse. The paintings occupy two canted sections, each subdivided by delicate blind tracery to give thirteen ogee-headed double bays to either side. Each double bay contains a pair of figures. The figures – the various Kings and Prophets of the Lord's family tree – appear to ride on the rolling waves formed by the undulating branches of the Tree itself, which springs from the loins of the now-missing figure of Jesse. Of the figures that survive, many retain a startling freshness, and all are of wonderful quality. The figures are arranged in affronted pairs, caught mid-action in a series of conversations. The space is alive with their colour and chatter, the gestures of their lady-like fingers.

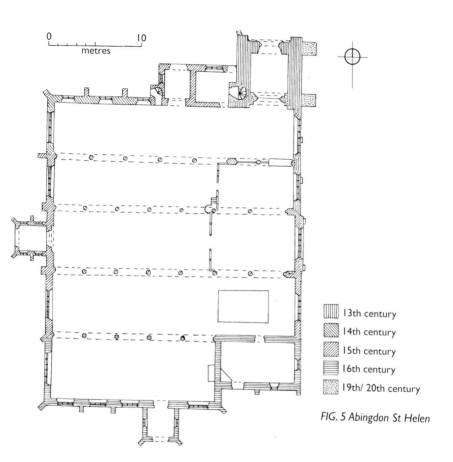

▦	13th century
▨	14th century
▧	15th century
▤	16th century
░	19th/ 20th century

FIG. 5 Abingdon St Helen

ALSO OF NOTE

C15 brass of praying man at W end of inner S aisle; lower portion of timber wall-post at W end of nave (set into W wall) carved with head of king; C15 stone corbels supporting wall-posts on nave piers; Mayor's Pew of 1707 at E end of inner N aisle with renewed lion and unicorn bench ends; early painting depicting family tree against S wall of outer S aisle; large number of mainly C18 wall and floor monuments, including wall monument to Elizabeth Hawkins (d. 1780) at W end of outer N aisle; C16 ceilings with tie-beams to S aisles; C16 brass to William Heyward (vicar) behind organ in inner S aisle; neoclassical pulpit of 1636 at E end of nave/ inner N aisle; carved wooden font cover of 1634 over Victorian marble font of 1851 (copy by H. P. Peyman of Norman font at Sutton Courtenay); variety of Victorian and later additions in chancel

Jacobean font cover

and Lady Chapel, including sedilia (chancel) and alabaster altar and marble
floor (Lady Chapel); c.1905 screen to Lady Chapel by C. R. Ashbee's Guild of
Handicrafts; C16 tomb to John Roysse in N wall of Lady Chapel; 1831 painted
and enamelled window at W end of outer N aisle depicting Evangelists; two-
storey C15 N porch to W of tower once housed exchequer room on upper floor,
and has carved panels with figures of Mary, John and Christ on Cross beneath
canopies; churchyard hemmed in by three sets of early almshouses, including
C15 Long Alley Almshouses to N.

● ● ●

ADDERBURY
ST MARY
Grand village church with fine sculpture and chancel

Adderbury is a village of rust-brown ironstone, its lanes
channelled by terraced cottages and the high walls of
polite houses. Its imposing church stands down a side
road, in a churchyard manicured and mown to the south,
wilder and wooded with yews to the west.

Adderbury from the south

   Despite outward appearances, perhaps, the evolution
of Adderbury church is a relatively uncomplicated one. An
early thirteenth-century cruciform church – a characteristic clearly visible from the plan (*see page 17*) – was considerably enlarged during the fourteenth century, when
the aisles were widened, a clerestory was added to the
nave, and a tower and spire added at the west end. The
current chancel and vestry were added in the early fifteenth century. The magnificence of the building is at least
partly due to the fact that the church was held by the
powerful Bishops of Winchester from an early date (one
of whom, William of Wykeham, appears in the form of a
head corbel over the east window).

   For all of the church's architectural refinement, several
developments have led to significant moments of visual dis-
comfort. Perhaps the most striking occurs at the transepts'
junctions with the chancel to the east and the side aisles to
the west, where the overlapping of later work has resulted
in windows being variously cut into. None of this detracts
from the joy of the exterior, however, which features work
of the highest quality – most notably in the chancel and in
the sculpted cornices that line the side aisles.

Junction of transept and chancel

Adderbury: the choir and rood-screen looking west

South side of chancel

Carved dragon on south aisle

The chancel was built between 1408 and 1419 and is one of the masterworks of Perpendicular architecture in Oxfordshire. The mason was Richard Winchcombe, who was also responsible for the Divinity School in Oxford. Both the Adderbury chancel and Oxford Divinity School feature elaborate, stepped buttresses with crocketed pinnacles. As well as being decorative, these reduce the load-bearing requirements of the walls, making possible the insertion of the huge windows that characterise this phase of English Gothic. The Adderbury windows are deeply set into especially fine surrounds, the hood-moulds over each forming continuous string courses that are even carried over the buttresses.

As well as stately architecture, the church displays workmanship, and specifically sculpture, of an altogether earthier character. Some can be found on the chancel, in the grotesques that lean perilously far out to leer or wonder at those passing below. Arguably more memorable, however, is the astonishing cast of figures that inhabits the cornices of the side aisles and tower. This is clearly the work of the same sculptor or sculptors who worked at nearby Bloxham, Hanwell and Alkerton. The figures include a dragon whose tail is tied in looping knots and whose muzzle is wrinkled in a growl. Elsewhere (but especially along the north aisle) figures play an array of medieval instruments, including the timbrel, buzine, psaltery and rebec. The compositions are expertly carved in deep relief, and are full of wit and ingenuity.

Of the other notable external features, the tower and spire also belong to the fourteenth century. The arrangement, with corner pinnacles, is like a less massive version of the earlier spire at Witney. Although an effective composition, it arguably suffers when compared with the more elegant example at King's Sutton, and the much taller and richer example at Bloxham, both nearby. A traditional local rhyme echoes the differences: 'Bloxham for length, Adderbury for strength and King's Sutton for beauty.'

With the exclusion of the chancel, the interior arguably fails to live up to the promise of the exterior, feeling bare and scraped of texture. Unusually, the aisles were made wider than the nave when the building was enlarged in the fourteenth century. Consequently, the nave, aisles and transepts now essentially describe one large, square space broken only by the arcades of nave and transepts. The nave arcades were reconstructed in the fourteenth century, probably incorporating the capitals from the thirteenth-century nave, and with all but the westernmost bay enlarged to give a nave of four bays rather than five.

The nave has a fine king-post roof dating from the late fourteenth or early fifteenth century. The tie-beams are supported by pairs of arched braces large enough to give an enjoyable sequence of rounded arches, with the three easternmost pairs of arched braces cusped (perhaps to 'honour' the now-lost Rood below). The easternmost clerestory windows of the nave became internal windows when a clerestory was added to light the transepts in the fifteenth century.

Nave roof looking east

The replacement of the west walls of the transepts with pairs of arches followed the widening of the aisles. The figurative capitals of the transept arcades are clearly related to those found at Hanwell and Bloxham (like those at Hanwell the variation between the capitals – and indeed the supporting piers – also raises the possibility of this being the work of more than one sculptor). The remaining transept walls contain significant clues to the church's thirteenth-century appearance. Flanking the later windows in the north and south walls are blocked lancets with slender shafts and stiff-leaf capitals, and in the east walls are the partial outlines of further lancets (two areas of stone in the north transept have been removed to reveal portions of painted window reveal).

Transept arcade capital

The fine rood-screen and rood-loft are an amalgam of fifteenth- and nineteenth-century parts. By 1866, only the lower portions of the original fifteenth-century screen survived *in situ*. A restoration of this date saw the reinstating of the original tracery to the rood-screen, and of a fragmentary vine trail to the bressumer of the rood-loft. The rood-loft (including the vaulting) is entirely Victorian. The design of the rood-screen is unusual for this part of the country, and a Winchester connection has been suggested; certainly, the tracery heads are closely related to those of the Lady Chapel screen in Winchester Cathedral.

The interior of the chancel beyond, which follows the architectural accomplishment of the exterior, represents

Chancel looking east

Choir stall poppyhead

a supreme example of Perpendicular surface decoration. Flooded with light from its huge windows, its walls carry an abundance of brittle stone carving, including reredos, sedilia, piscina, and canopied and pinnacled niches. Elongated corbels and label-stops in the form of carved heads hover gravely overhead.

The church was restored with great sensitivity during the nineteenth century, first by John Chessell Buckler in 1831–34 (chancel), then George Gilbert Scott in 1866–70 (nave, aisles and rood-screen). The most significant legacy of this programme is the window tracery, much of which was painstakingly recreated on the basis both of drawings of the original tracery here, and existing fourteenth-century work at nearby Bloxham.

ALSO OF NOTE

C14 N doorway with low relief foliage and flat series of attached shafts with carved heads, possibly by carver of N transept pier and capital (also, high up in E wall of N porch, reset triangular-headed piscina); C14 S door of more familiar type, but richly moulded and with tiny ballflowers to hood; probably C14 aumbry in N wall of N transept; large, double piscina in S wall of S transept; C15 brasses to knight and lady in SE corner of S transept; some possibly C13 cream and black encaustic tiles reset in floor in SE corner of S transept; panelling lining transept walls reuses that from earlier box pews; late C19/ early C20 choir stalls in chancel incorporate sole surviving C15 misericord (of man's head flanked by dogs); brass to Jane Smith (d.1508) in chancel; surprisingly few good monuments for so prestigious a church (some notable ones, including two C16 monuments once occupying now empty tomb recesses in aisle walls, have been removed); crenellated bay window of domestic character in E wall of vestry; C18 headstones in churchyard, especially to E and lining path to S porch.

• • •

BAMPTON
ST MARY
Large and complex town church with fascinating history

Bampton from the south-west

Bampton once lay at the heart of an Anglo-Saxon royal estate, in what was once the largest parish in Oxfordshire. The church was a Saxon minster, whose size by the second half of the twelfth century testified to its considerable significance as an early religious foundation. It stands at the west end of the town in a churchyard fringed by limes and yews, its fine spire clearly visible across the flatness of the Thames vale.

The evolution of Bampton church is one of the most complex and interesting of any Oxfordshire church. The early development in particular is still in doubt. While some accounts suggest that the current tower may have formed the west tower of a small church with nave and apsidal chancel (the stair turret being then external), more recent accounts propose a longer church with a tower not where we find it today, but where the west wall of the current nave stands (where the footings of a structure with projecting stair base have been found). Either way, in the late twelfth century, the church was remodelled to give a cruciform plan approximating with that we see today, consisting of a nave and chancel, transepts and a crossing tower – and all of this on a grand scale.

Outside, the most conspicuous remnants of Norman work survive in the south transept, and include the south doorway and the blocked arch in the east wall. The recently restored doorway is perhaps surprisingly elaborate for one in this location. It has radiating orders of zigzag beneath a hood with billet decoration. The richness of the doorway may be related to its proximity to an altar recess that existed against the east wall of the transept, and is still marked by the round arch visible in this wall.

Restored Norman south doorway

In the second half of the thirteenth century and the first quarter of the fourteenth, the church was remodelled in the Early English style and further enlarged. Possibly as early as *c.*1250, the tower was raised in height and the spire added. The spire has the unusual, perhaps unique, feature of a quartet of near life-sized figures at its base. In an act of synchronised plank-walking, they each

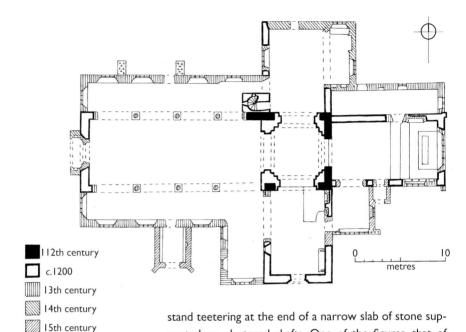

12th century

c.1200

13th century

14th century

15th century

16th century

18th century

FIG. 6 Bampton St Mary

Windows with cusped rere-arches

stand teetering at the end of a narrow slab of stone sup-ported on clustered shafts. One of the figures, that of John the Baptist, was felled by winds in 1991, and now stands inside the church, heavily weathered but dry at last.

Between c.1290 and c.1320, further alterations were carried out, most of them west of the crossing. The nave was rebuilt and given side aisles, and a south-west chapel was created. The fine, ballflower-studded west doorway, with its unusually proportioned, gabled porch, belongs to the middle of the fourteenth century. In 1497–99, the chancel was remodelled and the nave was given a clere-story – the latter being removed as part of Ewan Chris-tian's restoration of 1867–70.

The interior offers a mixed experience, with much of the interest concentrated in the north transept and chan-cel. The nave and aisles in particular, stripped of old plaster, are rather bare and lacking in texture (in this respect, the space echoes that of Adderbury to the north – as it does in the way the side aisles open into the transepts beyond). Despite the scraped walls, however, there remains much to admire. The nave has fine arcades of rounded piers and double chamfered arches, and is lit by windows in which the heads of each trio of lancets are outlined by cusped rere-arches flush with the inner wall face. Cusped rere-arches are locally distinctive, and are also found, for

Bampton: detail of the Decorated west doorway

Chip-carved Norman chancel arch

Wall monument in Horde chapel

example, at nearby Langford. The north and south doorways, like the lancets, also have trefoil heads.

Beneath the tower, earlier herringbone stonework is clearly visible. This may date from the eleventh century and represent fabric belonging to the east end of a previous nave (and not originally to a tower). Within the eastern tower arch, there is also a rounded Norman chancel arch with chip-carved decoration. Above (though now hidden by the floor of the ringing chamber) a blind arcade of round-headed arches with scalloped capitals survives (probably also Norman).

Around the crossing, the startling oddness of the plan form becomes ever more apparent. At the north-eastern end of the nave is the intrusive stair turret, which both halves the span of the final arch on the north side, and leaves but a narrow passage through which to access the north transept. Other Norman remnants, in the form of a door and part of a round-headed window, survive in the west wall of the north transept. On the east side of the north transept is a chapel to St Beornwald, arranged as a large recess framed by an expansive, thirteenth-century arch. This chapel, previously home to the saint's shrine, occupies the site of an earlier structure. It retains an empty but still lovely fourteenth-century canopied recess (possibly a shrine niche or Easter Sepulchre), the matrix of a lost brass (found buried in front of the niche) and a c.1400 stone effigy of a knight.

From the nave, the view to the south of the crossing – through the south-western chapel into the south transept beyond; through the fine c.1300 arch to the blocked twelfth-century arch in the east wall – is even less familiar. A door in the far wall gives access to a fifteenth- or sixteenth-century chapel and its collection of boldly carved seventeenth-century wall monuments to the Horde family.

Beyond the crossing is the remodelled chancel. This is home to further evidence of the church's Norman incarnation, and an array of interesting fixtures and fittings. In the north wall is a c.1200 round-headed doorway into the narrow vestry beyond, and hidden behind the altar in the east wall are two round-headed openings (possibly for an aumbry). Also in the east wall is a superb fourteenth-century reredos of Christ and the Apostles. It is reminiscent of the similar reredos at Somerton, and may be by the same carver (though at Somerton the figures are seated, and rather more animated and characterful).

The chancel also contains an impressive Perpendicular Easter Sepulchre in its north wall, a trio of brasses in its floor, and some early sixteenth-century choir stalls. The stalls retain two original bench ends and four misericords. One of these possibly depicts an Asp: a snake which blocks its large ears to resist the snake charmer, and is thus symbolic of the sinner's desire to block his ears to the Word of God.

Detail of Decorated reredos

ALSO OF NOTE

Medieval stone coffin with lid at W end of nave; square font with Victorian bowl on C14 arcaded base at W end of S aisle (bowl replaced C12 original, which had blind arcading, in c.1827); ironbound medieval chest in S aisle; weathered C14 stone effigy of woman in S transept (once in churchyard); monument to George Tompson (d. 1603) comprising dumpy stone effigy (similar to Richard Thorneton's at Westwell and of similar date) beneath pedimented canopy in S transept; several piscinae, including those in SW chapel and chancel, with stiff-leaf carving beneath bowls; probably C13 coffin lid or headstone with foliate cross mounted on N wall of N transept; restored C14 triple sedilia in chancel S wall with banded shafts and heads in quatrefoils and trefoils.

• • •

BLOXHAM
ST MARY
Magnificent Decorated church with wealth of carved detail

Despite strong local competition, Bloxham lays claim to both the finest steeple and the finest array of carved stonework of any Oxfordshire church. It stands imperiously at the head of the High Street, its sprawling bulk at first partly obscured by walls and trees. The church is closely related to Adderbury St Mary (much more so than at first seems the case) yet imposes itself both on its village and on the wider landscape in a way that Adderbury church does not and cannot, thanks to a loftier setting and a far loftier steeple. Bloxham's splendour may be attributed to a continuous history throughout the Middle Ages of first royal then rich local patronage. While significant parts of the church

Bloxham from the east

belong to the fifteenth century, and others to the twelfth (reused from a Norman church on the site), the church's character is defined by the additions of the fourteenth century, and in particular its carved decoration, window tracery, tower and spire.

The steeple is remarkable both for its architecture and its carved decoration. A local verse contrasts the height of Bloxham's steeple with the beauty of King's Sutton's, and although both are actually similar in height, their builders were bent on quite different visual effects. Whilst at King's Sutton the richness was made delicate and the masonry thin-walled and light, at Bloxham magnificence was the aim, with no effort made here to disguise the massiveness of the tower or the weight of its masonry; indeed, the chunky, stepped buttresses only serve to exaggerate these sensations as the eye travels down.

The stone carving, both architectural and decorative, is extremely fine, but is especially rich at the junction of the tower and spire. Here, a cornice of human and animal figures is fringed below with a pelmet of blind carving and crowned above by a balcony (or 'hollis') of wheel designs. The figurative carvings include, on the north side, a scene from the old nursery rhyme, *John, John, the old grey goose has gone* (in which the fox, having snatched the goose, is pursued by John and his wife, brandishing a cudgel and distaff respectively).

At the base of the tower is the extraordinary west doorway, with its peculiar stepped hood. Each of the twelve 'steps' is inhabited by the enthroned figure of an Apostle. To the left, the Blest clamber out of their coffins, while to the right, the Damned tumble into the jaws of hell. Overhead, Christ sits in Judgement, flanked by angels and the Instruments of the Passion. The doorway itself is closely related to the north doorway at Adderbury, and must be by the same carver. It has three elaborately carved orders, only here the fir cones on the outermost arch support roosting birds.

The church has some outstanding window tracery, the finest of it in the west windows of the side aisles. While the vertical lights of each window are handled in standard fashion, their heads have been given spectacular wheel designs. On the south side, in an act of geometrical

Details of west front sculpture

Bloxham: the Decorated tower and spire

Detail of north aisle window

East end of Milcombe chapel

playfulness, a Star of David has been subdivided to give a host of smaller triangles, three of which contain trefoils. On the north side, a Catherine wheel of star-like quatrefoils spins around a hub formed by the head of Christ. The remains of further sculpture, possibly once depicting the four Evangelists, can be seen immediately above, below and to either side of Christ's head. Instances of figurative sculpture in medieval window tracery are rare, but include the spectacular Jesse window at Dorchester.

Sculpture similar to that encircling the tower also lines the cornice of the north aisle. The depictions are full of invention and are brilliantly carved. A cat tries in vain to get a pair of monkeys off its back. Two dogs (one panting) dash towards a hare that cowers under foliage. A sow suckles her bottle-shaped piglets. A basilisk or cockatrice casts his mortal glare at a reeling dragon. A fox spars with a hare over a gaming board. The carvings belong to the first half of the fourteenth century, and are unmistakably the work of the same artist responsible for similar work at Adderbury, Hanwell and Alkerton.

While most of the exterior is fourteenth-century in date and Decorated in character, two notable parts are not. The Milcombe chapel on the south side of the church is fully evolved Perpendicular of the fifteenth century, and may be the work of Richard Winchcombe (who created the spectacular chancel at Adderbury). The evidence of the architecture suggests this is more likely than not. Certain details – especially the stepped buttresses topped with diagonally-set shafts, and the hollow-moulded window reveals in particular – are common to both churches. The other external feature conspicuously not belonging to the fourteenth century is the south doorway. This has a twelfth-century chevron moulded arch, reused here in the thirteenth or fourteenth century. Other stonework belonging to an earlier Norman church has been inventively reused inside the church.

Like the exterior, the interior also recalls Adderbury, particularly in the expansiveness of the space formed by nave and side aisles. As at Adderbury, the nave arcades' double chamfered arches appear to rest on earlier, and possibly thirteenth-century, capitals and piers (most are circular, but two on the south side have attached shafts and stiff-leaf capitals). Also like Adderbury, the north aisle opens into the north transept through arches resting on a finely moulded pier. This pier's elaborate capital, in the form of four figures with linked arms, is closely related to those found at Adderbury and Hanwell.

On the south side of the church, lit by four vast windows, is the Milcombe chapel. The aim here was to make as much of the wall as possible into window, and even then to carry the mullions down to floor level, in order to unify the treatment of the entire wall plane. As at Adderbury, the bays behind the altar have been subdivided to give a series of recesses forming a reredos (again supporting the theory that the architect responsible for the chancel at Adderbury also worked here). Crammed into the narrow strip of walling between the south windows are painted scenes from the life of a young, unknown martyr. He is shown bound by ropes as applauding onlookers watch on, the action played out against a chequerboard of faded greens and reds.

In a further parallel with Adderbury, Bloxham's chancel is divided from the nave by a rood-screen which, prior to its restoration in the nineteenth century, had been cut down to wainscot height. For this reason, only the lower

North transept capital

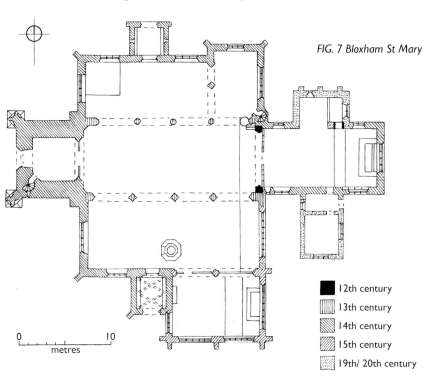

FIG. 7 Bloxham St Mary

- ■ 12th century
- 13th century
- 14th century
- 15th century
- 19th/ 20th century

0   10
metres

Restored rood-screen looking east

Reset Norman doorway in chancel

parts are substantially medieval (of *c.*1500); the mullions, tracery, head-beam and most of the paintwork above the middle rail are Victorian. Although faded and defaced, the wainscot paintings nonetheless represent a rare survival. While medieval panel paintings are relatively abundant on the screens of the South West and East Anglia, on no other Oxfordshire screen do original figure paintings of this type survive. Of the still recognisable figures, the Lion of St Mark can be made out to the left of the doorway, and the Eagle of St John to the right. The wainscot panels are also notable for their carved spandrels, which contain hunting dogs, green men, swans and a dragon.

The chancel itself is made memorable both for the fabric of the windows and for some of the glass they contain. In terms of date, the tracery belongs to the early fourteenth century. However, unusually, the masons chose to incorporate stonework originating in the round-headed arches of the earlier Norman church within the pointed arches of the three windows on the south side of the chancel and one on the north side. Given the expertise of Bloxham's sculptors in the fourteenth century, this may not have been mere expediency, but a reflection of genuine admiration for the workmanship of their predecessors. The quality of the twelfth-century work is certainly high, and full of the sort of life and detail they poured into their own work. Also in the north wall is a Norman doorhead with a tympanum of fish scale pattern, reset here in 1866 when the vestry was added (part of a sensitive programme of restoration by George Street).

The east window is an important early work by the firm that was to become Morris & Co., with William Morris together with Philip Webb and Edward Burne-Jones all having a hand in its creation. The design has two tiers of paired angels and saints in the main lights, ranged beneath further angels and Christ in Majesty seated on a rainbow above. The main figures wear their apparel and are posed somewhat as actors upon a stage. The palette is also striking, with acid yellows and greens against night-time blues and mauvey pinks. The window makes an interesting comparison with the even earlier east window by the same firm at nearby Middleton Cheney in Northamptonshire. The small window on the south side of the chancel is also by Morris & Co. (based on a design by Burne-Jones), as is the much later and less distinctive east window in the north aisle.

ALSO OF NOTE

C13 and C14 three-storey S porch, vaulted below and with priest's room above with fireplace and doorway into church accessed by stairwell inside S door; C15 font inside S door (similar to example at Idbury) with Jacobean font cover; C14 painted decoration to S-facing inner chamfers of S arcade; fragmentary C15 St Christopher with kneeling figure and mermaid on N aisle wall over N door; small fragment of Doom painting to top right of chancel arch (with flames of hell and monstrous face); array of medieval stone corbels, including commoners in N aisle and high status figures in S aisle; variety of mainly C17 and C18 memorial tablets and brasses attached to W wall of S aisle and N wall of N aisle; medieval (probably C14) wooden chest at W end of S aisle; three memorials to members of Thorneycroft family against W wall of Milcombe chapel (including reclining marble effigy of Sir John Thorneycroft of Milcombe Hall, d. 1725, which once stood against, and thus blocked, E window in Milcombe chapel); earlier nave roofline visible high up on W wall of nave; stained glass includes C14 fragments (including head of Christ) in tracery lights of N aisle window, and intricate 1886 memorial window by Charles Kempe in central window on S side of chancel; 1846 organ enlarged and re-erected on N side of chancel by J. W. Parker in 1867; relief-carved C17 and C18 gravestones in churchyard.

Morris & Co. chancel east window

Perpendicular octagonal font

• • •

BROUGHTON
ST MARY
Atmospheric parkland church with rare stone rood-screen

Broughton church stands in the shadow of Broughton Castle, the charismatic great house occupying a moated site just to the south. Both church and house are essentially creations of the early fourteenth century. But while the house was conspicuously updated in the sixteenth century and now wears a Tudor façade, the church has retained its fourteenth-century character, and still encapsulates beautifully the transition between the Early English and Decorated phases of English Gothic; the relative austerity of the former and the sculpted detail and animation of the latter.

The church consists of nave, chancel, and south aisle,

Broughton from the south

South aisle east window

Effigy of John de Broughton

and has a west tower with a neat broach spire. Although largely constructed from the local orangey-brown ironstone, some paler limestone has been used in decorative bands (for example, over the south doorway and several of the windows – as employed at Great Tew and elsewhere). Externally, numerous details catch the eye. Both tower and south aisle have friezes with much-weathered corbels (mainly small heads, flowers and ballflower). In the tops of the gable walls at both ends of the south aisle are pretty cinquefoil-headed niches with flower cusps. A range of window tracery can be seen, most of it fourteenth-century but not fully-fledged Decorated in style. The south aisle, for example, has geometric and intersecting tracery, rather than the curvilinear tracery found in the nave windows (including the restored six-light east window). The expansive Perpendicular window at the east end of the south wall is later.

The west doorway is a lovely example of early Decorated work. It has three moulded orders, the outermost hollowed out and enriched with ballflower, and the whole topped by an ogee hood, carved with leaves, which climb to a crowning finial. The south doorway, through which the church is entered, belongs to c.1300, but is plainer Early English in style.

The first space encountered on entering the church is the memorable two-storey south aisle. Here, windows of various shapes and sizes, painted hatchments bearing coats of arms, and an array of monuments, all jostle for space along the south wall. The effect is a happy jumble. In the south-eastern corner of the south aisle (partly overlapped by a later tomb surmounted by bears) is the ornate tomb recess and effigy of John de Broughton (died 1315). Although both were boldly recoloured in 1846, such tombs would have been richly painted and gilded, and much of this tomb's original colour apparently survived intact as late as 1805.

The south aisle is divided from the nave by a c.1300 transitional arcade of four bays. This has circular piers and moulded capitals of Early English character, but double chamfered arches typical of the Decorated era. On the western face of the pier nearest the font is a faded wall painting of the Crucifixion.

Broughton: view east towards the Decorated stone rood-screen

Detail of stone rood-screen

Chancel wall painting of Virgin

At the entrance to the chancel stands a fine and rare fourteenth-century stone rood-screen. In a chunkier version of timber screens of the period, the design comprises three crocketed ogee arches to either side of a central doorway, whose head is of flattened ogee form. The 'wainscot' takes the form of a plain dwarf wall. Carved on the cornice above, and on the mullions just above the springing points of the arches, are a number of little heads. Few comparable stone rood-screens survive today. The closest equivalent is probably the late fourteenth-century chancel screen at Bradford Abbas in Dorset.

Along the north wall of the chancel is a fragmentary cycle of wall paintings, possibly illustrating the Death of the Virgin. The westernmost image, showing the Virgin confronted by an angel bearing a palm branch, is the best preserved. The figures are beautifully drawn, the hands deftly articulating much of the scene's drama. In the south wall of the chancel are two fine alabaster effigies framed by a Perpendicular tomb recess. Intriguingly, the figures were probably not originally a pair, for while the lady belongs to the early fifteenth century, the man – thought to be Sir Thomas Wykeham (died 1470) – belongs to the late fifteenth century.

ALSO OF NOTE

Mid C14 effigy of knight on later chest tomb in NE corner of S aisle; brass to Lady Bishopsden (d. 1414) before altar in S aisle; C13 coffin lid on floor in bay between S aisle and chancel; stained glass includes three C16 panels in E window of S aisle (in 1611, Richard Lee recorded 52 coats of arms in this window) and collection of C19 glass, including E window by Clayton & Bell; C12 font with cable moulding at W end of nave and aisle; old and worn tiled floor, with several tiles retaining encaustic decoration; C18 gravestones in churchyard. Like Adderbury, Broughton was restored with sensitivity first by George Gilbert Scott, then his son George Gilbert Jr., mainly 1877–80.

• • •

BUCKLAND
ST MARY

Large cruciform church with spectacular Victorian transept

Buckland from the south-east

The village of Buckland lies within earshot of the busy A420 to the north-east of Faringdon. Pretty and well maintained but otherwise unassuming, it plays host to at least two surprising buildings. One of these is Buckland House: an accomplished Georgian mansion of 1757 by the younger John Wood of Bath. The house was once more doll's house-like but was enlarged in 1910. Another is the nearby church of St Mary: a strikingly proportioned cruciform church, whose chancel is almost as long as its nave.

The external appearance of the church is misleading, for the nave, despite its Perpendicular south window and crenellated parapet, is mostly Norman; the chancel, despite its tracery-free windows, mostly fourteenth-century. Between the two, both physically and date-wise, are the Early English transepts and tower. The south transept bears the date 1787, when various alterations were carried out, possibly including the insertion of the plain mullion windows in the chancel. As can be seen from the outer faces of the tower, the rooflines of both nave and chancel were once considerably steeper.

Original steeper rooflines on tower

The south porch is as large as the chancel of some churches. It probably dates from the thirteenth century, but was heavily restored in the late nineteenth century. Sheltering inside is the impressively large, if quite plain, Norman south doorway. This has two orders of roll mouldings springing from simple capitals and attached shafts, and just an overarching strip of saltire crosses by way of carved decoration. The north doorway, darkened by weathering and cloaked by yews, is similar, if perhaps slightly less tall.

Inside, the unusually wide Norman nave is soberly furnished with door-less eighteenth-century box pews. At the west end stands a sturdy Perpendicular font, and high over the chancel arch at the east end hovers a lofty gallery with balustraded front.

Beyond the chancel arch, the church's interior comes alive, most spectacularly in the south transept. This is one of the most startling and unexpected spaces to be found in any Oxfordshire church; a glittering box of colour to

rival anything left to church art by the Victorians. It was commissioned by William West, Director of the Great Western Railway, as a memorial to his wife Clara Jane, who died in 1888. The work was carried out by the firm of Powell & Sons, to designs by Henry Holiday (who was mainly a stained glass designer, but who was also responsible for illustrating Lewis Carroll's *The Hunting of the Snark*). The scheme is all-encompassing, taking in every available surface – including the floor and ceiling and all of the walling between, the stained glass, all the furniture and even the lighting.

The walls of the transept are covered in mosaics of gold, blue, green and red, depicting an array of apostles and prophets, martyrs and angels. The designs in the principal frieze echo those found in medieval and later stained glass, with the figures standing under elaborate architectural canopies. However, within the mosaic strip below window height is a series of lozenges whose imagery and line-work is more modern in feel. Here, next to sentimental depictions of angels and children, is a galleon under sail, a pair of whales whose flukes seem to have frozen solid in the icy air, and the cosmos seen through clouds reminiscent of the fanciful vapour trails of a Heath Robinson drawing.

Inevitably perhaps, the north transept is outshone by the south. However, it too holds much of interest. In the walls can be seen the remains of thirteenth-century lancets, still with much of their original browny-red pigment. The transept has several monuments to the Yate family. These include, tipped up against the north wall, a late sixteenth-century brass to John Yate and his wife, their twelve children huddling below; and an accomplished seventeenth-century tomb, in black and white marble, to Sir Edward Yate and his daughter. Set into the floor is the large indent of a foliate cross.

Transept mosaics by Henry Holiday

Like the transepts before it, the chancel comprises elements from several periods. The two tomb recesses belong to the fourteenth century. That to the north is in the form of a crude ogee with a pinched top, and is studded with ballflower; that to the south carved in low relief with clover, *fleurs-de-lis* and flowers. The triple sedilia and piscina – the piscina containing a later Italian alabaster relief, cut

Buckland: Victorian decorative scheme in the south transept

to fit – also belong to the fourteenth century. Overhead is a typically shallow-pitched and hefty Perpendicular roof, much enriched with carved bosses and shields. Many of the other fixtures and fittings are Victorian (including the choir stalls and lectern of 1871 by George Gilbert Scott). In a quirk of perspective, the church does not appear as long when looking west from the chancel as it does when looking east from the nave.

ALSO OF NOTE

Holiday's chancel east window

C12 ironwork and hinges on S door of nave; C18 pulpit beneath crossing (with trompe-l'oeil perspectives, cf. Shrivenham); several C18 slate floor monuments with elegant lettering beneath crossing; triangular niche in N wall of chancel containing heart burial to William Holcot (d. 1570); five medieval stained glass shields mounted in box frame on S wall of chancel; reredos of 1924 by Oxfordshire architect and writer F. E. Howard; array of C19 and C20 stained glass, including by Clayton & Bell (S window of chancel); Pre-Raphaelite style chancel E window of 1919 also by Holiday. Buckland has significant Catholic connections through the Throckmorton family, who commissioned the church of St George close by (an early work by Catholic architect Charles Hansom).

• • •

BURFORD
ST JOHN THE BAPTIST
Magical 'wool' church

Burford from the south-east

Burford has become the Cotswold destination *par excellence*. Yet despite what Pevsner memorably called, 'the cult of picturesque Burford', in few places in the country does so much of a small medieval town survive intact. Between the seventeenth and nineteenth centuries, Burford's status as a major centre of the wool trade waned. The main road once carrying traffic and trade through its heart moved away to the south, and the town quietly ossified. Instead of wholesale rebuilding (such as that which took place in nearby Witney), remodelling, re-fronting or leaving well alone prevailed in the post-medieval era. So it is that more than seventy medieval or part-medieval buildings survive in Burford. Pre-eminent among them is the church.

Although the lofty spire of the church is visible from a distance, the church's setting, down a side street at the bottom of the hill, is relatively discreet. Its location here probably follows that of a predecessor on the site, which may have been a minster church standing within a Saxon enclosure immediately south of the river Windrush.

Today, the church stands beyond almshouses in a grave-yard chock-full of bale tombs. Despite its size and status, it does not overwhelm – especially inside, where the lingering impression is one of intimate grandeur. Outside, the building is not easily read. The south elevation presents an unbroken, almost terrace-like composition of gables and walls, the architecture of which is overwhelmingly Perpendicular in character. But while the church was enlarged and remodelled in the fifteenth century, significant parts belonging to the twelfth and thirteenth centuries remain at least partly intact and legible.

Bale tomb outside south porch

The west wall of the nave and the lower two stages of the tower are the most conspicuous remnants of what must have been, to judge by the richness of the decoration and the length of the nave, an imposing Romanesque church. The Norman west doorway is a well-preserved example with a good array of beakheads, whilst the tower has several openings (some blocked) also framed by chevron mouldings. It appears, despite the addition of a south aisle and short transept by the end of the twelfth century,

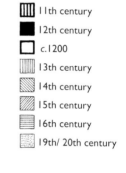

- 11th century
- 12th century
- c.1200
- 13th century
- 14th century
- 15th century
- 16th century
- 19th/ 20th century

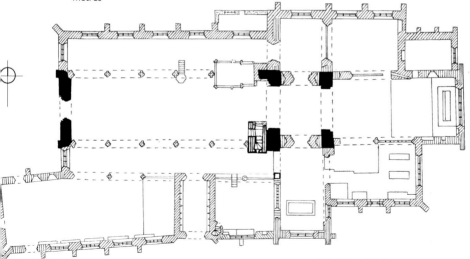

FIG. 8 Burford St John the Baptist

Norman west doorway

Perpendicular south porch

that the church did not become cruciform until the first half of the thirteenth century, when longer transepts were added and the chancel was lengthened.

The other major development at this time (probably in c.1200) was the construction of a freestanding chapel close to the south-west corner of the nave, by the powerful merchant guild. The chapel was built at a slight angle to the nave. Because of this, the decision in the fifteenth century to join it to the church inevitably resulted in compromises, most notably to the integrity of the recently-built porch. The porch is one of the glories of the church. Of three storeys, its component parts – the pinnacles that continue the lines of the buttresses, the narrow panel tracery, and the tall pedestals on which the figures stand – have all been calculated to give its architecture an insistent verticality.

As the guild chapel did not sufficiently overlap the nave, it was lengthened to the east (and shortened to the west: note the blocked lancet on the north side). This brought it against the porch, even cutting into the porch's western buttress. To the east, meanwhile, the porch is sandwiched by the chapel of St Thomas, and thus no longer stands proud of the façade, as it should (and still does, for example, at Northleach in Gloucestershire). The guild chapel, while largely Perpendicular in style, retains an Early English south doorway with a weathered Crucifixion above, and two lancets and a round-headed doorway on the north side.

Other work carried out during the fifteenth century, in an era when Burford reached its zenith as a wool town, included the rebuilding of the nave, the addition of a north aisle to the nave, a south chapel to the chancel, and a spire to the heightened tower.

The interior of the church is endlessly enticing. While nave and side aisles manage a semblance of familiarity, the eastern parts of the church are a warren of interlinked spaces filled, sometimes storeroom-like, with the clutter of the ages. Everywhere, the junctions between earlier and later work lie exposed to view: stonework that abruptly changes course, half-buried windows and discarded roof lines, monuments that pave the floors, climb the walls or fill entire rooms.

The rebuilding of the nave, together with the addition of the north aisle and the joining of the guild chapel, saw the introduction of fine new arcades, both to the nave and between the south aisle and the guild chapel beyond. These have piers of quatrefoil cross-section (with four attached shafts) and capitals similar to those found in several other 'wool Gothic' churches, including Chipping Campden and Northleach. In a pattern visible throughout the church, earlier steeply-pitched roofs were replaced with new roofs of characteristically shallow pitch in the fifteenth century, some with decorative arched braces. All this new work – arcades, windows and roofs – gave ample scope to the church's masons, who duly studded the interior with figurative sculpture in the form of label stops and corbels. Some of these carvings probably depict donors, local worthies, townsfolk and even the masons themselves. The best examples survive on the north side of the arcade to the guild chapel.

Nave arcade capitals

Further notable examples of the mason's art survive in the north aisle. The font is probably Norman, but re-cut in the fourteenth century. It is trimmed with ballflower and has a series of figures within rather squashed ogee niches (including a swaying St Catherine on the south side). To the east is the fascinating monument to Edmund Harman and his wife, of 1569. While the couple are absent, their sixteen children are well represented, carved in deep relief on the lower half of the monument. Although only two of the daughters survived their parents, the children are here shown full of life, wide-eyed and chubby-cheeked. The Amazonian figures above, possibly taken from a Flemish book of c.1540, are thought to be the earliest depictions in Britain of inhabitants of the New World.

Norman font with Decorated carving

The eastward view down the nave betrays another architectural compromise: the tower arch is proportion-ately too low for the remodelled nave. Both this arch and the one beyond should be at least as lofty as the adjoining arcades, and possibly would have been had it been struc-turally possible to so alter the tower's base. As it is (and this is surely a good thing) the tower's integrity as a piece of Norman architecture remains intact. Its nobility is clear from within, where round-headed arcades and windows, some chevron-moulded, line the walls. While the duck-ing down of the two tower arches does exacerbate the separation between nave and chancel, it is nonetheless

spatially appealing: in few other big churches is there such a pronounced sense of the various spaces having the quality of distinct rooms.

The demarcation between nave and chancel would have been even more pronounced when the rood-screen and rood-loft were still in place. The presence of these now-lost fittings is attested to by, amongst other evidence, the church's sole surviving medieval brass. Set into the floor beneath the chancel arch, this records the gift of the rood-loft ('rode soler') by John Spicer in the fifteenth century.

Wall arcade of Norman tower

Also bearing witness to lost medieval screens is the four-poster bed-like chapel of St Peter at the east end of the nave, together with the pulpit close by. The chapel, including the stone canopy, is part-medieval and is enclosed by screens incorporating early work, including from the dismantled rood-screen. The westernmost spandrel on the south side is carved with a sawfish or Serra: an evil fish-like creature drawn from the bestiary, whose serrated crest it uses to cut open and sink the ship of the Faithful. The chapel was restored in 1877–78 by George Street, who renewed some of the woodwork and designed the fittings. The pulpit to the west is also by Street, and also incorporates fifteenth-century screenwork (an expedient employed nearby at Widford and Swinbrook).

While the canopied chapel of St Peter is the smallest of Burford's array of chapels, the guild chapel (variously known as the Lady Chapel or Sylvester aisle) is the largest. This is dominated by the Sylvesters and their strikingly uniform chest-tombs. With the exception of the towering monument to Thomas Sylvester, most have similar backs, with strapwork and a merchant's mark in the centre. Arguably the chapel's two most interesting monuments are those at the west end of the north wall. The lower one (to Io Osbaldeston, died 1611) has foliage-clad caryatids; the upper one (to Richard Sindrey, died 1661) is hung with big swags of fruit similar to those on the Trinder monument at nearby Westwell.

Chapel of St Peter

The chapel of St Thomas stands immediately to the east of the porch, and is fenced off from the south transept by a rugged, part-medieval screen. It is memorably reached up a short flight of steps, being raised over an underlying crypt. This chapel was probably added in the

Burford: the south elevation

Monument in chapel of St Thomas

Whall window in south transept

fourteenth century; however, while the arch of the south window is consistent with this date, the attached shafts in the window reveals are more characteristic of thirteenth-century work. In the south wall is a fine piscina of *c.*1300 with little head-stops and a foliage-carved basin. The openings in the east wall, assuming they are original (the stonework at least looks Victorian), may have enabled those in the chapel of St Thomas to witness services taking place in the south transept (in which there was once an altar).

Evidence for the use of the south transept as a chapel is provided by the piscina in its east wall, and possibly by the image niche in its south-east corner. It was effectively disabled as a chapel when the massive chest-tomb was added in the fifteenth century. The tomb probably lost its brasses, and with them the identities of its high status subjects, during the Civil War, when Parliamentary soldiers occupied the building. On the north wall is a monument to master-mason and architect Christopher Kempster: resident of Burford, colleague of Christopher Wren, and designer of the magnificent Town Hall in Abingdon. The broad arch in the east wall (with Victorian cusping) may have been inserted to enable the masonry to be thickened, and thus strengthened, when the south transept was extended and raised in height in the thirteenth century.

When the two transepts were added, archways were opened through the north and south faces of the tower base. However, this weakened the tower, and in order for it to bear the weight of a third stage and spire it became necessary to reduce both archways to little more than doorways (further compartmentalising the spaces in this half of the church).

Like the south transept, the chapels flanking the chancel have also been intruded upon by later additions. In the case of the south chancel (Holy Trinity) chapel, built in *c.*1486, it is the organ that must be squeezed around. This chapel, like those to the west, has its scraps of old paintwork and its quota of monuments. The wall paintings include, under the east window, a sixteenth-century text from Romans, originally forming the backdrop to another now-lost altar. The monuments include superb wall-mounted examples from the seventeenth century: two cartouches flanking the east window, and two larger pedimented monuments on the south wall. One of the chest-tombs here is of the same type as those lining the south wall at the other end of the church. The south and north (St Katherine's) chapel are divided from the chancel by restored fifteenth-century parclose screens.

In 1625, the north chancel chapel was reduced to the status of a fitted box for the colossal Tanfield monument it now contains. This was evidently calculated to fill the space, minus just enough room for pilgrims (strictly one abreast) to make a circuit of the monument. The recumbent effigies are its least compelling features. They are neither as intransient nor as lifelike as they might be. The skeleton below also disappoints, failing to disturb as Alice of Suffolk's cadaver does at Ewelme. The canopy, however, must be enjoyed – or at the least admired. It is so grandiose (if architecturally muddled), so fanciful (note the cherubs' heads popping out of the ceiling) that one wonders how Sir Lawrence is able to keep a straight face.

Detail of Tanfield monument

The opening between the Tanfield chapel and the north transept, with its old clock parts and bells, was fenced off in the seventeenth century by an unusual screen. Evidently bodged together, it reuses fifteenth-century tracery below its middle rail, and what may be thirteenth-century work as cresting along its head-beam (it is similar to that surviving in situ at Chinnor).

The chancel next door is the most obviously restored part of the church. Here, Street replaced the shallow Perpendicular roof so characteristic of the church with one of steeper pitch. Hardman's east window of 1886 is more successful: an effective composition of blues and reds against a white ground. Two lancets (one blocked) on the north side, together with two sedilia and a piscina to the south, testify to the chancel's thirteenth-century origins. Meanwhile, two pinnacled niches flanking the altar bear witness to the church's later aggrandisement, looking like escapees from the south porch.

Detail of north transept screen

ALSO OF NOTE

Fragmentary C15 glass in tracery lights of nave W window and chancel E window; much C19 glass by Charles Kempe, including nave W window of 1869 with plenty of green; oddly proportioned reredos in Lady Chapel of 1911 by E. B. Hoare, with figures by Esmond Burton; painted Crucifixion over tower arch

Chancel east window by Hardman

and Adoration on reredos in chancel both by Clayton & Bell (1878); small C11 or C12 doorway with plain, recessed tympanum in W wall of tower stair turret to S of tower arch; primitive C11 or C12 sculpted stone slab (possibly depicting Flight into Egypt) high up on S side of tower stair turret; Transitional archway between earlier S aisle and S transept with stiff-leaf capitals; 1907 S transept S window by Christopher Whall, dense with figures but restrained in palette; C18 painted poor boards on W wall of S transept (including two shaped to fit in spandrels of arcade); numerous C17–C19 ledgers in floor of S transept; C15 stained glass fragments in N transept N window include head of woman with 'butterfly' head-dress, and head of St James of Compostela; unusual C19 painted memorial to Emma Durham (nurse to Tennyson) on wall in SE corner of N transept; C15 vaulted two-bay recess at E end of chancel N (Tanfield) chapel with some original colour; C15 squint through from Tanfield chapel to chancel beyond; C15 chimney at NW corner of N aisle; C15 image niche with later figure high up in W gable of nave.

• • •

CASSINGTON
ST PETER
Fine Norman church with lovely woodwork and glass

Cassington from the north-west

Cassington St Peter was built in c.1123 by the treasurer to Henry I, Geoffrey de Clinton. Happily sited, it forms a noble perspective when viewed from Church Lane, standing beyond a gravestone-free apron of green. The original twelfth-century church was altered and added to in the fourteenth century, and a better sense of its pre-Decorated appearance can be gained by imagining away the later spire and porches. Externally, the most conspicuous Norman features are the round-headed windows and doorways, and the corbel table.

The corbel table runs along both sides of chancel and nave, and forms a chunkily-carved gallery of heads, both human and animal. It also takes in the tower, where some of the stones were reused in the fourteenth century to support a frieze of blind quatrefoils. The north and south doorways and the north tower doorway are also Norman, as are the various round-headed windows which jostle for attention with the larger and more eye-catching Decorated windows in the side and east walls. Aside from the insertion of new windows, the most noticeable legacy of

Cassington: the medieval bench ends lining the nave

Curvilinear west window

Interior looking east

the works carried out in the fourteenth century (probably by the Montagu family as lords of the manor) was the addition of another storey and a spire to the Norman tower.

Further Norman work is visible inside, most notably in the finely moulded tower arches and vaulted chancel beyond. Given the richness of some of the church's stonework and the general finesse of its architecture, it is perhaps surprising that its Norman font is not of comparable richness, and takes the form of a plain tub.

The spacious nave contains precious early woodwork and delicate painted glass. The pews are rumoured to be of the thirteenth century, but are more likely to be of the fourteenth or fifteenth century. They are excellent, robust examples of rustic carpentry, their meaty bench ends moulded with simple chamfers. The church was sensitively restored by Bodley and Garner in 1876–77, and an opportunity to introduce Victorian pews in their place was happily passed over. Another significant piece of early woodwork is the south door, whose upper parts are painted with a faded sixteenth- or seventeenth-century depiction of the Instruments of the Passion (including images of the True Cross and Holy Lance, framed below by a bold Crown of Thorns-like frieze of interlace).

The stained glass in the nave is interesting for several reasons. Firstly, none of it originally belonged at Cassington (indeed, in 1825 the church was entirely devoid of stained glass). All of the current glass was brought in from elsewhere later in the nineteenth century. Some of the glass (together with the choir stalls and chandeliers) came from Christ Church in Oxford; but what of the rest? The source remains a mystery, but a connection with neighbouring Yarnton is a possibility. In the early nineteenth century, William Fletcher (Alderman of Oxford) gifted a large amount of fifteenth- and sixteenth-century stained glass to Yarnton church, including several sixteenth-century panels of Flemish painted glass of the same type as that found in the west window at Cassington.

The west window at Cassington is the richest in the church, with thirteen panels of grisaille glass depicting Biblical scenes, set within later red and yellow bordered glazing. The painting is deft and delicate, full of incident and detail. The other nave windows are relatively plain, but share a handful of panels, mostly roundels. Of these, several are fourteenth-century and of high quality.

The space beneath the tower — the crossing if this were a cruciform church with transepts — is given over to the choir, and contains the Christ Church stalls. Their refinement is in stark contrast to the hefty simplicity of the benches in the nave. Some of their blind decoration (including their broken pediments with ball finials) feels more Georgian than Jacobean. The delicate *c.*1500 rood-screen is largely original, but contains some replacement work (for example, to the tracery heads) pieced in as part of the nineteenth-century restorations. The treatment of the wainscot, with its blind tracery not subdivided to correspond with the open bays above, is unusual — as are the elevation squints cut through a couple of the loop lights below the middle rail (though holes of this type also survive in the screen at Stanton Harcourt).

Detail of west window

The little chancel beyond contains more good Norman and Decorated work. The twelfth-century ribs of the quadripartite vault spring from corner shafts of the same diameter, giving a simple, unbroken architectural frame to the chancel space. The east window belongs to the fourteenth century, and below and to the right of this is a double piscina — like a transommed and blocked up version of the east window.

Detail of c.1500 rood-screen

ALSO OF NOTE

Fragmentary C14 or C15 wall paintings to splays of nave E windows (possibly St Barbara or St Catherine on N side and St Margaret on S side, both beneath canopies) and over tower arch (Last Judgement); unusual brass memorial plaque with shrouded effigy of 1590 on wall to right of chancel arch; C18 chandeliers from Christ Church in nave; C18 altar rails with fancy balusters in sanctuary.

• • •

CHALGROVE
ST MARY
Modest village church with spectacular wall paintings

Chalgrove lies about ten miles south-east of Oxford. Like Kidlington and Yarnton to the north, the village has had to withstand swathes of new housing. However, also like them, it has an old church not yet overrun, but standing on the fringes – in this case ringed by a moat of gravelly path.

Chalgrove from the south

The church offers rather a mixed experience for the visitor. A neat and handsome exterior gives way inside first to a less-than-happy nave of skewed pews and recent clutter, but then to a fine chancel whose walls teem with tier upon tier of medieval wall paintings. Outside, the window tracery (almost all of which is either Decorated or Perpendicular in style) testifies to a structure at least much-altered during the fourteenth and fifteenth centuries. The chancel is particularly consistent, its windows containing finely moulded reticulated tracery. The neat three-stage tower belongs to the late thirteenth or early fourteenth century. Subsequently (presumably later in the fourteenth century) the nave roof was raised, as its ridge now cuts into the bell openings to the east. The tower carried a spire until 1727, when this was toppled by a storm.

Whilst the exterior is dominated by fourteenth- and fifteenth-century work, the nave arcades inside confirm that this was an aisled church at least as far back as the early thirteenth century. The Transitional south arcade, which has square bases and capitals, could be of c.1200; the north arcade, which has moulded and stiff-leaf capitals, appears more fully Early English in style, and must be later. While stonework was often originally painted in medieval churches, the white-washing of these arcades has done them no favours: better bare stone than the pallor of white paint.

Transitional arcade capital

The chancel comes as a real surprise (particularly given the shortcomings of the nave) for this is a rare example of an interior in which it is possible to gain a pronounced sense of the role played by colour in our medieval churches (others might include Kempley in Gloucestershire, Clayton in West Sussex and Claverley in Shropshire). The colour palette, although restricted to maroons, golden or brown

Chalgrove: the chancel wall paintings (south wall)

Detail of chancel wall paintings

ochres and charcoals (which tend sometimes to blue-black and sometimes to green-black) has been deployed in such a way as to give the impression of far greater variety (a trick that medieval painters were adept at).

The wall paintings are coeval with the chancel, and thus mid fourteenth-century. They depict scenes from the Lives of the Virgin (south wall) and Christ (north wall), together with the Last Judgement (west end of the south wall) and the Tree of Jesse (west end of the north wall). The windows have larger figures in the reveals, and are speckled with stencilled red flowers and topped with brocades of golden foliage. The workmanship throughout is superb, the compositions inventive and the line-work spare yet decisive. The Gothic figures, swaying and sinuous, might have stepped here from the pages of an illuminated manuscript. The walls are full of the ebb and flow of their toing and froing.

ALSO OF NOTE

Unusual, whitewashed font of c.1660 at W end of nave; late C17 rustic painted memorial to Quatremaine family on W wall of nave; polygonal, Jacobean pulpit at E end of nave; portion of C14 cresset stone in S wall at W end of nave; triangular piscina in wall at SE end of N aisle; fragmentary wall painting at E end of N aisle; C17 slate memorial to Winchcombe family on N wall of N aisle; some fragments of early glass in N windows; piscina and credence in S wall of S aisle; C17 bier with c.1500 chest at E end of S aisle; C14 piscina and triple sedilia on S side of chancel; C15 brasses to Barantyn family in floor of chancel.

Piscina and triple sedilia

• • •

CHARLTON-ON-OTMOOR
ST MARY
Unspoilt church with rustic interior and superb rood-screen

Lying between Oxford and Bicester, Otmoor is an area of low-lying wetland bounded by the 'Seven Towns of Otmoor', of which Charlton is pre-eminent. Prior to their draining in the nineteenth century, Otmoor's marshes flooded regularly, and Charlton, which stands on a slight eminence, must then have seemed like a haven on the edge of untamed wilderness. Local legend tells of a lost traveller using the tolling bell of Charlton church to guide

Charlton from the south-west

Charlton-on-Otmoor: the nave and rood-screen looking east

him off the moor. Today, the land around Charlton lies firmly under the farmer's thumb, its marshes put to grass. And yet the village retains a sense of isolation, seeming further away from other places than is actually the case, and having a memorable, slightly left-behind character.

South aisle Decorated window

The church stands on the high street and is outwardly unspectacular, with a standard composition of aisled nave, chancel, south porch and west tower (see *plan on page 13*). The original thirteenth-century church was extensively remodelled in the fourteenth century and is now, externally at least, an example of Decorated architecture at its most restrained. Enrichment, what there is of it, is concentrated in the window tracery and tower pinnacles. Elsewhere, discreet quatrefoils can be found: cut in low relief into the south aisle parapet, giving shape to three clerestory windows on the north side of the nave, and painted onto the underside of a nave tie-beam. Above the south door is a set of Perpendicular image brackets, closely related to a set at nearby Merton.

Whilst the exterior is unassuming, the interior is full of texture and unspoilt workmanship. The nave is especially enjoyable. Its arcades have double chamfered arches and octagonal piers, but rounded capitals (like those at Adderbury). They retain a significant amount of original red paintwork. Hiding behind the westernmost pier of the north arcade is the font, a plain twelfth- or thirteenth-century tub with a cover in the shape of a wigwam. The nave has a fine, ruggedly-carved medieval roof, with some timbers (including a number of wall-posts) left as little more than roughly worked tree trunks.

Nave roof looking east

The rood-screen is one of the finest in Oxfordshire, and is closely related to the one at Thame (indeed, they could be the work of the same carpenter, such are the similarities between the wainscots and mullions of each). In both cases, the comparatively robust Gothic common to late medieval church screens has given way to something more flamboyant and delicate, less architectural. The treatment is rather un-English (especially the loft coving, with its animated filigree), and could even be the work of a Continental carpenter: the combination of linenfold panels and distinctive patterned mullions can be found on a number of screens in the north-west of France.

At one time, the arrangement of the screenwork would have been quite different. We know from an early illustration that a screen tympanum (painted with the royal arms) still filled the chancel archway above the screen as late as 1822. This had been removed by 1846. From mortise holes visible in the upper face of the bressumer, it is also clear that the rood-loft was bounded on its western side by what was probably an elaborate parapet. The current Victorian paintwork is apparently based on traces of original paint (the colours used are broadly consistent with surviving paintwork on other screens). It might have been better either to have painted the whole screen (as it once was), or to have left it entirely unpainted. On top of the screen stands a cross of box branches. Placed here each May Day, this harks back to the ancient custom of dressing the Rood and rood-loft with garlands and branches during church festivals.

Rood-screen vine trail carving

Standing to the west of the rood-screen is an unusual and attractive pulpit, dated 1616. It is supported on a single baluster, like the stem of a wine glass. The chancel beyond, although lacking the interest of the nave, has several features of note, including a sturdy triple sedilia and piscina in its south wall, some fragments of medieval glass in the upper lights of its windows, and some medieval floor tiles on its altar steps. The richly carved seventeenth-century altar rails seem a little incongruous in such humble surroundings.

ALSO OF NOTE

Blocked C13 or C14 doorway in N wall of N aisle; medieval cambered tie-beam roofs to side aisles; small fragments of C14 paintwork in chancel; monuments in chancel include stone slab with foliated cross to John de Craneforde (rector 1369–) and brass of priest in cope to Thomas Key (rector 1467–75); pediment and shaft of medieval preaching cross in churchyard.

• • •

CHECKENDON
ST PETER AND ST PAUL
Unspoilt Norman flint church with rare painted apse

The village of Checkendon lies in the far south-east of
the county, in a landscape flecked with chalk and flint,
and wooded with beech. Its little Norman church is built
almost entirely of flint and topped with clay tiles. It seems
inconceivable that it could belong in the same county as
the rust coloured ironstone churches of Hanwell and Horley far away to the north.

Checkendon from the south-east

Despite appearances perhaps, the Norman church
is well preserved; for while the tower, porch and nave
roof with parapet belong to the fifteenth century, and
most of the windows to the fourteenth and fifteenth
centuries, the church remains otherwise largely as built
in the twelfth century. The most notable original part is
the rounded apse, complete with conical roof and round-
headed east window (*see plan on page 6*).

With walls of brittle, nubby flint, carved decoration is
limited to a south doorway of sandy limestone (now concealed within the porch, but once exposed to view). The
doorway has fine capitals. That on the left is carved with a
pair of beasts (possibly mantichores); that on the right, a
pair of eagles with the big-clawed feet typical of this creature's treatment in Romanesque carving. The tympanum,
which is later, is framed by a roll moulding and a hood
carved with fish-scale.

South doorway capital

The interior of the church is delightful. Much of its
satisfaction derives from its distinctive spatial qualities;
particularly its surprising small-scale grandeur, and the
growing sense of the special as one moves east, stepping
up through diminishing archways into ever smaller and
more precious spaces.

The well-proportioned, aisle-less nave is the most conspicuously altered part of the church. In the fifteenth century, its original more steeply pitched roof was replaced by
a flatter Perpendicular roof. The roof rests on corbels, two
of them in the form of crudely carved heads. Most of the
fixtures and fittings in the nave – the pews, pulpit, jaunty
floor tiles and some of the monuments – are Victorian. Set
into the wall to the right of the wall monument to Herbert

Checkendon: the interior looking east

Angel corbel on north wall of nave

and Maud Rothbart by Eric Kennington (filling the now-blocked north doorway) is a lovely small medieval corbel of a curly-haired angel holding a book.

At the head of the nave is a monumental Norman chancel arch. Like the south doorway, the arch has typical Norman roll mouldings. In the capitals, however, the earthiness of beasts gives way to the decorum of refined plant forms and ornate interlace. The differences in style between the capitals on each side of the arch suggest the work of two different hands. Furthermore, the fleshier foliage of the capitals to the south is closer in character to Early English stiff-leaf and feels later. The second arch beyond essentially echoes the first, though on a smaller scale.

Between the two arches is the choir, texture-wise the richest part of the church's interior. Here the walls are unplastered, the whitewashed flints lined up as if on narrow shelves of mortar. Below, the floor is tactile with brasses and the nibbled surfaces of medieval tiles. The fine brass on the south side is to John Rede (died 1404), the figure framed beneath a delicate architectural canopy. The brasses on the north side show Walter Beauchamp (*c*.1430) borne aloft by collared angels, and Anne Bowett (died 1490) standing in prayer.

Other interesting monuments occupy the walls here, including a Jacobean monument to Richard Braybrooke (died 1629) and his wife on the south side, the couple kneeling before one another; and a later one to Henry Knappe (died 1673) on the north side, with strange, bird-like putti below. On the north wall is a finely drawn fragment of wall painting. A man appears on the left-hand side, apparently leaning in to whisper something to his horse.

Up further steps to the east is the rounded apse, a cosy space with enough room for an altar and little else. Around its walls are thirteenth-century wall paintings in pinky-reds. Cut-out figures of Apostles tread as if across stepping stones through a sea of flowers, towards a pair of arches and the Kingdom of Heaven beyond. Overhead, Christ sits in Majesty, leafy tendrils curling from the legs of his stool. Turning round and looking west through the arches, the south door is visible at the other end of the church. Somehow it feels further from there to here than it actually is.

Wall painting of Christ in Majesty

ALSO OF NOTE

Plain octagonal C15 font at W end of nave; engraved glass window by Lau-
rence Whistler to Eric Kennington in S wall of nave (Kennington, d. 1960, was
artist friend of Lawrence of Arabia, whose 'The Seven Pillars of Wisdom' he
illustrated); eye-catching C20 mosaic wall monuments of St George to Moon
family on N and W walls of nave; variety of mainly C18 wall monuments
grouped at NE of nave and on S wall of choir; large floor monument to
Blackall family in porch.

• • •

CHIPPING NORTON
ST MARY
Stately 'wool' church with fine stonework and soaring nave

Chipping Norton from the south-east

The setting for Chipping Norton church, tucked away
near to the bottom of the hill on which the town sits,
seems at first incongruous, particularly given the ambition
and self-assertiveness of the building. However, before
c.1200, it was here that settlement was concentrated,
in the shadow of church and castle. Only in the early
thirteenth century was a new town centre and market
place established further up the hill, effectively shifting the
town's commercial and residential centre of gravity up
and away from the church.

Much of the church belongs to the thirteenth and
fourteenth centuries. However, its most celebrated parts,
the nave and clerestory, belong to the mid fifteenth century. Responsibility for their commission has traditionally
been attributed to John Ashfield (wrongly described as a
local wool merchant). In fact, the works are more likely
to be linked to the establishment of the town's Trinity
Guild in 1450. The clerestory is the most striking of any
Oxfordshire church. Glass has all but usurped stone, with
the wall itself reduced to a fine, grid-like lattice for the
glazing. Clerestories were a popular addition to English
churches at this time, but in few is the ratio of glass area
to wall area so high.

A range of mainly thirteenth- and fourteenth-century
windows light the chancel and side aisles. Of these, the
great Decorated window at the east end of the south
aisle is by far the finest: a brilliant composition of six lights

Decorated south aisle east window

topped by a wheel of trefoils that turns forever clockwise; the 'direction of travel' indicated by the five outermost mouchettes. Legend has it that the window was brought here from nearby Bruern Abbey at the Dissolution, but there is no evidence for this. Although it appears not to fit comfortably here – its head on the point of bursting up through the parapet above – the discrepancy is simply accounted for by the flattening of the pitch of the aisle roof in the fifteenth century.

Also on the south side is the unusual hexagonal porch, a handsome two-storey structure whose vaulted ceiling is made unforgettable by its carved bosses. Various mask-like faces hover in the shadows. One belongs to a bearded green man with the leafy tendrils of a vine sprouting from his nostrils (possibly identifying the figure as that of Christ); another belongs to a lion who sticks out his tongue irrev-erently, but without discrimination, at all who pass below.

Green man boss inside south porch

Inside, the barbarism of the porch gives way, in a most dramatic fashion, to the cerebral finesse of the nave: a soar-ing, light-washed space to rival the naves of Northleach or Chipping Campden. This is Perpendicular architecture at its most accomplished, and has been attributed by John Har-vey (*The Perpendicular Style*) to master mason John Smyth, on the basis of striking similarities between the nave piers here and in Canterbury Cathedral. The window tracery of the clerestory, the blind tracery of the triforium and the spandrels of the arches below are all treated as seam-less parts of an architectural whole. The narrow clustered shafts of the piers are carried from floor level, unbroken, up to the wall-posts of the roof high above. Throughout, the decoration is cool and crisp and precise.

If there is a problem with the nave, it is only that it feels proportionately too short for its height (but then this was an adapted rather than an entirely new space). The effect is most pronounced when looking west from the chancel step, and is accentuated by the fact that the north aisles are longer than the nave, and extend beyond its west wall.

The nave, both literally and architecturally, puts the rest of the interior in the shade. The side aisles, and espe-cially the cave-like chancel, seem gloomy by comparison, with less to remember them by. The north aisles are divided from one another by an arcade which follows the

North arcade stiff-leaf capital

Chipping Norton: the Perpendicular nave and clerestory

course of the earlier north wall of the church. The arcade incorporates earlier fabric, including fourteenth-century octagonal piers and a thirteenth-century stiff-leaf capital on its easternmost pier.

There are several interesting monuments – although perhaps not as many as one might expect for such an eminent church. At the east end of the north aisle is an early sixteenth-century chest-tomb to Richard Croft (died 1502) and his wife (died 1509). At the other end is a later chest-tomb to Thomas Rickardes (died 1570) and his wife. This latter is scored with old graffiti and probably once had a canopy. Other monuments cling to the wall above. Arrayed along the north wall are several brasses mounted on wood.

ALSO OF NOTE

Tower rebuilt 1825 (but some C12 fabric in E wall); C15 gargoyles around chancel; unusual C16 or C17 windows with un-cusped panel tracery in N wall; battlemented mausoleum on N side of church (erected by Henry Dawkins of Over Norton in 1800); surround of inner S door with band of large ballflower with stems; E clerestory window has rare traceried curtain arch; trio of canopied niches to N of chancel arch probably once reredos to earlier chapel enclosed by screens (cf. Burford); two further empty niches above flanking E clerestory window; C14 octagonal font at W end of S aisle with blind tracery on each face (cf. Lower Brailes, Warwickshire).

Decorated octagonal font

• • •

CHISLEHAMPTON
ST KATHERINE
Unspoilt small Georgian church

St Katherine's is a rare example of a complete surviving eighteenth-century church. Natty and compact, it might best be described as 'parochial classical' in style. And yet despite (indeed, partly because of) its lack of sophistication, it remains one of the most charming churches in the county. This enchantment might be the greater if it stood, not by the side of an alarmingly fast road, but in a parkland setting (like Rycote's or Wheatfield's perhaps).

In essence, the church is a simple, rectangular box with a pitched roof; and were it not for a handful of flourishes

Chislehampton from the east

Chislehampton: the west front and clock tower

(most obviously the jazzy little clock tower) its outward appearance might be quite forgettable. It was built in 1763 for Charles Peers of nearby Chislehampton House, and may be the work of that house's architect, Samuel Dowbiggin (though there is no documentary evidence for this).

Whoever it was, their deployment of the classical is certainly unusual. The western gable takes the form of an oddly proportioned scrolled pediment; four large urn finials, standing on the ledge formed by a continuous entablature, mark the corners of the church; and the ashlar quoins of the main structure are echoed in the rusticated quoins of the clock tower. The church was derided in the nineteenth century by the Gothic Revivalist, John Henry Parker, who was especially scornful of the clock tower, characterising it as, 'such as is usually placed on stables'. Parker was correct, but this needn't be taken as an affront.

The church is entered via a doorway which, if seen in isolation, could be mistaken for the side entrance to a Georgian house. Inside, further quirks become evident. The church is lit solely by a quartet of round-headed windows in the south wall. The other walls, including the east wall, are windowless. As with the outside, the architecture is classical but unconventional. For example, the pilasters lining the walls are not supported on moulded bases, but on console brackets (in order to keep them clear of the box pews below).

Interior looking east

The interior is a single undivided room, the only architectural acknowledgement of the sanctuary being a recess in the east wall. The sober furnishings (with the notable exception of the richer, Jacobean pulpit, which probably came from an earlier chapel) are all eighteenth-century, and original to this church. They include the plain, high-backed box pews (whose benches face both ways, like compartments in a railway carriage); a west gallery supported on Tuscan Doric columns; and the altar rails and altarpiece at the east end. The altarpiece is inscribed with the Lord's Prayer, the Decalogue and the Creed, with titles or first lines breaking into a flurry of curls, black on gold. Most of the memorials, together with the single piece of stained glass, are to the Peers family who built the church.

• • •

CHURCH HANBOROUGH
ST PETER AND ST PAUL
Village church with fine tympanum, nave and screens

The two Hanboroughs could not be more different. While Long Hanborough is new and sprawling – its growth fed by, and channelled along, a busy main road – Church Hanborough is its ancient backwater, bestilled and bypassed. Both have their churches, but only one is worth a visit. The church of St Peter and St Paul stands amid cottages and a pub, a twelfth-century structure wrapped in later fabric, each of whose building campaigns has gifted it features of the highest quality.

Church Hanborough from north-east

The proportions of the church when viewed from the north are a little odd. The stepped forms of chancel, short nave and west tower with spire rise up from behind a parapet-topped wall that runs unbroken from one end of the church to the other. The original Norman church probably consisted of a chancel (possibly with chapels), an aisled nave and a west tower. In the thirteenth century the chancel was remodelled and the porches added. In the fifteenth century the tower was rebuilt and a spire added, a clerestory inserted and the interior remodelled.

Externally, a number of round-headed windows and doorways betray the church's twelfth-century origins. Most memorable of all is the north doorway. Chunkily-carved, it has a delightful tympanum depicting St Peter flanked by the Lamb of God and the Lion of St Mark (the wing of the lion carved to look like the fingers of a stroking hand).

The church can be entered through this door or, better still, the west door beneath the tower, as this gives an enticing vista down the nave to the medieval screens and chancel beyond. Once in the nave, the full extent of the changes carried out in the fifteenth century becomes clear. The highly distinctive nave arcades, although of only three bays, are a match for those found in several larger and richer Cotswold churches (literally a match in the cases of Chipping Campden and Northleach, the nave arcades of all three being so alike that a common mason has been proposed). As at Chipping Norton, the remodelling of the nave must have profoundly altered the character of this space. The Norman arcade would have

Norman tympanum over north door

had rounded arches carried on heavier, shorter piers. The roof was then lower (note the weather-moulds above the tower arch), and there were no clerestory windows to light the space.

At the head of the nave and aisles is a fine and unusually complete set of medieval screens, whose deployment across the whole width of the church is more redolent of a West Country set than one found in the Midlands. What makes these screens especially unusual is the amount of late medieval colour that still clings to their timbers. Although fragmentary, the paint scheme echoes that found on a handful of other screens in England and Wales, with reds and greens alternating across the wainscot, gilding on the carved trails and spiralling along some of the mouldings in a 'barber's pole' pattern, and dark blue on the loft coving.

The screens' lack of uniformity suggests they are not of one build, as one might expect. It is also possible that they are the work of different carpenters or workshops; a theory given weight by the variation in decorative treatment of the screens. Related to this, although one might reason that both loft coving and bressumer, and thus rood-loft, originally extended unbroken across the whole width of the church, the evidence suggests otherwise. The bressumer of the north aisle screen is higher and of a different cross-section; its loft coving of steeper pitch, than that of the south aisle screen. It has been suggested by F. E. Howard (*Screens and Rood-Lofts in the Parish Churches of Oxfordshire*) that the south aisle screen is the earliest and the north aisle screen is much later.

The chancel was less heavily altered in the fifteenth century, and retains much that is recognisably of the thirteenth century, and Early English rather than Perpendicular in character. This includes the chancel arch with its clustered shafts and moulded capitals, the two lancets in the south wall, the footings of the jamb shafts originally flanking the east window, and the string course (which echoes that surviving on the south and east walls externally). Cut into the chancel arch is a series of mortise holes: five in its innermost face, and six smaller ones in its innermost chamfered face to the east. It is possible that the larger holes were for timbers that supported the

Perpendicular nave capital

Rood-screen vine trail carving

Church Hanborough: the south aisle portion of the rood-screen

Rood, while the smaller holes held timbers belonging to a screen tympanum.

The side aisles extend beyond the east wall of the nave to form short chapels flanking the chancel. Over the altar in the east wall of the north chapel is a pair of trefoil-headed niches, surprisingly and beautifully painted with white Tudor roses arrayed in a diagonal lattice against a red ground. In the south chapel, meanwhile, is the door-way and narrow, mural staircase to the lost rood-loft.

ALSO OF NOTE

C13 King and Queen label-stops on outside wall to either side of renewed E window; Norman S doorway (now hidden by boiler room) with tympanum with incised cross; unusual C15 octagonal font at W end of nave with Instruments of the Passion; C15 nave ceiling with eight large head-corbels of same date; restored C15 pulpit at E end of nave, on central stem with spreading ribs and blind tracery to panelled faces (cf. Charlton-on-Otmoor); fragments of C15 glass (Tudor roses against foliate background in SE window of S aisle); C15 rectangular aumbry in S wall of S aisle with original framing; arched recess with brass figure in winding sheet (Dr Alexander Belsyre, d. 1567) in S wall of chancel; C15 door to vestry in N wall of chancel with decorative ironwork hinges.

• • •

COMBE
ST LAURENCE
Picturesque church with fine stonework and wall paintings

Combe from the south-east

Combe once lay in the valley suggested by its name, but has long since climbed out. It now lies strung out across higher ground north of the river Evenlode. The outline of an early church survives down by the river, but the current church stands on an elevated site on the eastern fringes of the village. The setting is a lovely one. Approached by a rising, curving path, the church looks out over a cricket pitch to the north-east, and open countryside and wood-land to the south.

The church has a symmetrical plan, of chancel, nave, north and south porches, and west tower. The nave and tower represent well-balanced and largely unspoilt work of the late fourteenth or early fifteenth century, with matching three-light Perpendicular windows occupying the same three bays in the north and south walls, and an attractive parapet with blind quatrefoils. A painting of c.1816 shows the nave buttresses topped with pinnacles that match those on the tower, further animating the roofline of the nave, and creating a stronger visual relationship between nave and tower. Sadly, the pinnacles were removed in c.1820 during repairs to the roof. The chancel is earlier, and probably belongs to the early fourteenth century (though the windows, and most visibly the five-light east window, are later).

Parapet with quatrefoil decoration

The two porches are also interesting. Architecturally, the north porch is the finer of the two, having a well-moulded doorway, angle buttresses and a stone coped gable, topped with a fleur-de-lis finial with a date stone for 1395 (it was remodelled in 1595). Unusually, it is roofed in stone slabs. The south porch is plainer, but has a reused early twelfth-century round-arched inner doorway, indicating that an earlier church may have occupied the site. This porch, which is of similar size (if not status) to the north porch, may have been primarily for the use of the manor house next door (note the gate in the churchyard wall).

The interior of the church has a welcoming, roomy character, due to an unusually wide nave and chancel arch, with both nave and chancel being uniformly well-lit by expansive and mostly plain-glazed windows. The breadth of the chancel opening, which is fully as wide as the chancel beyond, has the effect of making the chancel seem more like an extension of the nave than a separate and distinct compartment in its own right.

Interior looking east

The main delights of the interior are the wall paintings and the carved stonework. Of the latter, three features are of particular interest. Set into the south wall of the chancel is a lovely trio of fourteenth-century sedilia. This robustly carved and happily proportioned example of Decorated workmanship has flower cusps that telescope back the full depth of the cinquefoil canopies above, and partitions pierced by trefoil openings.

In the south-east angle of the nave is a fine, Decorated image niche, probably slightly later in date. Sixteenth-century accounts mention an altar to 'Our Lady', which almost certainly stood before the niche and against the east wall of the nave; the niche itself possibly containing a statue of

the Virgin. It has been suggested that the niche may have been relocated tight against the south wall of the nave sometime in the fifteenth century, possibly to provide a visual balance for the rood-loft doorway on the north side.

Finally, on the north side of the nave, there is a rare and unusual fifteenth-century stone pulpit. Rather than standing on the floor, it is mounted on the wall with its base springing from a head corbel (thus recalling the refectory pulpits found in some abbey churches, including Beaulieu in Hampshire). The faces of the pulpit are divided into six compartments of blind tracery, each one different. This form of decoration is also common to fonts of both the Decorated and Perpendicular periods (including, for example, those at Faringdon and Chipping Norton).

Blind-traceried stone pulpit

The wall paintings, which date from the first half of the fifteenth century, were uncovered in 1892 having lain behind later paintwork for perhaps three centuries. Although fragmentary, they are full of interest. Over the chancel arch is a lively and crowded Last Judgement (or 'Doom'). The missing lower half of Christ was almost certainly painted on the upper parts of a screen tympanum. As is generally the case with Dooms, the fate of the Damned is arguably more compelling than the fate of the Blessed (by design perhaps, the didactic tradition then apparently favouring sticks to carrots). At Combe, the Damned are jostled and tipped into a gaping, toothy maw. Inside, a waiting devil sticks his tongue out at the congregation below and shrugs. The treatment is cartoonish, but the message unambiguous.

Below, to the left of the chancel arch, is a repainted Crucifixion. In it, blood pours from Christ's side as if from a tipped jug, drips from his forehead in a shower of beads, and runs down his arms in red tendrils. At the east end of the south wall is a fragmentary Angel of the Annunciation, looking across towards the niche that probably contained a statue of the Virgin. In the same wall, to either side of the south door, are several aquatic creatures that once framed a large St Christopher. These include fish, a mermaid and possibly an otter. The depictions are supple and dynamic, and represent arguably the most tantalising painted fragments in the church. The over-painting of the old figure of St Christopher with the Ten Commandments

Detail of Crucifixion wall painting

Combe: the Decorated triple sedilia in the chancel

is the clearest possible manifestation of the post-Reformation policy of replacing 'superstitious' images with the Word of God.

ALSO OF NOTE

Mid C15 glass in top lights of some windows in chancel and nave, including 30 almost identical cherubim with wheels (a reference to Ezekiel 10: 'And when the cherubims went, the wheels went by them: and when the cherubims lifted up their wings to mount up from the earth, the same wheels also turned not from beside them'); also, smaller fragments, including small birds, in nave E windows; C15 stairwell to N of chancel archway, with upper doorway at height of missing rood-loft (note painted flower, like ship's propeller, on 'ceiling' of upper doorway); much weathered, probably late medieval cross base in SE corner of nave, hollowed out for use as a font; handful of C14 encaustic tiles on floor in SE corner of nave; green velvet silk altar hanging in glass case on N wall of nave; C15 octagonal font at W end of nave.

Detail of medieval stained glass

• • •

COMPTON BEAUCHAMP
ST SWITHUN
Delightful chalk church with idiosyncratic interior

Compton Beauchamp church stands at the foot of the Berkshire Downs, a little white building in a landscape of chalk. Compton Beauchamp itself is less a village than a loose scattering of houses, and the church could be a private chapel, such is its size and its proximity to the house along whose driveway it is reached. The church stands in a sheltered churchyard beyond the house, accompanied by a number of hefty chest-tombs. Close by, a pigeon loft stands in a garden of remembrance like a summer house.

Compton Beauchamp from the west

Unusually, the church is constructed from chalk or clunch, with some sarsen stone in the tower and nave. Most of the surviving fabric, including the tower, chancel and possibly the north transept (though this may be slightly later) dates from the thirteenth century. The south transept was added in the fifteenth century (but rebuilt in c.1911). Windows from all three periods survive: plain lancets in the chancel side walls, reticulated tracery in the east window, and square-headed Perpendicular in the south transept. The tower, already diminutive, was made

Compton Beauchamp: the painted chancel

Sacred
to the Memory of
THOMAS LANGLEY
late Rector of this Parish
who departed this Life
May 11 1731 Aged 56 Years
In the Church Yard
near the North Wall of the Chancell
at her own desire
lieth the Body of ELIZ LANGLEY Widow of
THOMAS LANGLEY late Rector of this Parish
who departed this Life
May 11 1766 Aged 91 Years
Underneath
lieth the Body of ELIZABETH Daughter of
THOMAS LANGLEY and ELIZ his Wife
who departed this Life
Sept 23 1764 Aged 58 Years
Near this Place
lieth the Body of RACHEL Daughter of
THOMAS LANGLEY and ELIZ his Wife
who departed this Life
Oct 3 1749 Aged 37 Years
And near this Place
lieth the Body of ANN Daughter of
THOMAS LANGLEY and ELIZ his Wife
who departed this Life
Sept 4 1762 Aged 47 Years

Interior looking east

Painted owl on ledge of monument

to seem smaller still when the nave was raised in height in the fifteenth century.

While the neat exterior appears conventional enough, the interior is one of the most original and eccentric of any Oxfordshire church. This is due to the addition, early in the twentieth century, of carved fittings better suited to a Catholic church in southern Europe, and painted decoration that would be more at home as wallpaper in an Arts and Crafts house.

The woodwork at least is by the designer and artist Martin Travers, who restored the church in the 1930s at the behest of a local man, Samuel Gurney. Travers, like his patron, was Anglo-Catholic, and was responsible for several higher-profile commissions in London and elsewhere (most notably perhaps the reredos in St Magnus the Martyr, London Bridge). All the woodwork at Compton Beauchamp, minus only the pews, is his: the altar, altar rail, screens, Rood, font cover and the Madonna and Child in the tower alcove at the west end. The rood-figures and the Madonna and Child in particular look out of place here, like souvenirs from the Grand Tour. Travers was also responsible for the rather weak east window, which contains some early glass in its upper lights, including an Annunciation.

Despite appearances, the astonishing stencilled decoration in the chancel predates the woodwork. It was apparently carried out in *c.*1900 by Lydia Lawrence, a member of the Kyrle Society (which produced decorative murals for, among other places, schools and hospitals). While naturalistic vines ramble across the chancel walls, lilies and roses with the stylised quality of graphic art occupy the window reveals. It is hard to believe that the same person was responsible for both, so divergent is their treatment. As if all this lacked for interest, in *c.*1967 an array of fauna was added to the existing flora, including two kingfishers, two swallows, a bat, a dragonfly and – as if perched on top of the wall monument to the Langleys – a watchful owl.

ALSO OF NOTE

C15 octagonal font with quatrefoils inside N door; painted Georgian arms over N door; C18 wall monuments, including to Langleys and Hawkeswells in chancel, and to Rachel Richards (d. 1737) and daughter Anne (d. 1771) on opposing

sides of nave — the former with long and lovely inscription; C14 Crucifixion in
E window of N transept; painted and gilded plaque to St Swithun on S side
of entrance to chancel (by Travers); medieval pillar piscina and unusual bench
sedilia on S side of chancel; several C18 chest tombs to Langleys in churchyard,
most of uniform design and with big lettering (some with colour).

• • •

DORCHESTER
ABBEY OF ST PETER AND ST PAUL
Large abbey church with exceptional stonework and tracery

Dorchester, like Abingdon, is one of the early centres of
Christianity in Britain. A church was established here by
Birinus in the seventh century. Apart from some evidence
of Saxon fabric in the foundations of the north wall, the
earliest surviving parts (above ground at least) date from
the middle of the twelfth century, when the church was re-
founded as an Augustinian abbey by the Bishop of Lincoln.   *Dorchester from the south-west*
Dorchester is one of only two surviving monastic churches
in the county (the other one being Oxford Cathedral).

The current church is an unforgettable, in parts eccentric, building, most of whose fabric dates from the thirteenth
and fourteenth centuries, when the existing Norman cruciform church was dramatically enlarged and remodelled.
Disentangling the church's history is hampered both by its
self-evident complexity, and the loss of all archives relating
to its pre-Dissolution development.

Outside, the two most striking characteristics of the
church are its tremendous length, and the quality and
originality of its window tracery. Several key phases in the
development of Gothic window design are spectacularly
showcased, including geometric tracery of the late thirteenth century (north choir aisle), intersecting tracery of
the early fourteenth century (south wall), and curvilinear
tracery of the mid fourteenth century (sanctuary).

In terms of originality, while the south windows are
of a fairly standard type, those lighting the sanctuary at
the east end are quite unlike anything else to be found
in the county. Unusually, the tracery in all three windows
occupies not only the head of the window, but the whole
expanse of the opening.

Intersecting tracery in south windows

Geometric north aisle window

Furthermore, set into the base of the south sanctuary window, within deeply arched reveals, are four small windows of highly unusual, rounded-triangular form. Remarkably, these turn out to be integral to the sedilia within. The east window, bisected by an invasive but structurally necessary buttress, has reticulated tracery carried down to the sill, its pattern reminiscent of the winding tracks that raindrops make as they run down glass. The famous north window, studded with figure sculpture on the inside, is no more than a delicate, tree-like armature on the outside.

The windows lighting the north choir aisle, although less striking, are outstanding examples of geometric tracery. Of these, the larger of the two three-light windows is the finest. Here, as well as employing an attached shaft topped by a stiff-leaf capital in one of the window reveals, the mason has gone to the unusual length of having the tracery spring from still finer shafts on the inner reveals and mullions.

The north wall of the nave is the most substantial surviving part of the twelfth-century church, and retains one of its original full-height, round-headed windows at its west end. The two reticulated windows at its east end were inserted in the fourteenth century. The 'cloister' below, which houses a permanent display of stonework from the Abbey, was added in 2002 on the site of the former south cloister walk. No trace of the original cloisters and monastic buildings that once occupied the now denuded area to the north of the church remains (though the fifteenth-century abbey guesthouse survives to the west). The west tower, added in the fourteenth century but rebuilt in 1602, may have replaced a Norman central tower. It has corner turrets of flint and stone chequerwork (similar to Henley's) and is made to seem less mighty than it might otherwise be by the magnitude of the adjoining church.

Inside, the disparity between the western and eastern halves of the church is stunning – as if the building had been tipped up and all its riches had slid to the east end. The fifteenth-century south porch opens into a south aisle and nave beyond, whose relative lack of interest is entirely at odds with their scale. The aisle was added in the mid fourteenth century, causing the old outer wall of the south transept to become an inner wall (note the

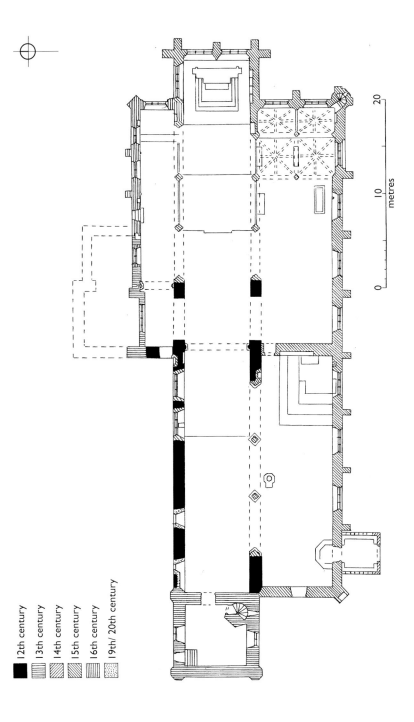

12th century
13th century
14th century
15th century
16th century
19th/ 20th century

metres

0   10   20

FIG. 9 Dorchester Abbey of St Peter and St Paul

drip-mould over the doorway to the north of the altar). The raised altar is explained by the presence of a vaulted charnel house below, built to take bones displaced from the graveyard by the encroachment of the south aisles.

Although comparatively bare, the western half of the church is by no means lacking in interest. The c.1170 lead font is among the finest surviving examples of English Romanesque metalwork. It is one of sixteen Norman lead fonts to survive in England, and one of five in Oxford-shire (the others being at Long Wittenham, Warborough, Childrey and Woolstone). The Dorchester font, however, is most closely related to the font at Walton-on-the-Hill in Surrey, with both featuring Apostles seated beneath a continuous arcade. For a time, the font was mounted on a Perpendicular octagonal stem with blind, cusped arches, rather than the current plain, cylindrical base.

Norman lead font of c.1170

On a pier close to the font is an incongruous piece of fourteenth-century sculpture, brilliantly carved with monks dozing among oak leaves. It looks like an overly heavy capital that has slid down its pier, and may have been relocated here (possibly from the monks' chapter-house) for use as a base for statues. The easternmost bay of the nave arcade contains the remains of the medieval screen that once divided the people's chapel from the monastic nave beyond. Set into the floor at its foot are scraps of medieval tiles.

Of the two halves of the church, the eastern half wit-nessed the more dramatic changes during the thirteenth and fourteenth centuries. The catalyst for some of these may have been the removal to Dorchester of the relics of St Birinus in 1225. The north choir aisle and a now-lost north chapel both date from this time. The north aisle has Early English attached shafts within, and a string course without, but was remodelled later in the thirteenth cen-tury when it gained its current buttresses and fine win-dows. It seems likely that there was a corresponding south aisle, but all traces of this were swept away when the cur-rent south choir aisle was added in the early fourteenth century. The addition of the south aisles together gave a south elevation of seven similar but not identical bays (note the change in buttress design and the slight increase in window height outside).

South pier carving of monks

Dorchester: the choir, sanctuary and great east window

Green man carving in south chapel

The south choir aisle was built to provide a fitting and spacious setting for a new marble shrine to St Birinus (constructed in 1320, destroyed at the Reformation, and replaced by the current shrine in 1964). The aisle is home to a pair of chapels and a large collection of monuments at its east end, all beneath a vaulted ceiling added by George Gilbert Scott in 1872 (though apparently intended by the medieval builders, as evidenced by the fourteenth-century vaulting shafts). On the south side of the south chapel is a dazzling piscina, its traceried gable roofed with leaves and flanked by tall pinnacles. With great ingenuity, a matching gable was inserted to frame the adjoining door in the corner of the chapel. Above this, the vaulting shafts spring from the head of a fearsome green man, and even the string course is terminated by a small head.

The south choir aisle contains an interesting and varied quartet of effigies. On the north side is the now-faceless fourteenth-century effigy of a bishop, the folds of his robes like a frozen waterfall. East of this, scored with graffiti, is a fourteenth-century alabaster effigy of a knight (possibly a member of the Segrave family) on a Decorated chest-tomb. Against the south wall is a third fourteenth-century effigy, of John de Stonor (died 1354). The platform-like canopy on his head makes him look like a caryatid (or 'telamon') tipped onto its back.

Centre stage, however, is taken by an astonishing late thirteenth-century effigy of an unidentified knight (possibly Sir John de Holcombe, or William de Valance). He is depicted as if startled awake, rolling over from lying on his side, at the point of unsheathing his sword. The moment is one of extreme physical tension, yet the composition and modelling are fluid. The knight's tunic ripples across his chest like a pool into which a stone has been dropped.

The floors of both the choir and south choir aisle are pock-marked with the indents of lost brasses, compelling in their own right, echoes of the figures and foliate crosses they once held. Just a couple of brasses now survive, including an undamaged brass of Abbot Bewfforeste (c.1510) in the choir. The surprise, perhaps, is not that so many brasses were taken up during and after the Reformation, but that any were allowed to remain.

Although its chronology is disputed, the choir arcade

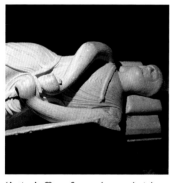

'Action' effigy of an unknown knight

was probably added at the same time as the south aisle, in the early fourteenth century. This is surely the finest arcade in the county, its clustered piers supporting moulded arches of supreme finesse. In c.1340, the chancel was extended through the addition of a rectangular sanctuary at its east end, and the new sanctuary lit by three memorable windows. All three have tracery studded with figure sculpture and hoods studded with ballflower, and all retain an unusual quantity of fine medieval stained glass.

Detail of choir arcade

The east window fills most of the east wall with a web of tracery. It was restored in the nineteenth century when William Butterfield added the rose window, and retains panels of fourteenth-century glass, including scenes from the Bible and the lives of the saints. The south window has twenty-one armorial shields of c.1300, most belonging to local noble families of the time. Below this stands the church's triple sedilia and piscina: a riotous composition of gables and pinnacles encrusted with figures, beasts and foliage. It is vaulted within and lit by the unusual little windows visible outside. Framed by tiny ballflowers, the windows are glazed with thirteenth-century medallions depicting scenes from the life of St Birinus.

Detail of great east window

The Jesse window on the north side of the sanctuary fully deserves its fame, depicting a single theme through a unique fusion of tracery, sculpture and stained glass. The figure of Jesse himself reclines on the ledge of the window, the trunk and limbs of the Tree spreading from his loins to form the tracery above. His descendants are presented both three-dimensionally, in figure sculpture at the intersections of the tracery, and two-dimensionally, in the stained glass. Of the sculpture, only Christ is lost, broken off the central mullion where this divides near the top of the window.

ALSO OF NOTE

C14 wall paintings at E end of S aisle, including small Crucifixion behind altar restored by Clayton & Bell in C19; head of medieval preaching cross on window ledge on S side of S aisle (cross outside S porch); some C14 glass in N window of nave, including three further armorial shields; doorway to roodloft on S side of chancel arch; C16 choir stalls with crozier and scroll with name of Abbot Bewfforeste on stall end; C14 piscina with traceried opening and crocketed gable in S wall of sanctuary; C13 arch with stiff-leaf at W end

of N chapel; opening with flue (possibly for baking communion wafers) in N wall of N chapel; triple aumbry in N wall of N chapel; mid C13 roundel of St Birinus in E window of N chapel; damaged C14 piscina with foliage-carved bowl and elaborately moulded hood in S wall of N chapel; collection of medieval and later ledgers and gravestones paving floor of S choir aisle; buttress at SW corner of exterior with C13 niche probably reused here in C14; buttress immediately E of sanctuary N window incorporates dogtooth moulding of C12 character; tower contains ring of eight bells: two C14, and all but one being original castings.

Decorated sedilia canopies

• • •

DUCKLINGTON
ST BARTHOLOMEW
Village church with superb Decorated chapel

Ducklington from the south-west

Ducklington lies just to the south of Witney, the village now almost a suburb of the town. Despite some nondescript later housing, the old core of the settlement to the south-east remains largely undisturbed; its church standing on a neat platform of a churchyard, overlooking a pond and thatched cottages.

The church might have remained no more than a likeable but unspectacular building of the late twelfth and thirteenth centuries, were it not for the dramatic remodelling of the north aisle in the fourteenth century. It is from this period that most of the surviving work dates: an original c.1200 plan form of aisled nave, chancel and west tower, with notable thirteenth-century alterations, including the chancel and a number of new windows. The east and west windows, together with at least the crenellated upper stage of the tower, belong to the fifteenth century.

Externally, the most striking characteristic is the north aisle tracery. While the windows in the south aisle are small and severe, those in the north aisle, as well as being larger, are among the loveliest and liveliest of any Oxfordshire church. The north aisle windows belong to the first half of the fourteenth century, and are examples of Decorated curvilinear tracery at its most animated. They are related to windows at nearby Witney (north transept) and Cogges (north chapel east window), and it is likely that all are the work of the same band of imaginative and highly

Ducklington: detail of the Decorated north chapel tomb recess

North aisle west window

South arcade waterleaf capital

gifted local masons. The outside of the north aisle is further enriched with three buttresses (also similar to those at Witney) which incorporate trefoil-headed niches, and a doorway topped by two orders of ballflower.

The interior, too, is lifted by the richness and artistry of the north aisle. Except for the nave, the rest of the interior is largely uneventful, though not without its pleasures. The piers and capitals of the south arcade (if not the arches above, which are probably later) are Transitional work of c.1200. The capital to the east is a good example of the mixing of motifs that are late Norman (the intersecting arches) and Early English (the nailhead ornament). The south arcade, lovely in its own right, appears archaic next to the north arcade, erected a hundred and fifty years later. This has clustered piers, whose mouldings are carried over the arches. Its hoods terminate in knotted serpents to the south and head corbels to the north (possibly depicting Edward III and his wife Philippa).

At the west end of the nave is a Norman font decorated with intersecting arches. It looks like a capital planted on a chamfered column base. Above is an open collar truss roof with three early dormer windows (not visible from the outside due to the aisle roofs).

While the south aisle has comparatively little to recommend it, the north aisle positively bristles with Decorated stone carving; the inside more than fulfilling the promise of the outside. Although the presence of a fourteenth-century arcade suggests that the aisle was a new addition at this time, the conspicuous widening and cutting away of the earlier window reveals indicates that this work in fact represents an ambitious remodelling of an existing aisle. Besides the tracery – which serves to enrich not only the exterior but also the interior – the aisle is also encircled by a necklace of ballflower, and inset with a series of recesses at its east end.

Of the recesses, three are now almost devoid of sculpture. The others, with the exception of the recess in the top of the east window (containing the Coronation of the Virgin) have been damaged, possibly during the Commonwealth. Of the surviving sculpture, two pieces are especially engaging. At the east end of the north wall is the Nativity, the swaddled Christ child borne aloft by the nuzzling forms of the ox and ass. Meanwhile, in the top of the otherwise empty uppermost recess to the right of the east window, two feet and the hem of a robe can be made out, as the ascending Christ is caught on the point of exiting this world.

At floor level in the north wall (and mercifully largely undamaged) is perhaps the richest pair of tomb recesses to be found in any Oxfordshire church. The niches are of cusped ogee form, their surfaces lushly carved with a Bacchanalian profusion of heads and vines. In the nook between the canopies, a figure sleeps. Given what may be a branch sprouting from beneath the robes of the figure, and the heads studding the canopies to either side, the carving almost certainly depicts the Tree of Jesse.

Sculpture in south wall of north aisle

ALSO OF NOTE

C17 polygonal pulpit at E end of nave (originally from Magdalen College, Oxford); C18 ledgers in floor of nave; fragmentary wall paintings in S aisle, including C14 Trinity on reveal of E window; fragments of C14 glass in E window of N aisle; restored chancel with C13 lancets, trefoil-headed piscina and credence in S wall, and gabled aumbry in N wall.

• • •

EASINGTON
ST PETER
Simple farmyard church with unspoilt, rustic interior

Easington church lies tucked away behind farm buildings at the end of a lane that rises up over open farmland. Fittingly, the construction of the roof shares much with local barn types, and the building was even used as a store for agricultural bric-a-brac in the first half of the twentieth century.

The church is more Welsh than English in its proportions, being small and low to the ground, with nave and chancel in one. It shows little by way of embellishment. Buttresses (especially on the north side) suggest that there may have been problems with the sloping site, and the chancel seems to have been rebuilt: its regularly coursed stonework contrasts with that found in the nave walls. The trefoil lancets and the three-light east window belong to the fourteenth century, but the two larger windows

Easington from the west

in the south wall are Victorian. The two fragments of zig-zag moulding over one of these windows, together with the north doorway with its unfinished quatrefoil decoration and possibly the font, are all that survive from a late twelfth-century church.

The interior is a delight: a chapel-like space, timeworn and welcoming, with high-backed benches and buttermilk walls. The floor is old brick and there is mildew around the font, as if a spring once broke here. The pulpit was remade in 1916 out of seventeenth-century panels (one is dated 1633). On the east wall of the chancel is a red-brown fragment of wall painting. The imagery, what there is of it, is hard to make out, but the plant-forms in the lower half appear to be pomegranates. Traditionally found on the hem of priests' vestments, the pomegranate is also the badge of Katherine of Aragon.

Interior looking east

Besides this, there is little else to see; and when the farm next door falls quiet, there is little else to hear. Just the loudness of the silence.

ALSO OF NOTE

Arch-braced collar-truss roof with curved wind-braces and tie-beams in nave; Queen-post roof in chancel; C14 trefoil-headed piscina in chancel S wall; reset medieval encaustic tiles in chancel floor.

• • •

EWELME
ST MARY
'Suffolk' church with extraordinary tomb and font canopy

Ewelme lies tucked away in a shallow valley at the edge of the Chilterns, its high street strung out along a chalk stream and a number of old watercress beds. The church and adjoining almshouses form a picturesque ensemble at the south-eastern end of the village, the church at the top of a slope and the almshouses tumbling away to the west. It is a place of monastic tranquillity.

Ewelme from the south

The village was home to Alice Chaucer, grand-daughter of the poet Geoffrey Chaucer. Following her marriage to William de la Pole, she became Duchess of Suffolk, and in c.1432 this powerful and wealthy couple endowed the

Easington: the nave looking west

church, almshouses and school. All three buildings remain exceptionally well-preserved.

The Suffolk connection at least partly accounts for the distinctive appearance of the church, which has several characteristics atypical for the county, particularly inside. Only the fourteenth-century tower was not a part of the rebuild, this having been retained from a predecessor on the site. The tower has unusually deep diagonal buttresses (owing to the sloping site) and is rectangular, rather than square, in cross-section.

The body of the church, comprising aisled nave and chancel, belongs to c.1432, and it is possible that builders from Suffolk were employed in its construction. The use of materials is striking, with brick – then a common material in East Anglia, but not in Oxfordshire – present alongside locally occurring flint and limestone. The latter, used separately throughout most of the building, come together in a chequerboard pattern (as at Dorchester and Henley) around the east end. The crenellated parapet is of brick – an arresting feature even now, and one that must have seemed even more so when the material was rare in the county.

Crenellated brick parapets

Entry to the church is through north or south doors, or via its western link with the almshouses below. Inside, it has more in common with the churches of the South-West or East Anglia, having no chancel arch, and a set of screens forming the sole division between aisled nave and aisled chancel beyond. Both the clerestoried arcade and

FIG. 10 Ewelme St Mary

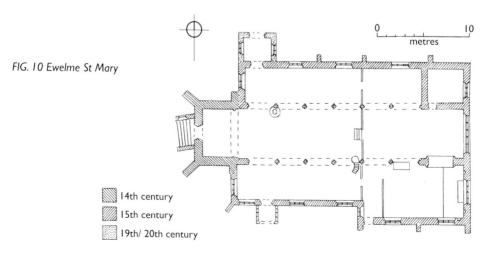

0   10
metres

14th century
15th century
19th/ 20th century

the shallow-pitched ceiling above run unbroken into the chancel. The sprightly arcade only comes to a halt just short of the east wall. The overall impression is of a light and open interior which, despite its spaciousness, retains a human scale and does not overawe.

The west end of the nave is dominated by the spectac-ular font cover; a Tower of Babel-like creation of tier upon tier of cusped and crocketed arches rising from a thicket of carved uprights. Perched on top, like a fairy on a Christ-mas tree, is the angelic figure of St Michael, and overhead is a counterweight in the form of a large Tudor rose. The font cover was given by John, Duke of Suffolk in 1474, and is similar to the equally spectacular covers at Ufford and Worlingworth in Suffolk. Standing on a stepped base below the cover is a perfectly good Perpendicular font, here made to seem incidental by what hovers above – a case of the vessel eclipsed by the lid that was made to serve it.

Font cover at west end of nave

The nave walls are enriched with figurative sculpture, including the bearded head of a king and several shield-bearing angels at the springing points of the arches. The ceiling corbels above include a squatting man and another seemingly on the point of vomiting. Evenly distributed along the paving of the nave and side aisles, meanwhile, are a number of brasses. Although incomplete and vulner-able to footfall, they remain happily free from the runners or mats that often conceal such monuments.

The screens at the east end of the nave and side aisles are also East Anglian in character, having lights that are taller and more slender than is typical for Oxfordshire screenwork. They were lowered in 1844, but restored to their original height in 1925. Unusually, the mullions are now of metal.

The chancel beyond is memorable for its east wall and its monuments. The east wall is lit by a typically shallow-arched and expansive Perpendicular window, surrounded here by a repeated IHS motif (the first three letters of 'Jesus' in Greek) and with an inscription underlined by foliage above. The IHS motif, although restored in 1843, is said to be faithful to the original scheme. The monu-ments include more brasses and a number of fine wall monuments. In a niche on the north side of the chancel is a small and delightfully eccentric monument to Henry

Wall monument to Henry Howard

Howard (died 1647), comprising two angels hauling a man in a shroud from an urn. As a fanciful allegory for rebirth, it is rather effective. On the opposite side of the chancel, eclipsing this in both size and ambition, is the extraordinary tomb of Alice, Duchess of Suffolk, a monument as rich and unflinching as she seems to have been.

The monument is carved from alabaster within a limestone surround, and is the work of a craftsman whose tool marks are those of an engraver. Alice is depicted not once, but twice: firstly, upon the chest-tomb, in the peaceful and familiar pose of one asleep; and secondly, visible through traceried openings at the base of the tomb, in the shocking and unfamiliar form of a decaying corpse. The 'sleeping' Alice has manly features and is simply clad in a long gown, her head resting on a pillow held by exquisite, blade-winged angels. Behind her head is an intricate canopy, whose carving-within-carving defies explanation.

Effigy of Alice of Suffolk

The cadaverous Alice beneath the tomb is a *memento mori* of the most explicit kind. Although caged beneath the crushing weight of the tomb, this second Alice is not quite alone. Astonishingly – and this can only be seen by getting on hands and knees with one's head close to the floor – painted on the underside of the tomb, a few inches from her face, are depictions of the Annunciation and St Mary with St John. The tomb itself is lined by shield-bearing angels, and has vestiges of its original colour scheme. It occupies a magnificent canted recess between the chancel and the chapel of St John, and is overlooked by further angels. Some of these are of stone, and line the recess itself; others are carved from wood, and perch like lookouts on the crenellated turrets above.

Detail of Alice of Suffolk's tomb

The wonderfully preserved chapel of St John provides the tomb with an altogether more intimate setting. The chapel is lined, wallpaper-like, with the IHS pattern. Just as with the chancel, it has a shallow-arched east window with painted foliage and inscription above. To either side of the altar are fine canopied niches, again with some original colour. The general richness is carried up to the ceiling, which has carved bosses at every intersection. Some of these are in the form of angels, wings outstretched as if on the point of dropping into the space below. The ceiling must have been painted once, and its current darkness

Ewelme: the tomb of Alice, Duchess of Suffolk

serves to compress the space somewhat. To the west of Alice's tomb are brasses to her parents, Thomas Chaucer and his wife Maud, inset into the top of a chest-tomb decorated with enamel badge-like armorial shields.

Encaustic tiles in chapel of St John

ALSO OF NOTE

C15 blind-traceried N and W doors, and door to vestry; painted unicorn-topped helmets with arms of Roets and Chaucers between arches on S side of chancel (related female figures on other side of arcade, in chapel of St John); cartouche to Francis Martyn (d. 1682) on N wall of chancel; collection of C15 encaustic tiles around altar in chapel of St John (further fragments around font at W end of nave); 1902 altar and reredos with gold and holly scrolls by Ninian Comper in chapel of St John; C15 pew with poppyheads to W of Chaucer chest-tomb in chapel of St John; collection of mostly C15 glass in E window of chapel of St John, including saints in main lights and armorial shields in tracery lights.

• • •

FARINGDON
ALL SAINTS
Large church with exceptional Early English stonework

Faringdon from the south-east

Of all Oxfordshire's major churches, Faringdon is the most self-effacing. Despite its prominent setting overlooking the market place, it sits long and low, its tower barely clearing the churchyard yews. This modesty is unintentional, result-ing from the loss of its spire during the Civil War, and the subsequent removal of the tower's upper stage. Although not evident from the market place, the church is happily aligned with the south front of Faringdon House to the north, providing the house with an eye-catcher of sorts across its lawns.

Most of the current church belongs to the end of the twelfth century and the first half of the thirteenth. To what extent the church's plan form – cruciform and with a cen-tral crossing tower – respects that of a Norman prede-cessor on the site is not certain. However, the lowermost parts of the west wall of the nave, at least, belonged to an earlier Norman church, and, given the status of the struc-ture as a minster church under the wealthy patronage of the Bishop of Salisbury, this would almost certainly have been a large structure.

From c.1200 onwards, the church was rebuilt from west to east, in a programme spanning the transition between the Norman and Early English styles. The north doorway, reset here when the baptistry was added opposite the south door, is clearly late Norman (of the end of the twelfth century). It has unusual decoration, with a boldly crenellated arch, and jambs with lotus flowers (scratched in on the east side but in deeper relief to the west). The south doorway, through which the church is entered, belongs to a Victorian rebuild. However, the extremely fine south door, whose ornamental hinges terminate in dragons' heads, belongs to the early thirteenth century.

Late Norman north doorway

Inside, the rounded nave arcades and clerestory windows are essentially late Norman. At the crossing, however, rounded arches have given way to pointed arches; and moving east again, the lancet-lit chancel is pure Early English, with no vestige of Norman remaining. The crossing, north transept and chancel all belong to the early thirteenth century. In the fourteenth century, a west aisle was added to the north transept, and in the fifteenth century, the north aisle and north transept chapel were rebuilt. In 1645, during the siege of Faringdon House, the upper parts of the tower and the south aisle and transept were all destroyed, the south side of the church being rebuilt only in 1853 as part of an extensive Victorian restoration.

- ■ 12th century
- ☐ c.1200
- ▥ 13th century
- ▨ 14th century
- ▧ 15th century
- ▦ 19th/ 20th century

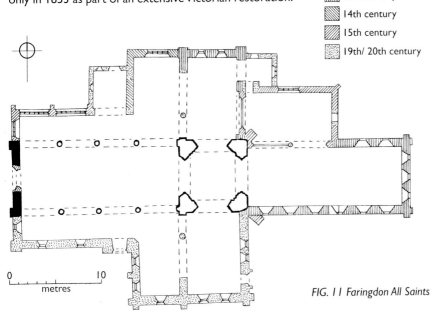

0   10

metres

FIG. 11 Faringdon All Saints

This earlier restoration, together with certain twentieth-century changes, has added to what was already a visually busy interior, and it must be acknowledged that the fine stonework and monuments must vie with other less worthy distractions for the attention of the visitor. The nave is arguably marred by the intrusive organ and internal porch, and the pews and flooring do little for the setting of the existing architectural stonework. Meanwhile, the south transept has rooms on two floors, boxed in with timber and glass, and including a kitchen and toilet: perfectly reasonable for the increased utility of what is evidently a well-used and much-loved church, but unfortunate nonetheless.

When the clutter is overlooked, there is much to enjoy. The nave arcades are of the highest quality and beautifully detailed. Their rounded arches have some decorative banding of light and darker stone. The spandrels between have little quatrefoil niches, which, to judge from those beneath the tower, once contained sculpture. The stiff-leaf capitals are crisply carved and of several designs, with those set against the west wall made richer by their foliate brackets. The bases are also carved, mostly with foliate spurs, but also with a tortoise (south side). The west end of the church is lit by a variety of windows, including a pair of big Perpendicular windows in the north aisle.

Stiff-leaf nave capital

The crossing stonework is even finer than that found in the nave. To stand beneath the tower and turn slowly through 360 degrees is to look upon a gallery of architectural stone-carving to rival that of any Oxfordshire church. While the stiff-leaf carving of the nave capitals reads as surface decoration for the underlying architectural forms, the fleshier and more assorted foliage of the crossing capitals, to varying degrees, defines the forms of these capitals – indeed, sometimes becomes the capital. In the north transept arcade is another fine capital, this one carved with oak leaves and acorns. Some of the acorn cups are empty, as if their acorns had fallen out and might be found littering the floor.

Crossing capitals

The north transept aisle was built as a chapel for the Unton family, and is lit by a fine reticulated window with cusped rere-arches (reminiscent of those at Langford and Bampton). It contains a fascinating collection of

Faringdon: the ironwork of the c.1200 south door

Detail of acorn capital

monuments, the earliest of which is the chest-tomb with alabaster effigies of Sir Thomas Unton (died 1533) and his wife Elizabeth (died 1536). As is often the case with such monuments, dogs serve to lighten the mood. Here, one is a pillow for his master's head, while another leaps playfully on a third at the feet of their mistress. Set into an unusual Purbeck marble monument next to this, there are rare palimpsest brasses to Sir Alexander Unton (died 1547) and his wives (copies of the reverses can be seen on the wall to the east).

The life-sized figure kneeling in prayer, with manly arms almost as thick as her tiny waist, is Lady Dorothy Unton (died 1634). She looks like a ship's figurehead, and originally belonged to a monument that may have included an effigy of Sir Henry Unton (died 1596), who is honoured on the wall monument behind. The fine wall monument above – again coloured – is to Sir Edward Unton (died 1583) and his wife. The standing monument to the right, with its billowing clouds of cherubs, is to Henry Purefoy (died 1687).

To the east, another chapel opens from the north transept. This one belongs to the Pye family, who held the manor in the eighteenth century. One member of the family, Henry James Pye, is notable for becoming Poet Laureate in 1790 despite his spectacular deficiencies as a poet (he was described by the historian Robert Blake as, 'the worst Poet Laureate in English history with the possible exception of Alfred Austin.') The chapel contains a number of unremarkable eighteenth-century Baroque monuments. Set into the floor, however, is a fine slate monument to Tobias Pleydell and his wife, its line-work elegant and spare.

A pair of arches open between the Pye chapel and the chancel next door (the western arch with Perpendicular tracery inserted in the nineteenth century). The addition of a chapel to the north robbed the chancel of what would have been a striking uniformity, with six lancets along each side wall and three more in the east wall. As it is, the chancel is still a memorable space. Unusually, it is marginally longer than the nave. Although heavily restored, it retains a fine triple sedilia and piscina in its south wall, and an interesting collection of old brasses, together with a couple of aumbries.

Green man poppyhead in chancel

ALSO OF NOTE
C15 roof to N aisle; C15 font with blind tracery decoration in baptistry on N side of nave; choir stalls with green man poppyheads in chancel; various interesting monuments in churchyard, including pair of damaged C18 wall monuments between E windows, and several chest-tombs (one with rare shroud-top to E of chancel).

• • •

FREELAND
ST MARY THE VIRGIN
Unspoilt Gothic Revival church with sumptuous chancel

Freeland from the south-east

Most churches are an accretion of parts, but not Freeland. Built in 1869–71, it remains a virtually unaltered time capsule of Gothic Revival architecture and decorative art. The architect was John Loughborough Pearson, designer of some of the finest English churches of the second half of the nineteenth century (including the spectacular Kilburn St Augustine). His patrons, the Taunton family, were dedicated Tractarians. The resultant church neatly embodies both their advocacy of High Church ritual and trappings, and Pearson's admiration for the Gothic architecture of northern France. Pearson also designed the adjacent vicarage and school.

The church consists of a nave, apsidal chancel, south porch and north-east tower. Externally, the tower is the richest and most visually arresting part of the church. It has bell openings with attached shafts and moulded hoods, a peculiar abstract 'corbel table', and a steeply-pitched saddleback roof. Today the church is approached from the south, meaning that the tower is partly concealed on the other side of the building. However, it is clear that Pearson intended church, vicarage and school to be understood as parts of a single composition, and the church to be viewed from the north-west (the tower forming a counterpoint to the now-missing small tower, or *flèche*, on the school to the north). This is confirmed by Pearson's own watercolour of *c*.1865–66, reproduced in the excellent guidebook to the church.

Although the outside is largely free of carved decoration, the treatment of the string courses is interesting.

'Stepped' string courses

Pearson makes no effort to resolve neatly the junctions of the mouldings between chancel and nave, and nave and south porch. Instead, he chooses to have the string course step down unevenly, then die into the east wall of the porch, only to re-emerge slightly lower down to align with the capitals of the outer south doorway. This approach continues inside, and may be an expression of Pearson's belief in 'truth in building'; that parts of a church are distinct from one another, and should be openly treated as such and not artificially resolved to a uniform whole.

After the plainness of the exterior, the treatment of the interior comes as a great surprise. The nave is simple and relatively unadorned, with low-backed pews beneath a dark, pointed barrel vault ceiling. Respecting High Church emphasis of the Sacraments, the font is prominently sited at the west end. One of only two components in the nave to be painted (the other being the pulpit), the font is the wellspring for the church's decorative iconography, which ranges from Christ's Baptism on the font itself, through to his Passion and Resurrection in the chancel – all played out in both stained glass and wall painting.

The chancel beyond is a virtuoso example of Victorian church art and architecture. For Oxfordshire, only the south transept at Buckland is of comparable richness. To fulfil the requirements of High Church practice, it has been raised above the level of the nave and made large enough for a choir and organ. It has a stone quadripartite vault, rounded apse and lancet windows with deep reveals, together giving it a strongly French Gothic flavour. Architecture and wall paintings have been treated as parts of a decorative whole, for example by using similar reds for the stonework of the wall shafts and the adjacent painted scenes; or by allowing the bare plaster or stone behind the scenes to show through and add their own colour.

Although the decorative scheme is intended to recall the spirit of the Middle Ages, the wall paintings and stained glass could only be English and could only belong to the nineteenth century. Both are the work of the firm Clayton & Bell, and the narrative wall paintings in particular owe more of a debt to the Pre-Raphaelites than to their medieval forebears. Indeed, with their blocky colour and stylised line-work, they have the quality of twentieth-century

Murals and glass by Clayton & Bell

Freeland: the choir and sanctuary looking east

graphic art, and look as if they were printed rather than painted onto the surface of the plaster. The effect, like that of the overall design of the church, is one of measured and contained richness.

• • •

GREAT ROLLRIGHT
ST ANDREW
Picturesque church with richly carved south aisle and porch

Great Rollright from the south-east

The village of Great Rollright does not so much occupy this rolling corner of West Oxfordshire, as range over its slopes. Its church seems on the point of drifting away to the north-east, yet remains, transfixed perhaps by the little manor house cupped in the valley below. Despite its modest size, the church features decorative and architectural stonework of great quality and originality. This is concentrated on the unusually rich south aisle and porch, much of it the work of an unknown but highly gifted sculptor in the fourteenth century.

This work represents the most notable in a series of changes witnessed by the church during the Middle Ages. In the thirteenth century, an existing Norman church on the site was enlarged and updated. A side aisle (and the resultant arcade) was added on the south side, and the chancel probably remodelled. In the fourteenth century, the south aisle was remodelled and the porch added. The west tower, clerestory and chancel windows all belong to the fifteenth century.

The south side of the church is lit by a striking collection of windows from the fourteenth and fifteenth centuries. Most unusual of all is the window to the west of the porch. While the vast majority of church window tracery, to a greater or lesser extent, employs standard patterns, this is a true one-off. Its segmental-arched top, its heavily encircled quatrefoils and its label stops (one in the form of an oak branch springing from a man's head) are all highly unusual features for a church window of any date.

The curvilinear tracery of the window to the east of the porch is of a more familiar type. However, the stylised flowers and plant forms (or paterae) lining the window

Detail of south window and cornice

Great Rollright: south window with carved cornice above

Panel-traceried south window

Norman tympanum over south door

reveals are, again, highly unusual. The square-headed windows in the east wall of the side aisle and the chancel are later and of a different character (Perpendicular rather than Decorated). Of these, the four-light window in the south wall is an especially delicate and well-resolved example of panel tracery. The tracery in the chancel east window was restored by George Street in 1852.

There is other stonework of note on the south side. Below the parapet is a cornice of stylised flowers and heads, the hair on some of the female heads resolved to wavy zigzags. At the south-east corner of the south aisle is an angle buttress with an ogee-headed niche: an unusually elaborate detail for a church of this size. Buttresses of a similar character are also a feature of the even richer fourteenth-century north aisle at Ducklington (though stylistic differences between the two extensions would seem to preclude a common workshop source). The two-storey porch also has pinnacles, but these are much eroded. The tower has eight further crocketed pinnacles aligned with the weather-beaten gargoyles jutting from the string course below.

Sheltering inside the porch is the Norman doorway and tympanum, the work of an earlier stone carver who delighted in pattern-making of restless variety. The doorway was reset here when the south aisle was added in the thirteenth century. To either side of the door are two attached shafts with deep scalloped capitals. These support two halos of decoration: an inner one of radiating chevrons, and an outer one consisting of beakheads, with a pair of mysterious, doll-like human figures at the right-hand end.

The remarkable tympanum is crammed with saltire crosses and roundels. However, a beast is also depicted here, together with two partial humans. It has been suggested by Mike Tisdall (*God's Beasts*) that this may be Leviathan disgorging (rather than swallowing) a human head; the person thus being delivered up from death and Hell. The head at the tail end of the creature could be read as that of a dead man wrapped in a shroud or winding cloth.

Inside the church, the chevron moulding over the north door is also Norman. The arcade and the chancel arch belong to the thirteenth century. The tops of the attached shafts of the chancel arch are peculiar, disappearing as they do into the hollowed-out undersides of the capitals above. This quirk probably dates from Street's 1852 restoration (a programme which may have also involved the addition of the neat, lean-to vestry on the north side of the chancel).

Standing against the east side of the chancel arch is a pretty rood-screen. This was brightly (but not inappropriately) repainted in the 1850s. It dates from the fifteenth century, though its covering of paint makes it almost impossible to ascertain what repairs, if any, have been carried out. It would be unusual if all of the fabric were medieval.

High above the chancel arch is a coved and painted portion of timber panelling, the panels divided up by ribs and bosses. This represents a survival even more precious than that of the rood-screen below. It also represents something of a mystery. Its location at least would suggest it is a celure: an extra-decorated portion of roof, forming a canopy of honour for the now-lost Rood below. However, its form is unusual for a celure (though a coved celure of similar form is known to have existed in the now-demolished church of St Martin's, Carfax in Oxford).

Painted rood-screen

In terms of its form and composition, the panelling looks much more like the coved underside of a rood-loft; in which case, what is it doing up here? The screen below offers some clues. When originally erected, the rood-screen would have stood against the western side of the chancel arch. The coving of the rood-loft (and the loft gallery above) would then have sprung westwards from the head-beam of the rood-screen (as it still does at Church Hanborough); the loft gallery being fixed against the west side of the chancel arch.

At some point, most likely during Street's restoration, the screen was moved to its current position on the 'wrong' side of the chancel arch, and the loft coving removed (though the coving might have been removed at an earlier date). This may have been done to address the perceived intrusiveness of the screenwork, or to expose the Early English shafts and capitals of the chancel arch (the move probably leading to the repair of the capitals). Whatever the timing of the removal of the loft coving, while it was deemed undesirable to leave it *in situ*, it was decided not to discard it altogether, but to retain it as a

Loft coving above chancel arch

curio, still on display but out of the way. The paintwork, although almost certainly refreshed, is essentially correct for the underside of a late medieval rood-loft, and may have been based upon existing paint remains.

ALSO OF NOTE

Faint imprint of quatrefoil in S wall of porch to W of lancet over doorway; sundial of 1658 set against parapet of porch above doorway; smallish C15 octagonal font inside S door; nave roof dated 1814, possibly incorporating earlier timbers; small brass to James Batersby (d. 1522) against N wall of chancel; unusual Perpendicular canopied piscina and credence shelf (with some renewed colour) in window splay in SE corner of chancel; much patterned Victorian decorative glass; C15 roundels in tracery lights of one S aisle window; stepped base and stump of medieval cross in churchyard; unusual lychgate (given by nine sons of Henry Randall, in memory of their mother, d. 1905).

• • •

GREAT TEW
ST MICHAEL
Refined parkland church with richly textured interior

Great Tew from the south-west

Great Tew is not quite the time capsule it first appears. Its seventeenth-century cottages were recast as elements in a picturesque landscape by Scottish horticulturalist, John Loudon, in the nineteenth century. Surprisingly perhaps, the church is tucked away further up the valley, barely visible from the main road. It is approached through one of the most unusual church gateways in Oxfordshire, along a straight path flanked by ha-has.

While the cottages of Great Tew are uniformly of the local gingery-brown ironstone, the church makes only intermittent use of this material. Aside from in the tower and chancel, pale limestone dominates. In a pattern seen elsewhere in the county (including at Broughton and Bloxham), the decorative potential of combining light and dark stone is sporadically exploited (for example, in the banding over the blocked doorway and windows of the chancel, and over the south door).

Before the Norman south doorway is reached, the overwhelming impression is of a fifteenth-century Perpendicular church. This is due in large part to the prominent

Great Tew: the interior looking east

clerestory and the west tower, which has *torchère*-like finials at the corners of its crenellated parapets, and a frieze of blind quatrefoils (like those at Church Hanborough). Also Perpendicular are the gargoyles along the north aisle. Centuries of sluicing rain have made the easternmost gargoyle nightmarish, its gaping mouth a hole torn through its head to the sky above.

After all this, the south doorway is quite unexpected. The most conspicuous survivor of a late twelfth-century church on the site, it has a deep halo of chevron carving, jamb shafts with fancy capitals and a later cusped inner arch in place of a tympanum.

Inside, the church is spacious, full of texture and washed by light from a multitude of plain-glazed windows. Despite outward appearances, the present building has a thirteenth-century core, as betrayed by its Early English nave arcades. The piers of the south arcade rest on square bases that may be survivors from an earlier Norman arcade. Meanwhile, the north arcade is striking for the contrast between the pale limestone piers and the darker, tigerish stripes of the later, possibly fourteenth-century, ironstone arches they carry. The church was certainly further altered and enlarged during the fourteenth century, when the north aisle was added, the south aisle widened (note the fourteenth-century aisle windows) and the present chancel arch inserted. Altars evidently stood at the east end of both aisles, as demonstrated by the large piscina in each.

Perpendicular bench ends

The nave, like the exterior, saw the addition of features in the fifteenth century that have overlain it with a Perpendicular character. These include the blind traceried bench ends (an unusually fine and complete set for Oxfordshire) and the hefty octagonal font standing just inside the south door. The timber partition now fencing in the vestry at the east end of the north aisle comprises a portion of the original *c.*1500 rood-screen. It has tracery heads of fleshy foliage (some repaired using plaster) and linenfold wainscot panels. The tracery heads are now blind due to the infilling of the previously open lights above middle rail height.

Detail of screen

On the south wall of the south aisle is a series of faded wall paintings depicting the Passion, only uncovered by conservators in 1988. Beginning top left with the entry into Jerusalem, and ending bottom right with the Resurrection, the narrative is arrayed across five tiers separated by foliate borders, with three scenes per tier. The guidebook speaks of an 'unskilled draughtsman', but much of the line-work here is deft (for example, in the Deposition scene immediately to the left of the Victorian wall monument). The paintings date from the fourteenth century.

South aisle wall paintings

The church is not without its disappointments, a number of which may be attributed to Thomas Rickman, who restored the church in the 1820s. His later ceilings, one of which cuts into the top register of the south aisle wall paintings, look cheap and show little sympathy for the architecture. In the chancel, Rickman was responsible for the reconstituted stone sedilia and piscina, and possibly also the recess housing Chantrey's superb marble figure of Mary Anne Boulton (work which entailed the infilling of a window in the south wall of the chancel to balance out that blocked up in the north wall for the monument itself).

The chancel is rescued by its late medieval brasses. The finest – to Sir John Wylcotes and Alice de Cheyne (1410) – is striking both for its size and refinement. The two figures are framed beneath elegant ogee canopies, with that of Alice made memorable by the seemingly endless folds of her dress.

ALSO OF NOTE

C13 S porch possibly reusing earlier two-light window; W capital of N nave arcade retains swaggy, C14 painted decoration; C18 hatchments to Tracy and Keck families on nave walls (cf. Broughton); 12 large C15 head corbels support nave roof; early C19 triple-decker pulpit at W end of nave; box pews in side aisles of same date; two worn c.1320 effigies in arched recesses in N wall of N aisle (lady to W of screen, and knight to E of screen in vestry – possibly Margery Dyve, Abbess of Godstow, and Robert de Vere); C15 doorways and stairwell to rood-loft in S wall of S aisle (note reveal in lower door frame for lost door); early C18 headstones in churchyard (including pair of Baroque headstones to E of chancel).

Baroque headstones

• • •

HANWELL
ST PETER
Little-known ironstone church with wonderful sculpture

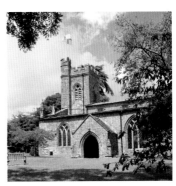

Hanwell church peers down on Hanwell Castle, the forti-
fied mansion built by William Cope, cofferer to Henry VII.
The castle's tower is one of four that once formed the
corners of a courtyard, and represents one of the earliest uses of brick in Oxfordshire (the house was begun
in c.1498). As lords of the manor, the Copes left their
mark on the church, with not all of their interventions to   *Hanwell from the south*
the betterment of the building. Despite this, the church
remains largely unspoilt, and is, thanks to its galleries of
stone carving, one of the most enjoyable in the county.
The carvings are closely related to work found in the
other north Oxfordshire churches of Bloxham, Adderbury and Alkerton.

Leaving aside the sculpted cornices of the chancel, the
outside of the church is relatively self-effacing. Most of
the window tracery – be it intersecting (south wall of the
south aisle), reticulated (east wall of the north aisle) or
geometric (east wall of the south aisle) – belongs to the
Transitional phase between Early English and Decorated
Gothic, c.1300–c.1350. Sprouting from the south-west
corner of the south aisle roof, meanwhile, is what looks
like a purely decorative pinnacle. In fact, this is the chimney to a rare fourteenth-century fireplace that survives
in the corresponding wall angle inside (note the gabled
openings for the smoke). A similar chimney survives at
nearby Horley.

The recently restored cornices that line the chancel
are of limestone, rather than ironstone; possibly because
the former was easier to work or was deemed less friable – certainly the stonework here has lasted better than
that found elsewhere on the exterior. In terms of quality,
the figurative carvings are the work of a master sculptor.
Cold stone pulses with life. The carvings themselves are
in high relief, with some elements (such as the knotted
tail of the winged dragon on the south side, similar to
the example at Adderbury) carved in the round. The fig-
ures are a mixture of real and mythical, human and beast.   *Detail of south cornice*
On the north side, a monkey peeps from leaves and a

Hanwell: figurative capital in the south arcade

mermaid is depicted as literally half-woman, half-fish. On the south side, the raised stick of a hunter echoes the antlers of a stag, and elongated figures are shown as if crawling or swimming along a pipe. On both sides, there are ballflowers the size of cabbages.

Unusually, the church is entered via an unprotected doorway on the north side (the only porch being on the south side). The interior is open and honest, marks of change left un-erased on its stonework: cuts in the tower arch caused by the sawing motion of the bell ropes; the hollowed-out nave wall where the rood-loft stairs once rose; the old roofline of the nave over the chancel and tower arches. You are never quite alone in this church. There is the insistent tick of the caged clock at the west end of the nave, and the carved figures, the silent watchers, girdling the capitals of the nave arcade and lining the walls.

It is these figures that illuminate the interior, especially the quartets of men and women inhabiting the capitals. All are depicted with elbows held high, pushing down as if levering themselves out of chimney pots. The capitals of the two arcades differ both stylistically and design-wise, with those on the north side crenellated. It has been suggested that two sculptors may have worked here. Judging by the rough capitals at the west end, at least some of the carving was carried out *in situ*, with the scheme never fully implemented. The capitals at the east end of the nave, rather than being left unfinished, were probably cut back at a later date (note the sleeve and fingers on the south capital). Sculpture-wise there is much else to enjoy, including the musicians who perch on the capital ledges of the south arcade, the grinning dog at the east end of the north arcade, and the green man label-stop on the north side of the east window in the chancel.

There are other memorable features besides. The raising of a tower over the existing arcade called for further support on the north and south sides of the westernmost bays, resulting in the insertion of two spectacular, accordion-like sequences of chamfered arches. At the east ends of the side aisles are notable tomb remnants. Behind the altar in the north aisle is a reredos, almost certainly taken from a fourteenth-century chest-tomb. In the floor of the south aisle is a coffin lid with foliate cross next to

Two of the nave arcade capitals

the effigy of an unknown lady. Also in the south aisle is a twelfth-century font from an earlier church on the site. Besides the familiar intersecting arches, the tub also has three small, carved heads on its south side.

It is only in the chancel that the hand of the Copes becomes at all conspicuous: pleasingly in the case of the stepped alabaster effigies of Sir Anthony and Lady Cope; less so in the case of the raising of the chancel floor to the height of the sedilia seats in 1776, to make room for a family vault beneath.

Effigy of Lady Cope

ALSO OF NOTE

Clock in recess at W end of nave with early crown wheel and verge escapement (apparently made in 1671 to designs of Sir Anthony Cope); elaborately moulded C14 lancet and trefoil-headed piscina with credence shelf in S wall of S aisle; C13 attached shafts in reveals of S aisle windows; plainer ogee and trefoil-headed piscina in E respond of N arcade; recess in S wall of chancel contains three Cope family funeral helms.

• • •

HORLEY
ST ETHELDREDA
Ironstone church with memorable interior and wall painting

Horley is a small, hilly village of rust-brown houses and cottages. Its church stands on elevated ground looking out over rooftops to the fields beyond, the squatness of its steeple-less tower denying it the landmark status the site would seem to guarantee. The church is built almost entirely of ironstone – all except for the attached shafts of its thirteenth-century doorways, which are of milky limestone and look like lengths of drain pipe.

Horley from the south-west

Although the individual parts of the church – aisled nave, tower and chancel – are not in themselves especially striking, the composition as a whole is distinctive. The tower squats between the nave and chancel, rather than standing at the west end, as is more common. This is explained by the fact that the church began life as an aisle-less Norman structure with a central tower. The tower is the most conspicuous surviving part from the late twelfth-century church, and retains its original

round-headed belfry windows in both east and west walls.

Both nave and chancel were heavily remodelled in the thirteenth and fourteenth centuries, with the addition of a clerestory and side aisles to the nave (the south aisle later enlarged), and new windows throughout. It appears that the chancel was rebuilt on the existing foundations, and evidently some fabric and features (including the piscina and aumbry) were reused from the original structure.

The church has an interesting and revealing array of window tracery. Much of it belongs to the remodelling of the thirteenth and fourteenth centuries, including the reticulated and intersecting tracery in the south aisle and chancel. The north aisle was rebuilt in the fifteenth century, and has some uncomfortable Perpendicular tracery (with awkward little transoms in the central lights and awkward upright bars in the flanking lights). Arguably the most arresting window is the one at the east end of the south aisle: a lovely, Decorated composition with a swirling wheel of mouchettes in its head. Several windows have renewed tracery, probably due to heavy weathering of the friable ironstone (note the battered and flaking west front).

Decorated south aisle east window

The interior comes as a genuine surprise, particularly in terms of its proportions; for the visual cues given by the squat tower outside are entirely at odds with the loftiness and shabby elegance of the interior. The sense of loftiness is imparted by the unusually tall-striding nave arcades, which have alternating round and octagonal piers supporting later double chamfered arches above. The arcade seems to have been remodelled in the early fourteenth century, at the same time that the clerestory was added. The roofline of the twelfth-century nave is still discernible on the east wall of the nave, above the rood-loft.

Scattered about the nave and side aisles are a number of medieval wall paintings, including the colossal St Christopher for which the church is celebrated. The figure of St Christopher strides purposefully along the north wall opposite the main entrance, Christ on his shoulder and a snatch of their conversation caught in two ribbons of speech. What the image lacks in finesse it makes up for in monumentality, but there is also detail and incident here: the almost-Romanesque curls of the Saint's hair and beard, the stencilled flowers falling like snowflakes to

Horley: detail of the St Christopher wall painting

either side of him, the gnome-like fishermen at his feet, and the fish themselves playing about his calves (two of them with the floppy ears of dogs). The painting dates from c.1450, and is similar to the St Christopher at Baunton church in Gloucestershire.

Of the other wall paintings, the most interesting is arguably that of a female saint cloaked in red, on the westernmost pier of the north arcade. This may be St Zita, who is generally identified by a purse and keys (a purse, at least, can be seen top right). However, it could also be St Etheldreda, who is said to have died of a throat disease, and who saw this as a punishment for wearing jewellery, specifically necklaces (note the proffered string of red beads), she being a pious woman opposed to her former love of such adornments. Also intriguing are the encircled crucifix-like 't's painted on the wall to the north of the chancel arch.

Female saint on north arcade pier

The church was the subject of intermittent and often comprehensive restoration from the seventeenth century onwards. The Rood, rood-loft and celure were added midway through the twentieth century by the architect Lawrence Dale. The rood-loft demonstrates a knowledge of certain medieval Welsh examples (specifically the loft at Llanegryn in Merionethshire). The composition, with the large Rood and attendant figures of Mary and John, is admirably bold, but would have been bolder still if it had been entirely, rather than only partly, coloured. The celure above strongly suggests that Dale knew Great Rollright, where a similar medieval canopy (or loft coving) can still be found.

Dale's Rood, rood-loft and celure

Beyond the rood-loft, the church narrows to a neck beneath the crooked and cracked beams of the tower's bell stage, before widening out again into the chancel. After the visual chatter of the nave, the chancel is altogether quieter: white walls and the mesmerising geometry of the east window, with its intersecting tracery and happy lack of stained glass. The roll moulding lining the walls dates from the late twelfth century, as do the little aumbry in the north wall and fine piscina in the south wall. The piscina has double-zigzag decoration, giving it the appearance of a miniature Norman doorway, and hinting at the lost richness of the original twelfth-century church.

Norman piscina in chancel

ALSO OF NOTE

Small but ornate C18 organ at W end of S aisle; rare medieval fireplace and chimney in SW corner of S aisle (cf. Hanwell); restored c.1200 tub font at W end of N arcade; C15 corbels to nave roof; remnants of medieval stained glass mainly in upper lights of aisle windows (includes donor figures of Henry Roworthe, rector 1416–20 and Archdeacon of Canterbury, and his successor, Master Robert Gilbert, rector 1420–26 and made Bishop of London in 1436, in N aisle); C15 carved stone standing upright at E end of S aisle may be from chest-tomb; C13 stone on floor to E carved with star of David over a Cross may be lid of child's coffin; reredos behind altar at E end of N aisle redolent of Eric Gill; pulpit painted in C20 with scenes from life of St Etheldreda; Romanesque chamfered abaci to W tower arch; C13 coffin lids to tomb recesses beneath tower; c.1500 brass indents to floor beneath tower for lady and six daughters, incomplete but retaining small brass of six daughters; fanciful C20 candelabra throughout church, with matching, spindly rood-screen; scattered carved stones, especially at W end of aisles, from earlier church; shallow niches in outer walls: two in W wall and one, with crocketed pinnacles, over S porch; several C18 headstones lifted clear of churchyard and set against wall of church (one to S aisle; five more beneath E window).

• • •

IFFLEY
ST MARY
Richly carved and wonderfully preserved Norman church

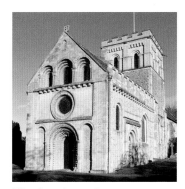

Iffley from the south-west

Like Kilpeck in Herefordshire and Barfreston in Kent, Iffley is one of England's celebrity Norman churches, instantly recognisable and admired for centuries for the quality of its stone carving. The church stands at the end of a lane, with the rectory and its memorable chimneys for company. It deserves a better setting, but is not as compromised as one fears on glimpsing it from the helter-skelter of Oxford's southern bypass.

The church was built in c.1175–82, evidently at great cost and possibly by Robert de St Remy, whose family held the manor at Iffley in the late twelfth century. Although subject to modest alterations (for example, in the thirteenth, fifteenth and nineteenth centuries) the original structure, of aisle-less nave, crossing tower and chancel, remains largely intact. Externally, the most obvious post-Norman additions include some of the windows

(Early English in the chancel; Perpendicular in the tower and nave), the crenellated parapet on the south side (of 1612) and the tower.

In the seventeenth century, the pitch of the nave roof and west gable was reduced, resulting in the uppermost side windows in the west gable being sliced into below the height of the capitals. This damage was undone in the first half of the nineteenth century, when first the gable was rebuilt and then the original pitch of the roof was reinstated. The uppermost blind window and the round window are both nineteenth-century, the latter inserted in 1856–57 by John Buckler to replace a fifteenth-century window that had apparently displaced the original round window. This was one of a number of Victorian interventions to the building characterised by marked sensitivity.

Outside, the carving is at its richest at the west end of the church, in the surrounds to door and window openings. The dominant motifs are chevrons and beakheads, deployed in radiating orders. The walls seem to have been unzipped to leave deep openings jagged with zigzags; or as if the layers of stone had been cut by pinking shears. The overall impact of this decoration is not lovely, but was not calculated to be; rather it is dazzling, restless and highly strung. The west door in particular, more so back then, might even have required an act of faith to pass through. There is something of a maw about it, the nightmarish crowding in of beakheads daring you to pass through.

Whilst zigzag is the dominant theme when standing back from the church, figurative carving becomes more noticeable closer to. As well as the beakheads (which appear of uniform design, but in fact display numerous variations of surface patterning) there is an array of figures both human and fantastical. Some are drawn from the Bible, others from the bestiary. They appear in the hood over the west door like charms in a bracelet, and most spectacularly on the south doorway, on its innermost capitals. Here, centaurs and horsemen tumble, and Samson prises open the jaws of the lion.

Intriguingly (and as if all of this were not enough) it is clear that the church was intended to be richer still, and that some of the decoration was never completed. This is most apparent in the corbel table running around the

South doorway

South doorway capital

Iffley: detail of the west front

nave and west front. At first sight the square blocks look as though they might be recent replacements. In fact they are original and were intended to be carved *in situ* (as just two of them were on the south side). Why the work was left unfinished is not known. Perhaps the patron became unwilling or unable to see such a costly project through to completion.

Today, the church is entered through the west door. It is likely that the varying degrees of richness exhibited by the various doorways reflect a ritualistic hierarchy, with the west door reserved for ceremonial occasions, and either the south door or the much plainer north door intended as the regular entrance. For a period up until 1820, the south door was protected by a porch.

Inside, the proportions are striking and unfamiliar, the lack of side aisles or transepts contributing to a narrow and elongated spatial quality. The nave, while offering enticing views eastwards, arguably suffers a little both from its plainness as a space when compared with the crossing and chancel beyond, and from the looming edifice of the organ (whose addition also led to the blocking of the south door). That said, the windows abound with more zigzag, and contain some enjoyable stained glass. This includes the lovely nineteenth-century west roundel by Hardman, to Eliot Warburton, 'lost in the Amazon January 4th 1852'; the twentieth-century south window by John Piper, with its deep, deep colours, its charcoal-eyed owl and its Jack-in-the-beanstalk stem; and the twenty-first century north window by Roger Wagner, depicting 'the Flowering Tree' mainly in blues.

Hardman's west window

Piper's south window

The nave also contains an unusual late Norman font inside the west door. Its huge, square bowl is made of black limestone or basanite, and supported on corner shafts (the three with spiral fluting are original; the plain fourth was inserted in the thirteenth century). It is reminiscent of Romanesque Tournai fonts (of which there are seven in England, the most famous being in Winchester Cathedral) and may belong to the group.

Moving east, the crossing is framed by a pair of superb and near identical arches. The outermost shafts to the west are of Purbeck marble (not a true marble but a shelly limestone), and call to mind the later use of this material for decorative effect in Gothic architecture (most notably large church and cathedral architecture). Apart from the ubiquitous zigzag, the arches also have what may be stylised lotus flowers in their outermost orders (though they have something of the sunflower about them).

Despite being remodelled in the thirteenth century – indeed, partly because of this – the chancel remains a wonderfully atmospheric, almost cavern-like space of two quadripartite vaulted bays. The western bay is original to the Norman church and has thick zigzag-moulded ribs. At the junction of the ribs is a fine carving of a curled-up dragon framed by beasts' heads and fir cones (not quite a boss, in that it doesn't project proud of the ribs). In this way, just as with the exterior, the potential monotony of the zigzag is relieved by the sparing deployment of naturalistic details.

Chancel arch looking east

The rebuilt eastern bay disappoints only in as much as we expect stonework to become more, rather than less, rich as one moves east. However, the ribs and window surrounds are finely moulded and the composition as a whole is a happy one. The original appearance of the east end of the church is not known. However, the gap between the two bays indicates that walling of some kind – presumably with an archway through – once divided the western bay from whatever lay to the east (a choir and apsidal sanctuary perhaps, as at Checkendon). The blind arches that bridge the gap between twelfth- and thirteenth-century work have been given some zigzag in order to make as seamless as possible the transition between the two.

Vaulted chancel

ALSO OF NOTE

Some early stained glass in N and S windows of nave, including late C15 shield on S side, and angels in upper lights on N side; rood-stairs with doorways to now-lost rood-loft on S side of nave to W of crossing; C13 triple sedilia, piscina and aumbry on S side of chancel (latter now containing recent angel sculpture by Nicholas Mynheer); octagonal C15 font bowl outside W door; base and shaft of medieval cross in churchyard to SE of church.

• • •

KIDLINGTON
ST MARY
Fine Decorated church with superb chancel woodwork

Kidlington from the west

Kidlington's spike of a spire is clearly visible from distance, but the church has a tendency to disappear closer to, when searched for through the sprawl of this town-like village. Given its proximity to all this, the church's setting on a limb to the north-east is unexpectedly peaceful and villagey. It stands in what must be the largest churchyard in Oxfordshire, with neat allotments of gravestones laid out to the north and west.

The church itself is an impressive and apparently consistent building of mellow limestone. Its character is overwhelmingly Decorated, the result of the remodelling of an existing cruciform church of the thirteenth century – possibly under the direction of Thomas of Kidlington, Abbot of Osney, 1330–73. This replaced a twelfth-century church on the site, a stubborn kernel of which endures in the form of the Norman tub font inside. In the fifteenth century, the nave was given a clerestory, the tower was raised in height and the slender spire was added.

St Mary's is characterised throughout by fourteenth-century workmanship of high quality – especially in the south porch and south chapel. The south porch is entered through a doorway studded with small ballflowers, and topped by a hood-mould of ogee form. This serves to funnel the eye up to the delicate image niche above, and to the figure sheltering inside.

The windows are also excellent, and the most conspicuous legacy of the remodelling that took place in the fourteenth century. Those lighting the nave, side aisles and chapels are dominated by crisply carved reticulated tracery of uniform design. Elsewhere, curvilinear tracery survives: delicate and sinuous on the north side of the nave; deeply cut and more muscular in the east walls of the chapels. The finest window of all is arguably at the east end of the south chapel. It features a wheel of cusped forms radiating out from a bearded head (echoing that found in the south transept west window at Bloxham). Most of the fourteenth-century windows have label-stops in the form of carved heads.

Reticulated south window

Kidlington: one of the medieval bench ends in the choir

Although a substantial amount of thirteenth-century fabric survives (for example, in the north and west walls of the nave, the transepts and the lower parts of the tower) visible clues to the appearance of the earlier church remain fleeting. Two lancets survive intact in the west wall of the north transept, while the jambs of blocked lancets can be seen in the west walls of nave and south transept. Two surviving doorways – one blocked in the north wall of the nave (which has stiff-leaf capitals) and another one still in use in the west wall of the south transept – also belong to the thirteenth century.

Inside too, Early English Gothic has been largely displaced by Decorated and Perpendicular. The nave is dominated by an arcade of fourteenth-century octagonal piers with double chamfered arches, and by a large fifteenth-century west window with panel tracery. This mix of Decorated and Perpendicular holds for the remainder of the church: crossing, transepts, chapels and chancel. Just as outside, fine fourteenth-century stonework abounds, including several piscinae and niches (the piscinae in the south chapel and transept, which have crocketed ogee heads, are especially good).

The eastern parts of the church are home to a superb collection of medieval woodwork. The north transept has a finely moulded Perpendicular ceiling, with cusped spandrels below the tie-beams and cusped openings to either side of the king-struts above. With the addition of the chapels, the various spaces east of the crossing were demarcated with an extensive set of parclose screens, again in the fifteenth century. These are of several fairly standard designs, some have been moved (including two from the eastern bays of the chapels in 1848) and all have been subject to varying degrees of restoration.

Medieval bench ends and screens

Without doubt, the most interesting woodwork of all is that now furnishing the chancel. The choir stalls, which have plain misericords, are probably earlier than the fronts, which were made up using Perpendicular bench ends from the nave in the nineteenth century. It has been suggested the stalls belong to the first half of the thirteenth century; certainly their severe plainness makes an early date, if not in the thirteenth century then the fourteenth, a possibility. Two benches with poppyhead finials survive. A date in the fifteenth century has been proposed, but these too could be earlier.

The bench ends, although misappropriated for their current setting, are probably the finest in Oxfordshire (a county that has relatively few good sets). There are twenty carved bench ends in all. Most feature elaborate blind carving that mixes cusped, leaf and flower forms, Perpendicular tracery and badges.

The best are those on the south side, carved with animals. The depictions include a snarling, floppy-eared dog, a ram (probably an allusion to the sacrifice of Isaac, and thus to the Crucifixion) and two evil fish-like creatures (a sawfish or Serra, and a sea monster or Aspidochelone swallowing a small fish and alluding to the unwary being snatched by the devil). At the east end is a beautiful carving of the 'Pelican in her Piety'. The pelican is shown in the act of opening her breast, so that her blood can bring back to life the dead offspring in the nest at her feet (a potent allusion to the piercing of Christ's side).

Pelican bench end

The east and south windows of the chancel retain a notable jumble of medieval glass, ranging in date from the thirteenth to the sixteenth century. It was gathered from elsewhere in the church and placed here in 1829. The panels include, in the bottom right-hand corner of the east window, what may be a fifteenth-century representation of St Frideswide performing a miracle (from Christ Church in Oxford). In the second panel from the bottom in the middle light is a much-corroded thirteenth-century king from a Tree of Jesse, and towards the top of the central light is an early fourteenth-century Crucifixion with a beautifully painted Christ. The fifteenth-century Seraphim above and to the right have wings crossed in front of their bodies, like those at nearby Yarnton and Combe.

Detail of chancel south window

ALSO OF NOTE

Unusual C15 rainwater heads of bell form to aisle and nave parapets; C17 sundial in gable wall of S transept; richly carved Jacobean pulpit at E end of nave; painted hatchments lining nave walls (cf. Great Tew and Broughton); various mainly C14 roof corbels, including in nave and attesting to earlier roof line, and in N chapel (lion with some surviving colour); faded medieval wall paintings on E wall of N transept, of Virgin and St Margaret, uncovered in 1892 (depiction of Seven Deadly Sins uncovered at same time, but prudishly re-covered); C14 or C15 encaustic tiles reset in chancel floor before stall fronts in C19; C15 triple sedilia in S wall of chancel; C19 communion rail set with C15 cusped panels; several medieval (probably C15) doors, including in N chapel; various floor and wall memorials, most of C18 and in chapels and chancel.

• • •

Langford from the south-east

LANGFORD
ST MATTHEW
Part-Saxon church with exquisite Early English stonework

Langford lies in the flatlands of the Thames vale, close to the Gloucestershire border; a compact village bound together by limestone walling. Its church stands slightly adrift, left behind when the village shifted north-west to the junction with the Lechlade road. The church deserves to be better known. As well as having Saxon fabric of exceptional interest in its tower and porch, it also contains beautiful and unusual Early English stonework in its chancel and nave.

The exterior is full of interest. The central tower represents the most conspicuous surviving part of a large Saxon church, possibly built by Aelfsige of Faringdon on the site of an earlier church (Aelfsige was a native landowner who appears to have flourished in Norman England). The size and quality of Langford church may partly be accounted for by the fact that the parish was a royal estate, as confirmed by the Domesday survey of 1086. What is less clear is the precise date of the fabric, for while the design of the tower is resolutely Saxon not Norman, it is quite possible that the church was constructed after the Conquest, during the hiatus that existed prior to the establishment of Norman architecture in England. Whether before or after the Conquest, however, a date sometime in the eleventh century seems probable.

The tower, although four-square and robust, has carved details of surprising delicacy. In place of capitals, the roll-moulded bell openings have strips of foliage (probably acanthus) carved in relief, with a palmette above each central pier. Midway down on the south side, there is also a weathered carving of two figures in tunics with arms raised above their heads, forming a shallow corbel of sorts (which

Langford: the view east through the tower arches

Saxon Rood over south doorway

may once have held a sundial). The tower also features the pilaster strips, or lesenes, so characteristic of Saxon architecture and found, for example, at Earls Barton in Northamptonshire and Barton upon Humber in Lincolnshire.

The two Saxon relief sculptures set into the walls of the south porch also present problems of interpretation. Over the entrance is a Rood group, perversely reassembled with Christ's arms upside down, and the figures of Mary and John switched. The latter now turn away, feigning indifference. Although relocated here when the porch was built in the thirteenth century, Saxon Roods were often located over entrances (as opposed to chancel arches), so the context here is appropriate and may echo the original location of the sculpture. On the east wall of the porch is a monumental (though sadly now headless) figure of Christ triumphant, tubular cloak pleated down the sides, arms outstretched like the wings of an aeroplane.

Suggested dates for the two sculptures range from as late as the twelfth century for both, to as early as the eighth century for the Christ (based on the type of long cloak he wears). In the case of the Christ figure in particular, it is possible not only that it was carved for another church, but that it was brought here from abroad (Normandy being one suggestion). Certainly, nothing quite like it survives anywhere else in England.

Of the remaining fabric, the aisles belong to c.1200 and the chancel to the second half of the thirteenth century. The enlargement of the church in this period entailed raising the chancel roofline, which now cuts uncomfortably into the bell openings. It also involved widening the whole church except for the tower, leading to a rather pinched 'waist' between nave and chancel (a recurring architectural problem for widened churches with central towers).

The chancel is an especially fine and instructive example of Early English architecture. Its windows represent outstanding examples of plate tracery; of the transitional phase between the plain lights of the Norman and Early English periods, and the traceried lights of c.1250 onwards. Each group of windows consists of a pair of lancets with a concave rhombus above, the head of each group framed by a string course. From windows such as these it is but a short step to windows whose lights are

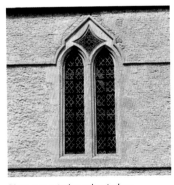

Plate-traceried south window

subdivided internally by bar tracery. The Langford windows are closely related to those in the east wall at Wyck Rissington church, just over the border in Gloucestershire (and may be the work of the same masons).

Except for the crossing arches, the interior of the church is dominated by Transitional and Early English architectural masonry of exceptional quality. It is entered via a south doorway framed by three orders of continuous roll mouldings beneath a hood studded with nailhead. This was added with the side aisles in c.1200. Inside, the nave arcades are uncommonly tall and elegant, their round piers topped with fleshy, stiff-leaf capitals. The capitals are topped with cross-shaped abaci bearing round, not pointed, arches (like those at Faringdon and Little Faringdon).

The view eastwards is a curious one. The pinch-point of the crossing tower gives tantalising glimpses through to the light-filled chancel beyond, while effectively uncoupling this space from the body of the church. The view is framed by a pair of tall, narrow arches. That to the west, the Saxon original, is resolutely plain and blocky; that to the east, of the thirteenth century, is of greater finesse, its roll-moulded arch forming a continuation of the responds that support it.

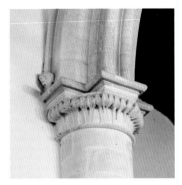

Early English arcade capital

The chancel beyond is crisply and subtly detailed, and largely free from the colour and clutter that might distract from the subtle stone carving. In a barely discernible sleight of the mason's hand, the hoods over the windows become progressively richer moving east, with first three then five further raised mouldings added to the string course and hollow moulding of the westernmost windows. The east wall is unusual for being lit, not by a single central window, but a symmetrical pair of windows.

Several anomalies suggest that the east end of the chancel was altered at a later date. The disjointed shafts flanking the east windows (which do not marry happily with the hoods above) together with the severed string courses both inside and out, confirm that this wall has been at least partly rebuilt. The current position of the blocked priest's door, which should not be this far to the east, suggests that the chancel may even have been shortened. However, apparently contradicting this are the original setback buttresses (similar to those at Wyck

Chancel looking east

Early English piscina in chancel

Rissington) at the north-east corner of the chancel. How likely is it that these would have been retained if the chancel was shortened?

Unsurprisingly, the chancel fittings are also of the highest quality. They include the finely moulded trefoil-headed piscina on the south side, and the rare six-compartment aumbry – indicative of the one-time wealth of the church – on the north side.

ALSO OF NOTE

Two pieces of C15 stonework in E wall of porch (uppermost one possibly from a piscina); remains of stairwell and blocked doorway to former room above porch on S wall of S aisle; rustic wall monument to Howse family of 1691 on S wall of S aisle; C15 octagonal font at W end of nave; C17 polygonal wooden pulpit on stone stem at E end of nave; C17 clock mechanism at E end of S aisle; window to E of S door with unusual, cusped rere-arch on wall-posts and head corbels (cusping looks later, possibly Victorian); C15 parclose screens to E end of side aisles (presumably once linked by rood-screen beneath W tower arch) – once open lights above middle rail now filled with later images; brass to Walter Prunes and wife (d. 1594 and 1609 respectively) beneath altar table in chancel; pair of flying buttresses erected 1574 on N side of church, evocative of monastic ruins; some original roughcast on N side of church; gabled stair turret on N side of tower; medieval cross base and shaft to E of church close to road.

• • •

NORTH LEIGH
ST MARY
Fascinating church with Saxon tower and fine north chapel

North Leigh from the west

North Leigh, like Yarnton and Kidlington nearby, unexpectedly harbours a wonderful church. This one, too, stands at the margins – in this case off to the north, barely attached by a thread of lane. The setting is a lovely one, the landscape falling away and widening out, to give fine views over open fields to woods beyond.

Something of the interest and variety of the church's interior is hinted at by its exterior. To the south is a curious stepping down of the aisle roofs, and to the west is an earlier roofline (indicating that the tower once stood within the body of the church, rather than at its west end). To the north are the distinct forms of two chapels: the smaller one deftly Perpendicular; the larger, robustly Georgian.

The church's evolution, as suggested by the tower in particular, is a complicated one. The tower is the earliest part of the building, and essentially all that survives of a sizeable pre-Conquest church (probably belonging to the first half of the eleventh century). Its bell openings have the round arches and baluster shafts found in other Saxon churches (such as Oxford St Michael and Earls Barton in Northamptonshire). The pre-Conquest church had an oblong plan form comprising a nave of two bays, a tower and chancel.

In c.1200, the nave to the west of the tower was abandoned, and the chancel to the east was converted into a new, aisled nave (as confirmed by the arcades, which have Transitional scalloped and waterleaf capitals). A new chancel was then added to the east – only to be replaced by another further to the east when the nave was lengthened by a third bay in the early thirteenth century. The responds of the thirteenth-century chancel arch survive in the chancel. The tower arch also belongs to this date.

In the early fourteenth century, both side aisles were remodelled and extended west to flank the tower, and a chapel built on the north side of the chancel. While the Wilcote chapel evidently belongs to the fifteenth century, the crocketed ogee arch in its south wall testifies to the presence here of a chapel a century earlier. Sometime in this period, the chancel division reverted back to its c.1200 position, enlarging the chancel by one bay at the expense of the nave.

Extensive alterations were carried out in the eighteenth century. Most of these were undone as part of Street's restoration of 1864, but the Perrot chapel on the north side of the north aisle was kept. Other later additions include the south porch (also by Street) and the extensions to the south aisle (one for the organ, the other a vestry). The church is entered through a Norman doorway, reset and altered to frame a smaller opening in the fourteenth century.

The legacy of this convoluted development is one of the most startling church interiors in Oxfordshire. The congregational space is disproportionately wide, probably

Transitional waterleaf capital

Perrot chapel arcade capital

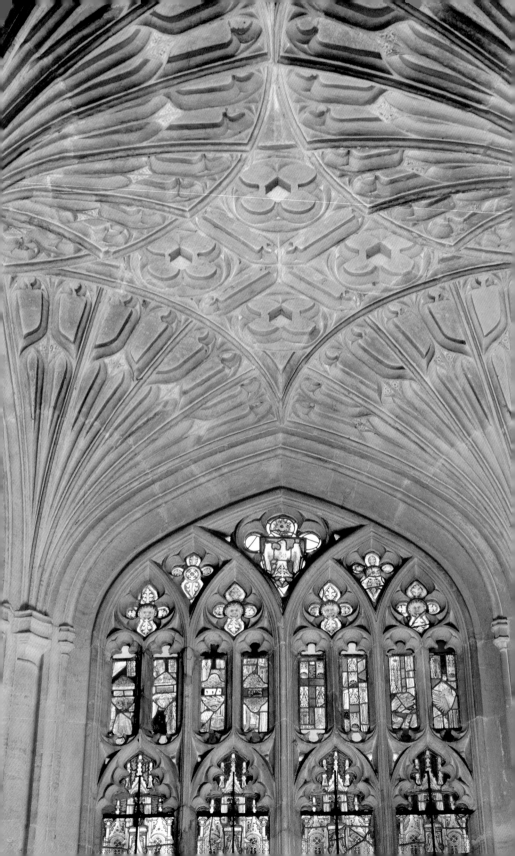

because the book-ending properties of the tower and chancel constrained any meaningful expansion east-west. The tower base, which lies within the body of the church, does not adequately read as a bay belonging to the nave, but as an encroachment upon it, further compromising the proportions.

The view eastwards is dominated by the striking chancel partition, comprising a stone rood-screen (designed by Street and inserted in the 1860s) with medieval Doom painting above. The screen, although odd-looking, is not without medieval precedent. It is reminiscent of the stone screens at Stebbing and Great Bardfield in Essex; or, perhaps more so, the flat-topped stone screen in Exeter Cathedral. The Doom was uncovered and restored at the same time the screen was added. The three vertical, floral strips presumably relate to the positions of the missing Rood figures. On the east side is a showy, Georgian plasterwork coat of arms. These are the arms of the Perrot family and not royal arms, so it seems unlikely (though not impossible) that these were ever displayed on the west side of the chancel division.

At the east end of the north aisle stands the Wilcote chapel, a cathedral-quality space whose presence in a village church is completely unexpected. Its Perpendicular fan-vaulting and panel tracery (with original glass in the upper lights) give it a casket-like richness. It was built by Elizabeth Wilcote and begun in c.1440. The architect may be Richard Winchcombe, who is thought to have been known to the family. The workmanship certainly bears comparison with that found at Bloxham and Adderbury. As well as being of comparable finesse, it also employs round wall shafts with hollow-moulded capitals similar to those found at Bloxham.

Chancel screen with Doom above

The Wilcotes themselves – Sir William (died 1410) and his wife Elizabeth (died 1445) – lie side by side within the superb ogee-canopied recess in the south wall. It seems that Sir William's effigy once lay in the centre of the tomb, and that only later did he make way for his wife. This would account for variations in the design and length of the effigies, and the fact that neither is properly fixed to the tomb. The figure of Elizabeth is full of charming details: the accordion folds of her dress, the song birds that circle her head.

Carved angel in Wilcote chapel

North Leigh: the fan-vaulted Wilcote chapel looking east

▥ 11th century

☐ c.1200

▨ 13th century

▨ 14th century

▧ 15th century

▦ 18th century

▦ 19th/ 20th century

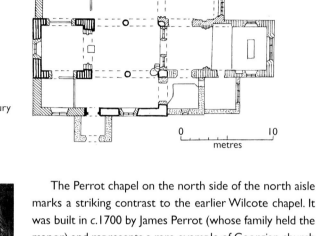

FIG. 12 North Leigh St Mary

0 _____ 10
metres

Engraved memorial plate

The Perrot chapel on the north side of the north aisle marks a striking contrast to the earlier Wilcote chapel. It was built in c.1700 by James Perrot (whose family held the manor) and represents a rare example of Georgian church architecture in Oxfordshire. The mason was Christopher Kempster, architect of the magnificent Town Hall in Abingdon. Besides its bold and quirky use of classical motifs, the chapel is notable for its rare, early eighteenth-century parclose screen and for its wall monuments to the Perrots and their descendants. These include several brass plates, taken from coffin lids and engraved in a lovely, looping script.

ALSO OF NOTE

Norman font, recovered from churchyard and re-cut in 1857 (displacing Georgian timber font then in use) at W end of nave; incomplete brass to Thomas Beckingham (d. 1431) in floor on N side of chancel; C13 trefoil-headed tomb recess in N wall of chancel; C14 piscina in S wall of chancel; Perrot chapel monuments include fulsome inscription to chapel's patron, James Perrot; coloured and damaged Jacobean wall monument to William Lenthall (d. 1596) and wife Frances with children below, on S wall of Wilcote chapel; similar wall monument to Robert Perrot (d. 1605) and wife Susanna with eight children below, on S wall of chancel; bale tomb and unusual coffin shaped tomb slabs outside S porch.

• • •

NORTH STOKE
ST MARY THE VIRGIN
Flint church with textured nave and refined chancel

North Stoke is a leafy backwater, lying between prairie-sized fields and a golf course to the south of Wallingford. The village is probably not much-visited. Its church, too, gives the impression of having been passed by, its interior passed over for updating, left undisturbed to ripen into characterful old age.

The present church, which belongs to the thirteenth and fourteenth centuries, probably replaced a Norman, and ultimately a Saxon, predecessor on the site. From the eleventh century until the thirteenth century, like nearby Checkendon, the church was in the ownership of the Abbey of Bec – a connection which may explain the distinctive Early English work in the chancel.

North Stoke from the north

Also like Checkendon, the church is built of flint and has a relatively plain exterior. The windows and walling differ between nave and chancel. The fourteenth-century nave has rubble stonework and is lit by two-light windows. The thirteenth-century chancel has squared and coursed stonework and is lit by plain lancets. The charming north porch, whose entrance is an archway of thick, silvery boards, was added in the fifteenth century. The fourteenth-century west tower suffered a partial collapse in 1669, and was only repaired in 1725 (note the date in brick on the west face).

On the outside of the church are two unusual mass dials. The first, and by far the finer of the two, has been set (probably reset) over the blocked south doorway. It takes the form of a disk (reminiscent of an old cartwheel penny) held by the hands of a figure whose head juts from the stonework above. Faded lettering can still be discerned around the raised edge of the dial. It may date from as early as the twelfth century. The second dial occupies a brick chamfer cut for the purpose into the south buttress of the tower. Its shape is more gravestone than sundial.

Mass dial on south wall

The inside of the church is mellow and time-worn, its contents a happy mixture of the rustic and the surprisingly refined. The nave was re-pewed and re-tiled in the

nineteenth century (though it retains three earlier pews in its south-west corner). Most of the rest of what survives, most notably the wall paintings and roof, belongs to the fourteenth century. The wall paintings are hard to make out, and perhaps are best enjoyed as a faded patina in concert with the pervading atmosphere, rather than legible narratives. They include the Martyrdoms of St Stephen (upper tier of north wall), St Catherine (lower tier of north wall) and St Thomas Becket (north side of chancel arch). On the south wall are scenes from the Passion, including the Betrayal, Trial and Flagellation in the middle tier. Overhead is a lovely queen-strut roof, whose heftiness is leavened by the animating effect of numerous curved wind-braces.

Detail of nave wall paintings

The chancel displays a level of architectural refinement the nave cannot claim, yet the contrast is quietly rather than starkly expressed. The chancel arch and the six lancets within have shafts and abaci of Purbeck marble (echoing the earlier use of this material in the tower arches at Iffley). The shafts are topped by a variety of lively stiff-leaf capitals. From the leaves of one a little face peeps out.

The choir stalls in the chancel were evidently cobbled together from a number of once-disparate bits of carpentry. On the south side, the west-facing boarding, rail and cut-off upright almost certainly once belonged to a rood-screen (the cut-off upright possibly forming a door-post). The equivalent boarding and rail on the north side again almost certainly once belonged to a screen – though apparently not to the same screen.

Stiff-leaf capitals and purbeck shafts

ALSO OF NOTE

Late medieval N door with original ironwork; plain C13 font on hexagonal base with Jacobean cover at W end of nave; remains of C12 pillar piscina at E end of nave; five-sided Jacobean pulpit with tester at E end of nave; C18 royal arms over chancel arch; memorial slab to Robert de Esthall, rector of North Stoke (1238–74) in chancel floor; medieval encaustic tiles at E end of chancel; headless C14 brass to Roger Parker at E end of chancel.

• • •

North Stoke: the nave looking east

Oxford St Mary from the south-east

OXFORD
ST MARY THE VIRGIN
Large city church with spectacular steeple and rich history

For its combination of architectural and historical interest, St Mary the Virgin is one of the richest churches in England. It superbly showcases the late Decorated and late Perpendicular phases of English Gothic architecture. It has performed the role of library, courthouse, lecture theatre, exam hall, tourist destination, and University and parish church for Oxford. And it provided the stage for such historical set pieces as the trial for heresy of Thomas Cranmer in 1556.

The church has an unusual plan form, and is only made to appear less odd than it might otherwise seem by the degree to which it has been assimilated into the adjacent architectural ensembles. To the south it forms an imposing continuation of the High Street frontages to east and west; while to the north it encloses one side of Radcliffe Square, its tower aligned, and in celebrated dialogue, with the dome of the Radcliffe Camera in the centre of the square.

The earliest part of the structure is the c.1300 tower. It appears, from window remains in the east and west walls of the tower's ground stage, and from the arch in its south wall, that the tower has always occupied this unusual location against the north side of the church. Seen from Radcliffe Square, the tower itself is a dignified and powerful structure, with large and deeply set bell openings, and sturdy, many-stepped angle buttresses.

In the first quarter of the fourteenth century, the tower was topped with a spire which remains one of the most enjoyably lavish in the country. At the base of the spire is a thicket of gabled and crocketed niches and pinnacles teeming with ballflower decoration and figures. The sculpture on this part of the steeple has been much-restored, both in the nineteenth century and more recently (a number of the original figures are now in the cloister of New College).

If there is a flipside to such encrusted decoration, it is only that the legibility of the underlying architecture can be reduced. This is the case at St Mary's, where it is not immediately obvious that the corner niches are simply upward extensions of the buttresses below, or that

Detail of Decorated spire

Oxford St Mary the Virgin: the Decorated spire

the pinnacles behind are aligned with the oblique faces of the spire. Ultimately, however, the design – part sleight of hand, part distraction through surface decoration – is a clever solution to the perennial dilemma faced by steeple builders: namely, how best to resolve the junction between a tower of square cross-section, and a spire of octagonal cross-section.

In chronological order, the next oldest portions of the church are the lowermost 'wings' immediately to the east and west of the tower, which belong to the first quarter of the fourteenth century. That to the west is a chapel; that to the east comprises the Old Congregation House on the ground floor, and the pre-Bodleian University library (the oldest purpose-built library building in England) on the floor above. Almost the whole of the rest of the church, including the chancel and the aisled nave, belongs to c.1462–c.1510.

Externally, the Perpendicular work is stately and richly detailed. All sides are lit by typically expansive windows, the bays divided by buttresses with pinnacles that visually tie the nave and chancel to the tower and spire built more than a century earlier. Nave, aisles and north chapel are all trimmed with an unusually elaborate parapet lined with figures and clambering beasts.

Detail of south parapet

The south or 'Virgin' porch is probably by local master mason, John Jackson, and was added in 1637. It is one of the most remarkable church porches in the country, a fanciful mishmash of classical and, in the case of its fan-vaulted ceiling, Gothic elements. The timing of its creation was unfortunate. With its twisted columns redolent of those in St Peter's in Rome, and its 'idolatrous' statue of the Virgin and Child, it proved a red rag to the Puritans, and was cited in the trial that led to the execution of the then-Chancellor of the University, Archbishop Laud.

Inside, the tone of the architecture shifts to pure Perpendicular: refined, crisply detailed and free of the festive sculpture that enlivens so much of the exterior. The nave has a fine arcade of six bays, with piers of reed-like shafts whose lines are carried over its two-centred arches. The clerestory above is also beautifully resolved. Between each window is a vaulted niche whose canopy forms a corbel for the ceiling above. The niches rest on a band

Detail of 'Virgin' porch

of oak leaves reminiscent of the carved trails found on rood-screens of the period.

The view west is dominated by a huge window that fills almost the whole end wall of the church above the height of the early nineteenth-century west gallery. The window is a fine one by Charles Kempe, of 1891. The unusual amount of frosty-white glass is particularly effective next to the cool stonework. There is other Victorian glass of note, including the only two windows by Augustus Pugin to survive in Oxford: the second window from the east in the south wall (of 1848), and the window at the east end of the south aisle (of c.1843). Where the west window of the nave is silver, the latter is gold.

Nave looking east

The south aisle is also home to numerous monuments, including several fine eighteenth-century cartouches. On the north side of the north aisle, beyond a simpler arcade of two bays, is a chapel built in 1328 by the founder of Oriel College, Adam de Brome. This contains several worn indents for brasses in its floor, and one to de Brome himself mounted on a twentieth-century base.

The view eastwards is dominated by a choir screen and organ. In themselves they form an impressive enough

⬚	13th century
⬚	14th century
⬚	15th century
⬚	16th century
⬚	17th century
⬚	18th century
⬚	19th/ 20th century

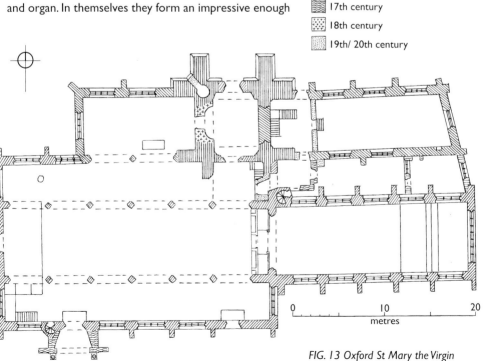

0   10   20
metres

FIG. 13 Oxford St Mary the Virgin

Choir and sanctuary looking east

Medieval poppyhead in choir

composition, but do little for the spatial dynamics of the interior as a whole. They have the effect of segregating the nave from the chancel beyond, interrupting what could have been a commanding vista, and stifling eastward momentum towards the high altar.

Cut off from the nave, the grave and stately chancel feels like a college chapel in its own right. The woodwork lining the walls is all original, and includes desks with blind-traceried fronts and worn poppyheads; the panelling behind carries lovely, delicate cresting. At the east end, the triple sedilia, piscina and reredos (minus the original figures; the current ones were added in the 1930s) also belong to the late fifteenth century.

A number of spaces in the church have been appropriated to serve its role as a tourist destination. Beneath the low-slung vaults of the Old Congregation House is a coffee shop, while in the base of the tower is a gift shop giving access to the tower gallery. The gallery gives fine views across the rooftops of Oxford, and a different perspective on the Radcliffe Camera, whose proportions seem happier from up there.

ALSO OF NOTE

Fine nave pews, galleries, canopied pulpit and Chancellor's throne below W gallery, all by Thomas Plowman, of 1826–28; Perpendicular style font of 1828, also by Plowman, at W end of S aisle; oak organ loft of 1673, faced with stone screen by Plowman; C17 painted shields in windows of de Brome chapel; small brass of Edward Shemock (d. 1581) to W of tower door; small brass of Malina Boys (d. 1584) and twelve children; array of worn indents, tablets and memorial slabs set into floor at W end of chancel; C15 roof corbels in chancel; fragments of C15 stained glass in chancel E window; refined and extensive collection of C17 and C18 wall memorials, including to John Wallis or Waills (d. 1703) at E end of S aisle; to William Doble (d. 1675) in S aisle; to David Gregory (d. 1708) at W end of S aisle; to Charles Holloway (d. 1679) on S side of chancel; and another Charles Holloway (d. 1695) on N side of chancel.

• • •

OXFORD
ST PHILIP AND ST JAMES
High Victorian church of great subtlety and invention

The church of St Philip and St James is one of the master-works of George Edmund Street, diocesan architect for Oxford from 1850 until his death in 1881. Built in 1860–66, the church is the most ambitious and accomplished of Street's six Oxfordshire churches. At first glance an essay in the pared back Gothic style of the thirteenth century, it ultimately reveals itself to be triumphantly of its time; its distinctive architectural voice Street's alone.

St Philip and St James from the west

The church fronts the Woodstock Road, and is sur-rounded by the fashionable Victorian villas whose original occupants it was built to serve. The exterior is beautifully judged. Sparing use has been made of contrasting bands of ashlar-cut sandstone in order to disrupt the uniformity of the coarser Bath stone, giving the impression that the whole structure may have been cut from the sediments of a rock face. While the exterior is otherwise largely devoid of surface decoration, variety in form and in the deploy-ment and scale of form ensure that the architecture, upon which the building must therefore rely for its effect, is never monotonous.

The west front is a bold and assured composition, with a gabled porch, a trio of big lancets and a huge encircled quatrefoil above. The latter establishes a key motif, simple and geometric, variations upon which are found through-out the building – most strikingly in the plate-traceried clerestory windows. While these appear to follow a regu-lar pattern (round opening with lancets; round opening without lancets; round opening with lancets, and so on), the openings are actually of six different designs, with the design of any given window never matching that of the equivalent window in the opposite wall. In contrast, the ground floor elevations are regular, with paired lancets lin-ing the side aisles.

South elevation

The crossing tower and spire, far from being treated as an appendage to the church, are integral to the com-position as a whole, particularly in views from the Wood-stock Road (this care taken over the composition of west front plus tower and spire is a characteristic the church

shares with Gilbert Scott's church at Leafield). The treatment of the tower – bold and simple, with big lancets – echoes that of the west front; only here, in order to make explicit a greater thickness of wall (and thus to suggest strength and solidity) the reveals of the bell openings are markedly stepped.

Up to now, the architecture has been essentially Gothic in character and restrained in expression. Only in the spire does a note of whimsy creep in. Over the lucarnes are unusual canopies supported on pairs of attached shafts. Each canopy is roofed with an inverted fish-scale pattern, with the 'scales' imprinted rather than raised (like a plaster cast of fish-scale tiles). Owing to the gradient of the spire and the splaying of each pair of shafts, the individual shafts are borne at different heights and are thus of different lengths. While the openings have trefoil heads, the outer arches have Romanesque-style chevron mouldings. The canopies emerge from the faces of the spire like figures emerging through walls.

Detail of spire

The interior, inevitably compromised by its conversion to a library, has also been handled with great ingenuity. In order to minimise the disruption to sight lines of the arcades, Street had them pushed out towards the aisle walls, then curve in to meet the chancel arch (a feature discernible but not conspicuous from the outside). The result is a generous nave, and a slight funnelling of the view eastwards towards the altar. The irregularity of the clerestory becomes more pronounced inside, where a misalignment of the six clerestory windows with the four bays of the nave arcade becomes apparent. The space is roofed with a timber barrel vault, which, respecting the clerestory rather than the nave arcade, is also divided into six bays.

Detail of clerestory looking east

Although the church is cruciform, the shortness of the transepts and the handling of the crossing ensure that, spatially and dynamically at least, these lateral features are of limited bearing only. Indeed, due to the pushing outwards of the nave arcades, the church doesn't even feel much like an aisled church, let alone one with pronounced transepts. The nave arcades have short, thick piers with boldly carved Corinthian capitals carrying broad arches above. They impart a human scale to the space, which contrasts with the more upright proportions of the narrow

Oxford St Philip and St James: the south elevation and steeple

and soaring sanctuary beyond. This more rarefied space is more highly wrought, with an array of attached shafts carrying a rib vault above, and tall, tightly packed windows lighting the three-sided sanctuary beyond.

For the interior, Street made even greater play of colour and texture. The palette includes pink for the nave piers; black for the sanctuary shafts (echoing this use of marble in English cathedrals); contrasting bands of dark stone in the arches (like those in the arcades of some north Oxfordshire churches); pale grey for the capitals, bases and clerestory roundels, and warmer grey for the walls. The treatment of the stone ranges from highly polished in the nave piers, to ashlar-cut in the arches and windows, to rougher dressed in the walls. The contrast between the sooty-grey ceiling and the pale stonework below is particularly striking and successful. The one space conspicuous for its lack of colour is also the one part for which Street was not responsible: the little vaulted southeast chapel, added by Sir Charles Nicholson in 1920–21.

Stronger and brighter colours are provided by the stained glass. Much of it is excellent, and the interior actually benefits from the glass being the work of several practices, each with distinct stylistic traits; it only adds to the visual interest and variety established by Street. The best of the glass is arguably in the aisle and clerestory windows. The aisle windows are by Clayton & Bell, and display the clean, graphic quality that characterises the work of the practice. They are especially effective here, framed by limewashed masonry.

Aisle glass by Clayton & Bell

ALSO OF NOTE

Despite conversion to library, principal fittings by Street survive in situ: marble reredos (altered by Burlison & Grylls in 1883) with coloured figures depicting Christ at Gethsemane; pulpit with shafts echoing nave piers; font with Arts & Crafts-style font cover with metal strapwork framing and wooden panels (the uppermost ones with lancet/ quatrefoil lights echoing those of clerestory); brass lectern with pierced and coloured gables; arguably intrusive 1896 rood-beam and rood-figures by Micklethwaite & Somers Clarke; sculpture includes high relief affronted pairs of St George and Dragon in doorway to N of chancel arch, with pietà above, and low relief medallions in clerestory spandrels.

Street's font cover

• • •

RADLEY
ST JAMES
Surprising church with timber arcade and fine stained glass

Many churches are instantly enticing because of their setting or appearance. Radley church is not one of them. It stands on a busy junction and is outwardly unexceptional. Despite appearances, however, it has a colourful history and is full of interest. It was heavily damaged in fighting during the Civil War, yet retains a rare medieval timber arcade and a spectacular collection of mainly sixteenth-century heraldic glass.

Radley from the south

The current structure dates from the thirteenth and fourteenth centuries, but was so heavily rebuilt during the fifteenth century that differentiating which parts belong to what date cannot be done with certainty. Suffice to say, much of the visible fabric belongs to the fifteenth century, and most of the conspicuous features – including tower, crenellated parapet and windows – are Perpendicular in style. The current lopsided plan is the result of the loss of the north transept and aisle during the Civil War in the 1640s, when Royalist troops were garrisoned at Radley. A new north wall took their place.

Outside, there are a handful of noteworthy features. The chancel eaves carry a fleuron frieze, and at the corners are renewed fourteenth-century diagonal buttresses with pinnacled tops. On the south side of the chancel is the humped form of a seventeenth-century burial vault, and in the north slope of the nave roof a small dormer.

Inside, the nave might be humdrum were it not for the remarkable arcade which divides it from the south aisle. This consists of four hefty, chamfered (octagonal) oak posts set on stone bases, with pairs of arched braces deployed to form Tudor arches between. Pairs of longer arched braces span the nave and support the king-post roof above. The posts themselves – massive, plain and relatively crude – seem more likely to belong to the fourteenth century than the fifteenth. In c.1902, the original oak chancel arch was replaced by the current stone one, and the nave roof was restored (retaining some early timbers, including the tie-beams). The work was carried out by John Oldrid Scott (son of the famous George Gilbert).

Stepped diagonal buttresses

Wooden piers similar to those found at Radley are by no means unique. However, on the rare occasions that these are encountered, it tends to be in parts of the country with a stronger tradition of building in wood, such as Cheshire and Essex. In these counties, a small number of churches retain timber arcades, including Marton and Holmes Chapel in Cheshire, and Shenfield and Theydon Garnon in Essex. Arguably the loveliest timber arcade of all is at Llantilio Pertholey in Monmouthshire. Here, the faces of the piers are richly carved with cable moulding and encircled quatrefoils.

Wooden nave piers

Aside from the piers, the nave also has an excellent font at its west end, and pulpit canopy at its east end. The font is Norman (probably of c.1180) and comprises a drum-shaped bowl supported on four colonettes (at least two of which have been renewed). The bowl is carved with a continuous arcade whose bases, shafts, capitals and arches are unusually rich and varied for so early a date. The pulpit canopy is a superb example of late Gothic work (probably of the early sixteenth century), with panels of linenfold and blind tracery behind the pulpit, and lacy openwork lining the canopy itself. It was reputedly brought here from the House of Commons, where it formed a canopy over the Speaker's chair, by Speaker William Lenthall in the 1630s. Whether or not this is true, it was clearly not made for here.

Detail of Norman font

The chancel beyond has more woodwork not originally intended for this church. The elaborate backs of the choir stalls, conceived as six bays of panel tracery cut into by crocketed ogee arches, do not marry stylistically with the stalls below, and apparently came from Cologne (gifted to the church in 1847 by Sir George Bowyer). The stalls themselves are a fine set from the seventeenth century, their arms and feet carved with guilloche pattern, their misericords with cherub head brackets, and their front rails with big poppyheads.

Beyond the choir stalls on the south side stands a huge alabaster monument by master mason Nicholas Stone. On a broad, stepped tomb base lie the effigies of Sir William Stonhouse (died 1631) and his wife, both in ruffed collars, heads on luxurious tasselled pillows. On the side of the tomb base below, on a similar pillow, are four babies

Radley: the west window, possibly depicting Henry VII

Heraldic glass in south wall

swaddled in red (who, according to the text, 'have been sent to the sky ahead'). At the head end, forming a tragic addendum to the monument, is the figure of Sir William's eldest son, John, who died not long after his father. The monument as a whole is one of the finest of its date in the county, and is notable for the amount of original colour (especially red, green and gold) that survives.

The windows of both the nave and chancel contain a remarkable set of Royal heraldic glass. Again, this is not original to the church, and was given in 1847. The glass was inserted and added to with great skill and sensitivity by Thomas Willement, who led a return to medieval techniques of glass production in the nineteenth century. The arms include those of Henry VI, VII, and VIII, and Richard III, set against diapered backgrounds (with crowned 'R's in the case of the west light of the nave north window, which has the arms of Richard III). The outermost lights of the east window contain Biblical scenes – the southernmost light possibly showing the return of the Prodigal Son.

The most compelling window in the church, however, can only be appreciated properly by climbing the spiral staircase at the west end. Here, looking back at us, is the beautifully painted face of an alert young man who may very well be the first of the Tudors, Henry VII.

ALSO OF NOTE
S door inscribed 'Rodericus Lloid 1656'; C13 piscina in wall of S transept; several wall monuments, including C19 marble triptych with urn to members of Davis family to W of organ, and another featuring compass, canon and anchor to Admiral Sir George Bowyer on N wall of chancel; possibly Norman (though re-cut) altar with intricately carved oak reredos of 1909; C17 chest-tomb in churchyard to SW of S door.

• • •

RYCOTE
CHAPEL OF ST MICHAEL
Fine Perpendicular chapel with theatrical fittings

The first glimpse offered by Rycote chapel is of a crenellated tower rising among trees; the first impression that of a building whose size and architectural ambition are more akin to those of a parish church. The impression remains only partly intact when approaching the west door, when the narrowness of the building – its lack of side aisles – becomes apparent.

Rycote from the west

Externally, Rycote chapel is pleasing both for the measured proficiency of its architecture and the fact that it belongs entirely to one build (it was consecrated in 1449). Add to this a lovingly tended formal setting close to the recently restored remains of a great house, and it would probably merit a visit even if it held little of interest within.

Although in no sense ornate, the chapel's Perpendicular architecture is lifted above the ordinary by a number of finely judged decorative touches, a handful of which are almost whimsical. The west face of the tower has a fine, canopied image niche with a small window behind (of devotional rather than practical use). The hood-mould over the window below is terminated by the shields of Quatremayne and Englefield. Richard Quatremayne, buried at nearby Thame, was the founder of Rycote chapel. Also from the west, the staircase turret can be seen projecting from the south-east corner of the tower. Charmingly, the five small windows in its angled face are of five different designs (from the bottom: trefoil, rectangle, quatrefoil, lancet and loop light).

The body of the chapel is continuous, with no obvious demarcation between the nave and chancel. The side walls are divided into bays of irregular width by stepped buttresses that break through the eaves of the pinky-red tiled roof, and are topped by sometimes fancy pinnacles (the diagonal end-buttresses being topped by the fanciest of all: a pair of greyhound-like heraldic beasts). The bays each contain identical two-light windows, again irregularly spaced. In the north wall is a fairly elaborate doorway which, given its position and richness, was almost certainly intended for the occupants of the big house.

Heraldic beast at east end

Inside, the eye is drawn first to the seventeenth-century woodwork, and particularly the canopied pews for which the chapel is celebrated. However, this should not be at the expense of the medieval woodwork. Above, the original close-timbered wagon roof extends unbroken over nave and chancel. Paint remnants between the rafters suggest that this was richly painted (probably as part of the seventeenth-century scheme). The nave pews, and chancel choir stalls with their blind-traceried fronts and poppyheads, also belong to the fifteenth century. The other medieval timber fitting, the rood-screen, survives only in part. The wainscot was incorporated into the east wall of the canopied pews, but everything above the middle rail (including the rood-loft) is now missing – apart from some lengths of brattishing mounted on the north wall of the nave.

In the first half of the seventeenth century, the interior was dramatically remodelled. An array of new timber fittings was introduced, together with a somewhat theatrical paint scheme. At the west end of the nave, a gallery carried on Ionic columns was inserted. The underside of this is continuous with the ceiling beneath the tower, and both are decorated with clouds and foil stars. On the south side of the nave is the pulpit. This too belongs to the seventeenth century; however, whilst the panelling is carved with archetypal Jacobean blind decoration, the form – square rather than hexagonal – is unusual.

Detail of Jacobean pulpit

The two great pews hogging the front of the nave are unforgettable. They are less about seeing from as being seen in, and in the case of the south pew in particular (traditionally added for the visit to Rycote of Charles I in 1625) there is a tangible sense of a set having been dressed for a performance. Physically, both pews take as their starting point the old rood-screen, whose upper lights were replaced with an arcade of rounded arches carried on columns. The pews were then formed by boxing in the areas to the west with panelling topped by a continuation of this arcade (though the proportions of the arcade differ in each case). While the design of the two great pews is extravagant, the actual seats within take the form of surprisingly plain benches.

The south pew is topped by an ogee canopy supported on columns with Ionic capitals; the columns spaced one

Rycote: the view east from the west gallery

South pew arcade

Gallery of north or 'Norreys Pew'

for every two bays of the arcade beneath. The canopy has crocketed ribs above, and carved figures in the 'spandrels' formed between the edge of the canopy and the square frame on which it sits. At least two of the figures are now missing: a Virgin and Child occupied the top of the canopy until at least 1883, and another figure one of its corners into the 1920s. Inside, the vaulting of the canopy was evidently painted (like the chapel ceiling, a portion has been repainted to suggest how it might have looked). Below, eight-petalled flowers decorate the wall panelling, those at the centre of each panel within garlanded frames.

The north pew (also called the 'Norreys Pew' after the family then living at Rycote) wears a different hat to that of the south pew: a gallery with parapets on three sides decorated with much-renewed panels of delicate, almost Moorish, fretwork. This gallery is supported at its northern end by wall-posts resting on the window sills, and at its southern end by columns within the pew itself. It is accessed via the original rood-loft stairs, and was probably intended as a sort of minstrel's gallery. Once again, the panelled interior features a repeating design, this time a delicate scrollwork motif in gold. The north wall is also panelled floor-to-ceiling, with each panel painted with a portrait or scene within an oval frame. Most have largely disappeared, but the ghostly face of a lady still peers down from the central panel in the top row. The same billowing clouds that play across the ceiling beneath the west tower and gallery reappear on the ceiling here.

ALSO OF NOTE

Re-cut C12 font on C15 base at W end of nave; fragment of painted glass on N wall beneath tower; fireplace (probably for Communion wafers) in N wall of nave, possibly coeval with fabric but with later grate (flue rises within W buttress on N side of chapel); old tiled floor to nave set with lozenge-shaped C18 memorials; memorial to Alfred St George Hamersley (d. 1929) with lettering by Eric Gill on S wall of nave; fragment of wainscot of C15 rood-screen on W side of N pew; marble bust memorial to James Bertie, Earl of Abingdon (d. 1699) on S wall of chancel; late C17 altar rails in sanctuary; Baroque reredos of 1682 behind altar (early C17 reredos now beneath tower); trefoil-headed piscina in S wall of chancel.

• • •

SHELLINGFORD
ST FAITH
Classic, small village church with good Norman stonework

Shellingford St Faith is a child's picture of a church: a simple two-box silhouette with a steeple at one end, a porch and a handful of windows. The setting, too, is a happy one, the church and a cottage range together funnelling views up to the south porch and a mighty cedar standing in the churchyard beyond.

The church belongs to the late twelfth century, but has been variously altered down the centuries – not least in 1625 when it was heavily restored and a spire added to the tower. The nave and chancel are both original to the Norman church, at least in terms of footprint (the chancel was largely rebuilt in the fourteenth century; the nave in the seventeenth). The tower, with its tall lancet windows, belongs to the early thirteenth century. However, the spire had to be rebuilt in *c.*1848 following a lightning strike. The windows are of various dates, with most of those in the chancel belonging to the fourteenth century. The nave and tower crenellations look Perpendicular, but are probably seventeenth-century. The south porch was added in 1625 (and carries a date stone). Both inner and outer doors – the outer ones like spike-topped saloon doors – belong to the seventeenth century.

Detail of the south porch

The chancel and nave both retain significant Norman fabric, including three interesting doorways. The arch over the south door has sophisticated chevron moulding, the stonework apparently unzipped to reveal a roll moulding within. This feature is late Norman in character. However, the dogtooth hood-mould above and the stiff-leaf capitals and shaft rings of the attached shafts below are Early English in character. The priest's doorway in the south wall of the chancel (which was probably reset here sometime in the fourteenth century) shares the Transitional character of the south doorway, having shaft rings on both its inner and outer shafts. It also has low-relief figurative carving, including leaves, but only on the eastern half of the arch. The north doorway – which is no longer visible from outside, due to the later vestry – is also Norman, with an arch of beakheads.

Norman priest's door in south wall

The interior, although relatively plain, contains a number of interesting features, including a further good example of Norman masonry in the chancel arch. This has attached shafts and carved capitals. Again, these are Transitional in character, the capitals on the north side being of trumpet form and with stiff-leaf carving. The attractive font cover, complete with knobbly finial, is Jacobean, as is the restored pulpit. There are a number of significant monuments at the east end, including a couple to members of the Packer family (one of whom, John, was responsible for the church's restoration in 1625). There is also a typically theatrical marble affair to Sir Edward Hannes, physician to Queen Anne, on the north wall of the nave.

Norman chancel arch looking east

The church has some interesting stained glass, including a strangely compelling Victorian window on the south side of the nave. Early glass (probably belonging to the fifteenth century) survives in the east window of the chancel and the middle window in the south wall of the nave. In the case of the east window, the fragments were placed here largely in an act of safe-keeping, rather than in an attempt to articulate in any meaningful way the elements depicted, be they pieces of architecture or drapery. The middle window in the nave is less of a jumble, having four early canopies and a handful of early pieces (including the head of a king) incorporated into a pair of new figures.

To the east of this is an unusual window of 1889 featuring a Madonna and Child flanked by a pair of saints. The figures are heavily modelled and densely coloured. The effect is rather graceless, and the flanking figures in particular come perilously close in appearance to pantomime dames (or were they actually intended to be men?) While the general draughtsmanship of the glass is competent enough, the artist clearly struggled with hands – the interlinked fingers of the right-hand figure being especially clumsy.

Detail of 1889 stained glass

The church benefitted from a sympathetic reordering of its interior in 1948 by Frederick Etchells (co-author of *The Architectural Setting of Anglican Worship*).

ALSO OF NOTE

1960s organ and lighting in nave; C14 indent to now-missing canopied brass in chancel floor; archway in N wall of chancel (with intrados of quatrefoils)

Shellingford: the church as seen from the south-west

once opening to now-lost chapel or tomb recess of c.1400 (possibly to John of Bledbury or Bluebury, priest, d. 1372); C17 altar tomb to S of chancel to Alicia Clayton, wife of Richard, rector, d. 1643.

• • •

Shorthampton from the south

SHORTHAMPTON
ALL SAINTS
Little box-like church with fascinating wall paintings

Shorthampton, like Easington to the south, is little more than a farm and a church in the middle of nowhere. For both churches, an unforgettable sense of place is arguably their defining feature. Of the two, Shorthampton is the more exposed. While Easington hunkers down behind barns, Shorthampton stands before field and sky, taking all weathers.

The church consists of a nave and chancel, south porch and east belfry. It has an unusually boxy appearance, deriving from its shallow roofs (hidden behind a parapet in the case of the nave), its lack of a tower or spire, and its square-headed windows with flat hood-moulds. Most of the visible fabric belongs to the fourteenth and fifteenth centuries. However, parts of the church date from the twelfth century, including the blocked round-arched doorway high up in the west wall (probably the original north door, moved here to give access to a now-missing west gallery), and the small round-headed window in the north wall of the nave. The porch, which has an unusual trefoil-headed doorway, belongs to the nineteenth century; as does the little belfry rising between nave and chancel.

Once inside, it is the wall paintings that catch the eye. However, there are other striking features besides, including the doorway-shaped squint in the chancel wall. While the unusually small double chamfered chancel arch probably belongs to the fourteenth century, the adjacent squint belongs to the fifteenth century. At this time the nave was widened southwards, and a second altar set against the wall to the south of the arch (note the remains of the piscina and credence shelf in the nave wall). An opening was then cut through this wall to allow those seated on the south side of the nave to witness the celebration of Mass

Shorthampton: Wall painting of the Miracle of the Clay Birds

Nave looking east

East window with fields beyond

in the chancel beyond. The box pews in the nave belong to the eighteenth or nineteenth century.

The wall paintings, though incomplete, form an intriguing group and include a couple of notable rarities. On the inner face of the squint to the south of the chancel arch is a probable depiction of the Miracle of the Clay Birds. In this apocryphal tale, the infant Jesus is reprimanded by Joseph for sculpting a dozen sparrows out of wet mud on the Sabbath. Jesus responds by commanding the birds to take flight. Meanwhile, the figure on the reveal of the southeast window of the nave has been identified as the little known Tuscan Saint Sitha (or Zita), whose piety brought her initial hostility, before eventual acceptance. Although various other figures and scenes can be discerned, the lasting impression is of tantalising scraps of narrative: clumps of rushes in rippling waters; a faceless figure holding a staff; the fringe of a dragon's wing; thick reds, grey-blues and grey-greens, smudges of yellow.

After the visual commotion of the nave comes the serenity of a chancel bestilled by light. There are no wall paintings here, but an extraordinary perspective: a Bible stands open on the altar. Beyond this, a window. Beyond, field and sky.

ALSO OF NOTE
Four medieval head corbels supporting wall-posts of ceiling.

• • •

Somerton from the north-west

SOMERTON
ST JAMES
Village church with fine reredos, screens and monuments

Somerton St James stands among terraced cottages and cherry trees, on a hillside overlooking the Cherwell valley. It is full of carved incident – some in wood but most in stone, and much of it not immediately obvious. Most of the fabric and the best features belong to the fourteenth century, but parts survive that date from the twelfth century to the sixteenth.

The exterior testifies to a number of building campaigns, and reflects the presence locally of both ironstone and limestone. The two are sometimes used to decorative effect, for example in the banding on the west wall of the nave. The fourteenth-century tower is mainly ironstone, but high up in its north face is a pale, ogee-canopied limestone niche containing a weathered, cream-washed Rood. The windows are mainly Decorated or Perpendicular, with those in the chancel, including the reticulated east window, fourteenth-century. The boldly crenellated parapet crowning nave, aisles and tower is Perpendicular work of the fifteenth or sixteenth centuries.

Crucifixion on north side of tower

Inside, the nave is a bit of a hotchpotch, its arcades mismatched, and its aisles lit by a variety of windows. The north arcade has Transitional round piers of c.1200, but was updated in the fourteenth century with the addition of the current pointed and double chamfered arches. The fourteenth-century font is of unusual size and shape, and may have begun life as the base of a stone cross (now upturned). The three-light window in the east wall of the north aisle contains glass by Christopher Whall of 1893, with foliage in a mosaic of greens, and a dozing St George at the base of its central light.

The most memorable feature of the nave is arguably the sculpture associated with its fifteenth-century roof. The surviving stone corbels are especially well carved, full of life and humour; one, on the south side, could be of a lion or a bearded man, but is most like a Chinese Dragon. Meanwhile, in the shadows of the roof, at a junction of ridge-beam and rafter, broods an owl. To the medieval mind (as described in the bestiary) this was not the wise bird we think of now, but a creature associated with the darkness of ignorance.

The view eastwards is dominated by an outstanding fifteenth-century rood-screen, carefully restored in the nineteenth century, but missing its vaulting and rood-loft. The lower portion (the wainscot) is mostly new, but the rest is almost entirely original. The deep band of tracery beneath the middle rail is a rare feature found on just a handful of surviving rood-screens (for example, at Cherry Hinton in Cambridgeshire and Llanegryn in north-west Wales). The carving here and in the panel-traceried heads is excellent. In a county rich in medieval screens, this is one of the best.

Rood-screen tracery heads

The restoration of the rood-screen was part of a sensitive and high quality restoration of the church carried out by John Sedding in 1891. His hand is perhaps most apparent in the chancel, where the roof and probably the choir stalls – their fronts carved with a happy menagerie of local fauna – are his. The chancel also contains arguably the church's greatest treasure. Set into the wall behind the altar is a wonderful c.1400 stone reredos, carved with a depiction of the Last Supper. This is medieval sculpture at its most engaging: humane, animated and full of charm. Each deeply-cut figure is caught mid-gesture, each with toes peeping out from under the swaggy drapery of the table cloth. It is reminiscent of the reredos at Bampton, and the two may be related.

Detail of Last Supper reredos

On the south side of the chancel and nave stands the Fermor chapel. This is divided from the nave by a pair of fifteenth-century parclose screens, and from the chancel by a c.1600 (or later) parclose screen. The ill-fitting westernmost screen was inserted between these piers at a later date, and almost certainly once extended across the aisle from north to south, in order to enclose the chapel at its western end (note the cut-off head-beam behind the central pier), thus originally leaving a single-bay space to the west of the chapel.

Arguably the most interesting monuments in the Fermor chapel are the alabaster effigies of Thomas Fermor and his wife Bridget Bradshaw (of c.1580). The bill for the tomb survives, recording that Richard and Gabriel Roiley of Burton-on-Trent were the makers, charging forty pounds. The monument is made memorable not so much for the portraits at the head end, as for the dogs at the foot end. While Thomas's dog seems on the point of relinquishing its role as footrest by tipping over the side, Bridget's dog – a tiny creature with a studded collar – busies itself untying one of the knotted ribbons on the front of her dress. Paint traces here and there are all that remain of a once lavish scheme.

Detail of Bridget Bradshaw's effigy

Thomas Fermor and his descendants were steadfast adherents to the Roman faith: a leaning that got the family into trouble from time to time, and ensured that Somerton became one of the leading Roman Catholic centres in Oxfordshire.

Somerton: the restored Perpendicular rood-screen

ALSO OF NOTE
Medieval limestone gargoyles on tower; blocked C12 doorway in S wall of nave; C14 or C15 N door; two probably C14 bench ends in chancel; C14 triple sedilia in chancel; large collection of mainly C16 and C17 monuments and inscriptions in Fermor chapel, includes brasses to William Fermor (d. 1552) and his wife Elizabeth Norreys, and large monuments to Sir Richard Fermor (d. 1642/43) and Sir John Fermor (d. 1625); group of medieval encaustic floor tiles at E end of chapel; medieval preaching cross in churchyard.

• • •

SOUTH NEWINGTON
ST PETER AD VINCULA
Village church with exceptional wall paintings

South Newington from the south

South Newington lies midway between Chipping Norton and Banbury, on a main road that winds laboriously between cottages. The ironstone church stands on higher ground, overlooking the snaking curves of the road and the little river Swere below.

Externally, the dominant features of the church are Perpendicular in style. The most striking of these is the south porch. This is crowned by a contrasting limestone parapet with oversized crenellations, and is made spiky and memorable by the pinnacles that poke through, echoing those of the tower beyond. Above the doorway is an unusually tall, canopied image niche, reminiscent of those on the south porch at Burford.

Although the tracery hints at earlier phases of development, it is only inside that the church's evolution becomes intelligible. The two central bays of the north arcade have late twelfth-century round arches and a cylindrical pier. These belonged to a late Norman church consisting of a nave, north aisle and chancel. In the late thirteenth century, the nave was lengthened by one bay to the west, and the south aisle and probably the west tower were added (note the lancets at the west end of the south aisle and the Y-tracery bell openings in the tower). The church was further extended in the fourteenth century, when the aisles were enlarged and the chancel rebuilt (the ogee-headed piscina in the south wall of the chancel belongs to this date). In the fifteenth century, besides the south porch and

Scalloped late Norman nave capital

South Newington: wall painting of the murder of Thomas Becket

the matching uppermost parts of the tower, a clerestory was added to the nave, and a new east window inserted into the east wall of the chancel.

The church contains not one, but two sets of medieval wall paintings: the north aisle paintings for which the church is celebrated, and a later series of completely different character in the nave. The north aisle paintings date from c.1340, and are exceptional both for their technical attributes and their subject matter. The majority of medieval wall paintings use lime- or tempera-bound pigments applied to dry, rather than wet, plaster (in other words, a secco rather than a fresco technique). However, the north aisle paintings at South Newington have been painted in oil-based pigments (though possibly with some tempera as part of the emulsion).

St Margaret and dragon

The paintings illustrate the Martyrdoms of St Thomas Becket and Thomas of Lancaster at the west end of the north aisle; the Annunciation with St James and the donor Thomas Gifford below on the splay of the east window in the north wall; the Virgin and Child with the donors Thomas Gifford and his wife Margaret Mortayne on the north wall to the east of this; and St Margaret slaying the dragon on the splay of the east window. The draughtsmanship throughout is extremely accomplished, the figures displaying the graceful elongation that characterises Gothic drawing of the period. Figure illustration of this kind is best preserved in contemporary English and French illuminated manuscripts, and it is interesting to note that the oil-based pigments used by the artist are of a type sometimes found in manuscript illumination, suggesting a knowledge, if not a working knowledge, of this art form.

Two of the depictions are notable for their rarity: the murders of Becket and Lancaster. Whilst the Martyrdom of Becket was a popular subject for painters, and can still be found in many churches, in perhaps only two depictions does Becket's face remain intact. The scarcity of the image owes much to its purging from churches by Henry VIII, who saw Becket as symbolic of the Church's resistance to the Crown. This depiction of Becket probably survives because it was whitewashed during the Middle Ages. Even more precious is the image to the east. This is probably the only surviving depiction of the murder of

Murder of Thomas of Lancaster

Thomas of Lancaster. Lancaster led rebels against Edward II and was implicated in the killing of Edward's favourite, Piers Gaveston. This scene, although frustratingly incomplete, remains riveting. The stealthy murderer tiptoes up behind the kneeling figure of Lancaster, like a pantomime villain forever frozen mid-crime.

At the eastern end of the north aisle are the relatively complete depictions of the Virgin and Child, and St Margaret. The Virgin stands swathed in green-blue over red, in elegant *contrapposto*, head tilted towards the miniature adult Christ at her shoulder. The figures inhabit a delicate cinquefoil-topped surround. Around them, leafy red tendrils eddy. The figure of St Margaret, although engaged in the act of impaling the dragon at her feet, is similarly serene and at ease. In a pleasing act of compositional precision, the artist has St Margaret's staff running diagonally from the top left-hand corner of the frame to the bottom right, precisely slicing the composition in two.

Virgin and Child

The wall paintings in the nave are also interesting, if only because a comparison between these and the north aisle paintings highlights just how accomplished are the latter. The nave scheme is fifteenth-century or later, and includes scenes from the Passion of Christ along the north wall. The narrative is played out in a comic strip-like series of rectangular frames, the figures crudely drawn and dumpy. Despite being unable to compete with his north aisle predecessor, the nave artist appears to have been consciously referencing the former's work, using the diamond chequerboard pattern of the Becket image as a background in some of the frames. The mutilated Last Judgement over the chancel arch is thought to be part of the same commission.

ALSO OF NOTE

C12 font with band of zigzag at W end of nave; fragmentary stained glass, including C14 symbols of Evangelists in upper tracery lights of chancel windows, and armorial glass in S aisle; C18 or C19 numbered box pews in S aisle; C15 corbels supporting nave roof; various interesting C16 and C17 framed documents in aisles, including affidavits for 'Acts of Burial in Woollen', and documents relating to non-payment of ship money; a nearby alley is called Tink-a-Tank: an old name possibly referring to sound of sanctus bell.

• • •

Sparsholt from the west

Chancel south elevation

SPARSHOLT
HOLY CROSS
Characterful village church with extraordinary effigies

Sparsholt church is no beauty. It stands, dishevelled, at the southern end of the village, its walls a mishmash of windows and buttresses. The fabric is chalk and sarsen stone, but shot through with some ironstone laid in contrasting courses in the nave walls (and visible where the roughcast has come away at the west end of the nave). What the church lacks in architectural purity, however, is more than offset by the interest of its interior, which contains some of the most remarkable tomb effigies to be found anywhere in England.

The current church dates from the late twelfth century. The most conspicuous original parts are the north and south doorways. These are round-arched and essentially Norman in character, but with some Transitional features, such as stiff-leaf capitals. The blocked south doorway, with human faces rather than beasts' heads terminating its hood, is perhaps the later of the two. The west tower is thirteenth-century and carries a later broach spire. The handsome chancel, which has tall Decorated windows and a fancy parapet, belongs to the fourteenth century, as does the surviving south transept.

Inside, the aisle-less nave is broad and barn-like. Its best feature is arguably its fourteenth-century roof, which has big carved spandrels, and arched braces integrated by their mouldings with the tie-beams to form continuous almost-rounded arches. Over time, more windows were added to light the nave, including two-light windows in the fourteenth century, and three-light windows (over the doorways) in the fifteenth century. The windows retain fragments of fourteenth- or fifteenth-century glass, including the figures of a donor and Christ in Majesty on the south side.

While the chancel screen at the head of the nave is Victorian, the parclose screen fencing off the south transept belongs in part to the fourteenth century, making this a notable survivor. Only in thirteenth- and fourteenth-century screens (of which just a handful survive) do the mullions take the form of turned shafts supporting a carved

Sparsholt: fourteenth-century effigy in chancel tomb recess

South transept parclose screen

Oak effigy in south transept

board below the head-beam (as here); rather than extending up to the head-beam and having tracery heads inserted between, as is the case in fifteenth-century screens. The current head-beam and wainscot are later.

In the south wall of the south transept are two magnificent fourteenth-century tomb recesses, each containing a rare and beautiful oak effigy of a lady. A third effigy, this one of a knight, lies aligned with the west wall of the chapel. The recesses are of the cusped ogee form beloved of the period; though here, unusually, the cusps seem to have been pulled into that shape by heads carved as if craning to get a closer look at the effigies within. The left-hand effigy rests on a fine chest-tomb, animated by the nine little figures arrayed in a variety of dance-like poses along its visible side.

The two female effigies in particular are wonderfully carved. Despite plenty of peripheral interest – lions as footrests, angels holding pillows – it is in the folds of drapery that the carver seems to have lost himself. Here, there is apparently no bending of the wood to his will, but rather, through deference to it, a sense of easing from it what had always lain concealed within its grain. The effigies represent Joan and Agnes, the two wives of Sir Robert Achard. Sir Robert, who is represented by the third effigy, is thought to have been responsible for the enlargement of the church in the fourteenth century. His effigy, as well as being damaged, is altogether stiffer, as if newly pulled from ice. On the opposite side of the church, the north transept was pulled down in the late eighteenth century, leaving a blocked squint as the most telling reminder of its previous existence.

Two further Decorated tomb recesses, similar to those in the south transept, can be found in the chancel. However, their effigies – a knight on the south side and a cleric on the north side – are of stone and nothing like so arresting. The recess on the south side adjoins an excellent triple sedilia and piscina, again with crocketed and sprouting ogees and pinnacles. The chancel also contains a collection of fifteenth-century bench ends incorporated into a set of later benches. The ends are of two distinct types: the first one rustic and with shallow cusped lights; the second one expertly carved and with a variety of decorative and figurative elements, including a cleric preaching from a pulpit. Up above, the chancel roof is supported by a terrific set of corbels, including one apparently depicting a kneeling man with a dog on his back, tugging at the man's hair.

ALSO OF NOTE
Medieval N doors with original hinges; plain C12 font at W end of nave; wall monument to John Pleydell (d. 1591) and wife on N wall of nave; painted Georgian arms over N door; polychrome Jacobean wall monument to George Hyde (d. 1623) on E wall of S transept; several medieval brasses in chancel, including fragments mounted on boards on S wall (cf. Chinnor).

Tomb recess in chancel south wall

• • •

STANTON HARCOURT
ST MICHAEL
Cruciform church with superb chancel and rare screen

There is more to Stanton Harcourt than first meets the eye. While much of the village is humdrum, at its core there survives an uncommonly interesting group of buildings associated with what remains of Harcourt Manor. This includes one of the finest medieval domestic kitchens to survive in England, and a fifteenth-century tower (possibly by Oxfordshire master mason William Orchard)

Stanton Harcourt from the north

in which Alexander Pope completed his translation of the Iliad during the summers of 1717 and 1718. The crenellated tops of Pope's Tower and the Great Kitchen answer that of the church tower from the other side of a tall crenellated wall, giving to the picturesque ensemble a vaguely martial air.

The early size of both church and parish (the latter once incorporated Northmoor and South Leigh) suggests this may have been an important ecclesiastical centre. By the twelfth century, there was a substantial church on the site with a large nave and a central tower. In the thirteenth century, transepts were added and the chancel was rebuilt, becoming in the process almost as long as the nave. The chancel is lit by trios of lancets beneath a continuous string course, and remains the finest and most consistent part of the church, particularly inside. The unusual stair turret, which narrows to a blunt spike, also belongs

Norman south doorway

Perpendicular Harcourt chapel

Memorial to Earl Harcourt

to the thirteenth century. Over its door, the names of two eighteenth-century churchwardens are proprietorially displayed. Vestiges of the Norman church survive in the nave (the part least affected by later changes). These include the north and south doorways and two pairs of windows, all with round heads and roll mouldings.

Further alterations took place at the behest of the Harcourts in the fifteenth century. These included the addition of larger Perpendicular windows in the nave and transepts, a south chapel to the chancel, and an upper stage to the tower. The south chapel, possibly also by William Orchard, is enlivened by a fancy parapet pierced with quatrefoils, pinnacles rising from stepped buttresses and a cornice decorated with grotesques. Although tucked away behind the church, it acts as something of an antidote to the prevailing tone of Early English restraint.

The interior is initially unpromising, but gives way to an embarrassment of riches east of the crossing. The nave, cloaked in roughcast and largely devoid of tracery and carving outside, is no less bare inside. The space is only relieved by an excellent fifteenth-century nave roof with traceried spandrels and cusped braces. In the 1840s it became clear that the nave was not always so bare: during the re-plastering of the walls, the remains of an extensive series of fifteenth-century wall paintings were briefly uncovered.

Moving east to the crossing, while the north transept is now given over to the vestry, the south transept and chapel to the east are the sole preserve of the Harcourts. Entry to their domain is marked by the sentinel figures of two Williams flanking the entrance to the south transept: the one glowering, the other imperious. The brilliance of their careers – one rose to Chancellor of the Exchequer; the other to Field Marshal – is presented as a challenge to their descendants, or to anyone else stumbling into their line of sight. The south transept also contains a typically flamboyant Baroque wall monument, together with a more discreet chest-tomb.

The Harcourt chapel itself (alas, not generally open to the public) was originally conceived as a chancel aisle with an open arcade of two arches, and a further arch into the transept at its west end. The two arches into the chancel were bricked up in c.1700, to give further wall space

Stanton Harcourt: the c.1260 rood-screen and chancel beyond

against and upon which to set monuments. Architecturally, aside from the large windows, the chapel is essentially plain inside. The richness of the space comes almost
solely from its collection of monuments. Arguably the
most interesting of these are the colourful chest-tombs
with effigies to either side of the altar. On the south side
is Sir Robert Harcourt (the likely builder of the chapel in
the fifteenth century) and his wife Margaret Byron. On
the north side is another Robert. This one was bearer, at
the Battle of Bosworth, of the standard whose tattered
remnants hang above.

The chancel – in contrast to the Perpendicular Harcourt chapel it once opened into – is undiluted Early English of c.1260. As well as being beautifully proportioned
and detailed, it is unusually well-lit for the date. Eleven of
its original complement of fifteen lancet windows survive,
all with attached shafts and rere-arches giving the appearance of short arcades (single shafts in the side windows,
clustered shafts in the east). In the south wall is a large
piscina and credence shelf, inventively set into a widened
portion of window reveal, and with a drain echoing the
shafts of the east window.

Remarkably, the chancel retains a considerable amount
of its original browny-red paintwork: on the arches, the
shafts of the east window, and the north wall around the
fourteenth-century effigy of Maud de Grey. Further colour survives on the tantalising, walled-up fragment in the
south-west corner of the chancel. The guidebook suggests
this may have been a window. However, given the arrangement of its arches, a recess of some kind seems more
likely – at least originally (if it were further to the east,
sedilia might be a possibility).

Remnants of chancel paint scheme

The chancel contains two of Oxfordshire's greatest
church treasures: the rood-screen and the shrine of St
Edburg. The rood-screen is coeval with the chancel, and
one of just half a dozen to survive from the thirteenth
century. Of these it is by far the most complete and unaltered. Its design echoes that of the windows in the east
wall beyond, with arcades of turned shafts topped by
cusped arches. The sliding bolt and hasp on the eastern
side of one of the doors, if not original, are almost certainly medieval. The haphazardly-cut holes in the wainscot

are later, and were made as squints to enable members of the congregation to witness the Elevation of the Host while kneeling before the screen. Suggestions for the identity of the nun-like figure at the screen's southern end have included several saints. The guidebook, however, plumps for Queen Adeliza, wife of Henry I and probable founder of the church.

Squints cut in rood-screen

Standing against the north wall of the chancel is the shrine of St Edburg. Unlike the screen, this is not original to the church. It was acquired by Sir Simon Harcourt from Bicester Priory at the Dissolution in c.1537. The shrine itself, comprising the canopy and shafts, dates from c.1300 and is carved from Purbeck marble. The limestone base is later. Despite its damaged and incomplete state, it remains a supreme example of Decorated stone carving – made still more precious for the survival of much of its medieval colour. It has been tentatively attributed to Alexander of Abingdon, who is best known for his figures on at least one of the so-called Eleanor crosses, erected by Edward I in memory of his Queen.

Shrine of St Edburg

The shrine abounds with naturalistic carving: in the heads that peer down from the cornice; in the little figures in their corner niches, whose toes curl over the edge; and in the crisply carved capitals, which include a kingly head (possibly that of Edward I) together with oak leaves and acorns. The shrine is vaulted below and would have supported a reliquary above. The base on which the canopy stands is carved with Emblems of the Passion, lending weight to the theory that the shrine was appropriated at Stanton Harcourt as an Easter Sepulchre (and possibly accounting for its continued survival).

ALSO OF NOTE

C15 font (restored in C19) at W end of nave; C13 piscina in form of head in SE pillar of crossing; other monuments in Harcourt chapel include C14 chest-tomb with cross and heads of bishop and king set in top, adjoining chest-tomb of Robert Harcourt to N of altar; brasses to Thomas Harcourt (d. 1460) and Nicholas Alterton (d. 1454); wall tablet to Simon Harcourt (d. 1720) with epitaph by Pope on N wall; wall tablet to Simon, first Earl Harcourt (d. 1777) possibly by James Stuart; C19 chest-tombs with effigies at W end (George Simon Harcourt, d. 1809, by Coade on N side; Archbishop Edward Vernon Harcourt, d. 1847, on S side); C15 pinnacled piscina in S wall; wall memorial

Medieval glass in chancel

to Robert Huntingdon (d. 1685) on N wall of chancel (blocking lancet) with epitaph by playwright William Congreve; effigy of Maud de Grey (d. 1394) with later colour in recess in N wall of chancel; floor brasses to Ellen Camby (d. 1516) and Henry Dodschone (d. 1519) at E end of chancel; four black marble floor monuments with fine lettering at W end of chancel; fragmentary remains of C13 glass in S windows of chancel, including both grisaille and coloured glass; moulded edges of chancel wall plates with brattishing at junction of wall and ceiling; C18 wall monument with epitaph by Pope to John Hewet and Sarah Drew, both killed by lightning in 1718 (during Pope's stay at Harcourt Manor), on outer wall of S transept; blocked C12 round-headed door on N side of chancel; C20 war memorial by Oxfordshire architect-writer F. E. Howard to N of nave; handful of notable gravestones and chest-tombs in churchyard.

• • •

SWINBROOK
ST MARY
Windrush valley church with unforgettable monuments

Swinbrook from the east

Swinbrook church stands on high ground on the western side of the village, watching the Windrush beyond the rooftops. Seen from the opposite side of the valley on misty mornings, it seems to hover over the village.

The outside of the church is made distinctive by two features of unusual proportions: the east window and west tower. The Perpendicular east window is disproportionately expansive for the gable wall it inhabits. Its size was presumably intended both to compensate for the lack of windows in the side walls of the chancel, and to ensure that the spectacular monuments within were adequately lit. Such a window would not be out of place in a church twice the size or larger.

The curious tower meanwhile, added to the church in 1822, is disproportionately small. At the eaves level of the nave roof, the west wall of the tower has been left off (thus preserving the integrity of the west window and now-blocked doorway below). The upper part appears to be carried on a pair of tall buttresses. Both features, east window and west tower, exert a powerful influence on the composition as a whole. With both imagined away, the building becomes a different structure altogether, self-effacing and without pretension: closer to its *c.*1200 appearance.

The two square-headed Perpendicular windows on the north side of the nave, while unable to compete with the east window, are also interesting. They belong to the fourteenth century and have hood-moulds studded with unusually small and delicate ballflower decoration (reminiscent of that found at nearby Taynton).

While the outside of the church is dominated by features dating from the fourteenth and fifteenth centuries and later, the interior betrays a much earlier core. The arcades and the chancel arch feature good Transitional work of c.1200, including a number of scalloped and stiff-leaf capitals.

In the chancel, meanwhile, washed with light from the east window's wall of glass, are two of the most remarkable monuments to be found in any English church. Both monuments are to members of the Fettiplace family, who lived in a great manor house next door (this was sadly demolished in c.1806). Both take the form of a trio of effigies on shelves framed by a classical architectural surround, and both reach from floor to ceiling. The left-hand monument is the earlier of the two, and was commissioned by Edmund Fettiplace (died 1613) for himself, his father and grandfather. The right-hand monument was commissioned by another Edmund Fettiplace (died 1686) for himself and two of his ancestors.

Scalloped nave capital

Although compositionally alike and divided in date by less than a century, the monuments differ markedly, most notably in their treatment of the figures. The earlier Fettiplaces have a board-like stiffness and hold near-impossible poses, with only a cushion under each elbow for relief. The later Fettiplaces, by comparison, have a flesh-and-blood softness, and lounge in comparative comfort on basket weave mattresses. In the later monument, there is also greater differentiation of the figures, and a sense that the sculptor was engaged in, or perhaps was simply more adept at, portraiture.

Also in the chancel, there are five medieval choir stalls with misericords (possibly brought here from Burford Priory). The carvings, particularly those on the armrests, are hugely characterful. They include a superb two-headed, two-tailed dragon-like creature with webbed feet, and a morose fish with scales like the petals of a flower. The

HEARE LIETH THE BODYE OF WILLIAM
OF ALEXANDER FET IPLACE SQVIER HEIS
HEYROFSEOMVNOASHFIELD KNIGHT HTXISS

ETIPLACE E SQVIER SONNE ANDHEVR
OWSE DELIZABEF ASHIELDA GREES NO
E S SONNS HE DECERS OTEI ORVSOFMAN CO

HEARE LVE FITI BODY OF ALEXANDER
NVE FET IPLA CEE SQVIER FE WASFIRSTESPO
ESQVIER FENTO CORITV A SH LI QUE HAD IS VE 80

ETIPLA CES ONNEA HEVRE OF ANTHO
ISLAN AN OSNICHERA WIF FERIH LONAL
ANSANOTOVCFE VI IVN LORD OF ZIEO EO

former may be a Salamander, as depicted in the bestiary: a poisonous winged beast with forked tail, sometimes symbolic of Satan in disguise.

ALSO OF NOTE

C15 font at W end of nave; post-medieval pulpit at E end of nave with blind tracery panels probably from wainscot of C15 rood-screen; two-light E window in S aisle with medieval glass once found in chancel E window (inscription tells of relocation of glass here after German bomb exploded in nearby field); numerous other monuments and plaques to Fettiplaces throughout church, including marble bust with drapery and cherubs to yet another Edmund Fettiplace (d. 1743) on chancel S wall, by James Annis; two brasses on floor of chancel: quartet of John Croston and wives to N, and Anthony Fettiplace (d. 1510) to S with griffin emerging from behind head; C17 and C18 lichen-splashed bale-tombs and headstones in churchyard; graves of Nancy and Unity Mitford to W of porch.

Memorial window in south aisle

• • •

THAME
ST MARY THE VIRGIN
Large town church with superb woodwork and monuments

Thame from the south

Thame is one of the earliest centres of Christianity in England. Surviving accounts together with recent archaeological investigations suggest a Saxon minster church probably existed here by the eighth or ninth century. The current church belongs mainly to the thirteenth century. It was built by the Bishops of Lincoln (who controlled the diocese from c.1086) to serve what had become a sizeable and vibrant market town. As the town grew so did the church, with significant enlargement and remodelling taking place during the fourteenth and fifteenth centuries. Despite some heavy restoration, this remains a church of great charm and character.

Externally, the church forms an imposing architectural entity, its massive crossing tower visible from distance. Closer to, windows attest to the main phases in the church's evolution. The north wall of the chancel is lit by plain Early English lancets of the thirteenth century, together with a slightly later geometric window to the west of these; the side aisles have Decorated tracery of

Swinbrook: the Fettiplace monuments in the chancel

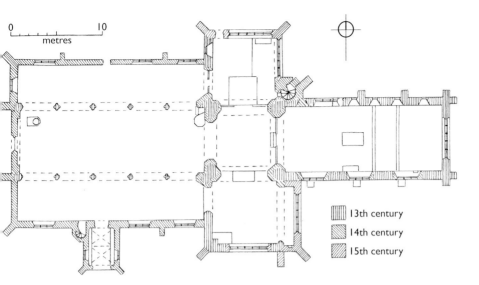

```
0          10
   metres
```

13th century
14th century
15th century

FIG. 14 Thame St Mary the Virgin

the fourteenth century; the transepts, grid-like Perpendicular panel tracery of the fifteenth century; and other windows contain post-medieval tracery (including some replacement work of the nineteenth and twentieth centuries). The transommed west window of the nave was inserted in 1673.

With much of the stained glass destroyed during the Commonwealth by Parliamentary soldiers quartered in the church, the majority of the windows are plain-glazed. While the loss of the coloured glass is a cause for regret, it has resulted in the interior being flooded with light – much to the benefit of the architecture and fittings. Unusually, all parts of the church are almost uniformly well lit by natural light.

Decorated south aisle window

The church is entered through a vaulted two-storey south porch. Inside, the nave has beautifully proportioned and moulded arcades of c.1260, with quatrefoil piers and double chamfered arches. The recent removal of the Victorian pews has at least served the arcades well, revealing their bases and allowing fuller expression of one of the glories of this interior.

The crossing is also Early English; its massive piers and triple chamfered arches a reminder of the colossal weight they must bear. There are two particularly fine screens here. The first one, the parclose screen to the north

Early English nave arcade

Thame: the effigies of Lord Williams and his wife Elizabeth

Tracery of north transept screen

transept, possibly belongs to the fourteenth century. Certainly the mullions, which take the form of octagonal piers terminated by capitals below the level of the tracery, are consistent with fourteenth-century work (in the fifteenth century, screen mullions generally had vertical mouldings that extended unbroken from the middle rail up to the head-beam above). The reticulated tracery heads are also characteristic of the fourteenth century. It is possible that this screen was originally the rood-screen, and was moved to its current position when a new rood-screen and associated fittings were introduced in the early sixteenth century.

The current rood-screen has two rows of linenfold panels in the wainscot, and a series of jazzily carved mullions above. Both are features of the closely related rood-screen at Charlton-on-Otmoor, and the two screens may even be the work of the same (possibly Continental) carpenter or workshop. The mullions in particular express a shift in taste from sober Gothic to livelier Renaissance decoration (mullions of this type survive elsewhere in England, including in the churches at Foy and Llandinabo in Herefordshire).

Thame is fortunate to still retain its churchwardens' accounts dating back to 1442. Among other things, these detail the rebuilding of the north transept midway through the fifteenth century. This work saw the reconstruction of the north wall, and the insertion of one of the huge new windows that was to light each transept. The south transept must be of a similar date, but is slightly larger due to the east wall having been rebuilt further to the east (note the line of the original wall). Richard Quatremayne, builder of nearby Rycote chapel, founded a chantry here in 1447. He is shown with his wife, Sybil, and one Richard Fowler (possibly their godson – the couple were childless) on a brass on the top of the fine tomb on the north side of the transept.

The chancel is the part of the church that most obviously belongs to the thirteenth century, and the part that feels most conspicuously Early English in character. The composition must have been both more striking and more harmonious when all twelve lancet windows still lined its walls – as they once did at Faringdon – and the east wall perhaps contained a set of graduated lancets, rather than the late thirteenth-century geometric window it now contains.

The chancel contains an extremely fine set of choir stalls, whose chestnut-brown timbers have mellowed to a leathery sheen. The stalls, some of which were gifted to the church in 1529, feature the same profuse linenfold panelling as the rood-screen, and were probably part of the same commission.

Choir stall poppyheads

The chancel also contains a fine collection of monuments. These range from humble vernacular plaques, through to the exquisite marble chest-tomb to Lord Williams of Thame (died 1559) and his wife Elizabeth, centre stage. The carving is highly naturalistic, the work of a sculptor (possibly of the Southwark School) whose coaxing of these two people from blocks of solid stone is a kind of miracle. The tomb was damaged during the Civil War and subsequently repaired in the seventeenth century, when a new unicorn and greyhound were added.

ALSO OF NOTE

C19 stained glass in W window of nave, W window of N aisle (by Morris & Co.) and chancel (some by Clayton & Bell); C15 nave roof corbels; unusual font (now in N aisle but once at W end of nave) made up of at least two fragments: C12 base with cable-moulding, and re-cut C13 octagonal bowl with leaf decoration (with Jacobean cover); c.1500 partial wall painting of pietà on SE pier of tower; C13 effigy of priest set into S wall of S transept; access to now-missing rood-loft high up in N wall of chancel (position of floors to lofts once crossing transepts also visible); sprawling churchyard with avenues of dwarf sycamores and array of gravestones (an especially poignant one, leaning out as if to catch the eye of passers-by, reads: 'Heare lies Neare Two of my Children Deare. Robert aged 2 years 10 mon Mary 2 days 1668').

Gravestone to Robert and Mary

• • •

Uffington from the south-east

UFFINGTON
ST MARY
Unspoilt Early English church with fine stonework

Uffington village lies in the shadow of White Horse Hill: 'the boldest, bravest shape for a chalk hill that you ever saw', according to the Reverend Thomas Hughes (whose grandson, another Thomas, wrote *Tom Brown's Schooldays*). The church is clearly visible from the hill, a tiny landmark in the sweeping flatness of the vale. Its prominence might have been greater still, but for the felling of its spire by a storm in the eighteenth century.

The loss of its spire has been the most dramatic of unusually few changes witnessed by the church in its 750-year history. Consequently, it remains almost as it must have looked when first built in c.1250: an example of Early English Gothic at its most pure, and a building of peerless workmanship. The only major alteration to the original plan was the loss of the sacristy from the north side of the chancel. Other alterations have been minimal, resulting in little damage to the overall harmony of the composition, either inside or out (*see plan on page 10*).

The architectural consistency of the church is well expressed by the rare survival of almost all of its original lancet windows. These are deployed in twos and threes, and are framed above and below by continuous string courses. Later windows include the reticulated fourteenth-century window in the south wall of the chancel, and the three lancets at the west end of the nave (whose oddly flattened heads are probably a result of a rebuild in the 1670s, which saw a flat roof temporarily cover the nave).

Aside from the unusual octagonal tower, the most striking external features are the three porches and the three gabled bays that protrude from the east walls of the transepts. The south porch is one of the finest in England for its date, and is uncommonly rich in sculpted detail for a parish church. The treatment of the gable is especially distinctive. This is topped by an unusual moulded coping and flanked by angle buttresses topped by gablets. The buttresses have beautifully moulded niches with later figures. Rising from the buttresses are the stumps of now-lost pinnacles (or pinnacles that were never completed).

South porch

Uffington: the interior looking east

Porch and altar recess on south side

The much-weathered relief sculpture includes a pair of creatures in the apex of the gable. The left-hand one may represent a Salamander: a creature the bestiary describes as being able to pass unscathed through fire, and which thus came to be used symbolically to evoke the good Christian (who might pass unscathed through the fires of temptation).

The two other porches, although discreet by comparison, are no less interesting. The porch on the east side of the south transept is unusually elaborate for such a location. It has a pair of almost-rounded arches springing from attached shafts, the inner and outer archways linked by a short tunnel-vault of sorts. Above is a large and deeply cut quatrefoil.

Also breaking from the east walls of the transepts are three gabled bays (one from the south transept and two from the north) each housing an altar recess within. Although the recesses are evidently at least partly original, the date of the triangular-headed windows in the gable walls of each remains unclear. With their plain mullions extending into un-traceried window heads, they recall the transept and chancel windows at Buckland, which were probably inserted in the eighteenth century. It is possible, however, that the Uffington windows were added in the 1670s, at the same time as the unusual west windows.

Several of the characteristics outlined above at least raise the possibility that a monastic foundation or minster church may have existed here; one perhaps established by Abingdon Abbey, which owned Uffington manor during this period (though no other evidence for such a foundation here has been found). If a monastic foundation had existed here, it might account for the unusually elaborate doorways giving access to the transeptal chapels and the chancel (possibly for the use of monks). It might also account for the previous existence of a sacristy forming a separate annex to the chancel.

Inside, almost all of the interest lies east of the nave (though the nave at least lays claim to one of the loveliest eastward vistas of any English church). Although the nave is aisle-less (and thus devoid of the resultant arcades) three arched bays do exist in the transepts, opening into the altar recesses. Again, the workmanship here is exceptional, with clustered shafts supporting intricately moulded pointed arches. In the south wall of each altar recess is a trefoil-headed piscina. The Communion vessels for the chapels were presumably kept in the quadruple aumbry – looking like a blocked-up window – in the north wall of the north transept. On the west wall of the south transept, meanwhile, is the church's best monument: a ruddy-cheeked effigy to John Saunders (died 1638) within a coffered and part-gilded marble niche.

The chancel is one of the finest spaces of this or any date in any English church: a sculpted casket in warm, creamy stonework, whose multitude of attached shafts and pointed arches give it a bounding grace. The current ceiling is of timber, but the easternmost bay was vaulted in stone, or was at least intended to be (note the springers for the ribs in the angles of the sanctuary). The treatment of the side walls of the chancel differs markedly. While the north wall has three pairs of lancets above a level string course (the central lancets are blind owing to the sacristy once being on the other side of this wall), the string course on the south wall steps down from east to west. It does so in order to accommodate the fabulous sedilia to the east and the later and larger Decorated window to the west.

Clustered shafts and capital

Chancel looking south-east

ALSO OF NOTE

External roughcast render later applied to protect friable masonry; 11 port-hole-like roundels beneath lower string course once held metal Consecration crosses (a twelfth almost certainly belonged in wall of lost sacristy); S door has fine medieval ironwork; vaulted S porch has ribs springing from angle shafts, and early coffin lid mounted on E wall; 1920 font at W end of nave (in memory of John Jenkins, killed at Gallipoli in 1915); close by is early stone coffin; small Perpendicular font in S transept; oak chest in S transept made up of panels from C15 rood-screen; early clock mechanism in N transept; medieval banded muniment chest in N transept; small, round-headed recess to E of sedilia in chancel may survive from C12 church; four head-corbels supporting wall-shafts in chancel, comprising man, lady, lion and dragon.

• • •

pray☩e to ☩he loue of walter Curſon and
☩oo☩e ☩of thꝭ ☩he la☩dꝑe ☩le ☩and ☩the
who☩le bodyeꝭ ☩le ☩yn the ☩aꝝgulꝑne
☩yyple ☩yn ☩the ☩eſe ☩of ☩☩ ou☩ ☩lꝛd

WATERPERRY
ST MARY THE VIRGIN
Atmospheric little church with fine brasses and glass

Waterperry from the west

Waterperry church has seen it all. For roughly a thousand years it has stood here in some form, unbowed by change, while the world has turned. Today it wears an apparently unfinished wooden tower, and must jostle for the attention of the passer-by with the adjacent gardens, art gallery, shop, museum and restaurant. Those who do find their way in are rewarded with an interior whose interest is out of all proportion to that suggested by what is visible outside.

Outside, what can be seen by the general visitor remains limited. The west front – on the south side of which is the current entrance – forms part of a continuous wall; the south, east and north walls, meanwhile, lie beyond on a part of the site not accessible to the public. The west front gives little away, and what it does give away is misleading anyway. There is a Perpendicular window, a stocky tower above (part-boarded, part-stone), and a shallowing of roof pitch to either side, suggesting a pair of side aisles. In fact, the church is far earlier than the window suggests, and has only the one side aisle.

Inside, the true antiquity of the church – at least of some of its fabric – is betrayed by the chancel archway. Clearly visible over the later, fourteenth-century pointed arch is a partly blocked rounded arch. This has square imposts characteristic of Saxon work. Excavations done in the 1950s uncovered the foundations of a small apsidal east end beyond, and it is thought that the western extent of an earlier nave may be marked by the westernmost of the nave piers. The arch in particular points to the presence on the site of a small pre-Conquest church, possibly altered in the twelfth century to give it an apsidal east end (this being more a Norman than a Saxon feature).

In the late twelfth century, the church was extended to the west and the south, in a partial rebuild that doubled the length of the nave and saw the addition of a south aisle. The easternmost of the two nave piers, seemingly with a round capital enclosed within a scalloped outer casing, is Transitional work of the end of the twelfth century. The square-ended chancel (which more

Transitional nave capital

Waterperry: south window, depicting Walter Curson and his sons

than doubled the footprint of the earlier apsidal east end) belongs to the thirteenth century. Unusually, its lancets are capped outside by little hood-moulds. At the same time or a little after, the nave was again partially rebuilt, this time widening it to the north.

Most of what attracts attention inside – the monuments, brasses, stained glass and furniture – is later. On the south side of the south (or Lord's) aisle is the Fitz Elys tomb, dating from the fourteenth century. Its fine, Decorated canopy shelters a cross-legged Robert Fitz Elys, whose family held lands at Waterperry from the twelfth century until the sixteenth. Some green pigment survives in the folds of his cloak, and well into the nineteenth century the Fitz Elys arms were apparently discernible on the shield. The four surviving head corbels – two supporting the chancel arch (one with hair like bunches of fingers) and two now mounted on the north wall of the chancel – also belong to the fourteenth century.

The church's greatest treasure, however, is one that many visitors will reasonably overlook, as it lies beneath the larger of the red carpets on the floor of the nave. This is the brass to Walter and Isabel Curson, whose descendants held the manor at Waterperry. Eight tiny sons huddle together below the figure of Walter, just as seven daughters once did beneath the figure of Isabel. Bordering the figures and their shields is a marginal inscription punctuated by skulls and crossbones.

Brass to Walter and Isabel Curson

What adds enormously to the interest of this brass is the fact that the Cursons were not the first to be represented by it: for this is a rare palimpsest. The brass began life laid in a London church in c.1440 to serve the memory of Simon and Margaret Kamp; only to be taken up at the Dissolution, sold on and reused a century later to serve the memory of the Cursons. The doctoring entailed a new head and shoulders being grafted onto the body of Simon, and his shoes being rounded off (as per current fashion). More remarkably, Margaret was sliced off at the waist, the sheet of brass flipped over, and the reverse engraved with an image of Isabel. A copy of the now-hidden brass to Margaret can be seen in the south aisle, giving this lady with billowing sleeves a second chance to be thus remembered.

To the west of the Curson brass is a smaller and earlier brass to Isabel Beaufo, of c.1370, with hair zigzagging in distinctive fourteenth-century style (a trait the depiction shares with head corbels at Great Rollright). Isabel's feet have been lost; as have those of the unknown man (probably another Curson) represented by the much cruder brass in the south aisle.

For such a small church, Waterperry has an excellent collection of stained glass, some of it early. The glass filling the three lancets in the north wall of the chancel, although much decayed, is probably coeval with the windows themselves, and thus of the mid thirteenth century. Most of the remaining glass dates from the fourteenth and fifteenth centuries. Donors kneel in the north windows: a man in blue and a lady in green, set against a background of oak leaves and acorns. One of the tracery lights above contains a fine depiction of Christ in Majesty.

The most striking glass of all is in the south window, over the Fitz Elys tomb. Here, in an echo of the palimpsest brass, the figures of Walter and Isabel Curson kneel before an incomplete Virgin and Child in the central light. Their offspring, radiant in sapphire blue, kneel in bunches behind.

Donor figures in north windows

ALSO OF NOTE

Current W entrance of 1820 replaced S door (visible inside); internal porch made up of 'Gothick' panelling from chapel in Waterperry House; C15 font at W end of nave with earlier, possibly C13, base; C18 box pews in nave; Jacobean pulpit with sounding-board dated 1677, with reading desk dated 1632; C15 or C16 doorways and staircase to rood-loft in NE corner of nave ('the rode light of Waterperry' — the candle for rood-beam — is recorded in accounts for 1527); arms of George II on wall of S aisle (with inscription to 'Richard Rippington Church-warden 1757'); handful of C14 tiles on floor of S aisle; fine Jacobean wall monument to Sir Francis and Anne Curson on S wall of chancel (with two sons and four daughters below); moving wall monument by Chantrey to Anna Maria Rooke Greaves (d. 1819) on N wall of chancel; C17 chest in chancel with top haphazardly cut with initials; aumbry in N wall of chancel has medieval hinges; C18 barley twist altar rails in chancel (possibly also originally from chapel in Waterperry House); medieval cross base and shaft in churchyard.

• • •

Westwell from the south

WESTWELL
ST MARY
Tiny village church with lovely font and rustic monuments

Westwell stands on the brink of Gloucestershire, little-known and apparently remote, despite being only two miles from Burford. Happily, it remains less scrubbed than other Cotswold trophy villages nearby.

Like Widford, Easington and Shorthampton, Westwell church offers pleasures that are out of all proportion to its size: a picturesque setting overlooking the spring which gave the village its name, a handful of captivating details, and a simplicity which, in contrast to many larger churches, allows the eye to breathe.

The church is small and simple; a two-cell Norman building with Early English and Victorian additions. The thirteenth-century chancel is lit by narrow, mismatched lancets, and probably represents a rebuild of an earlier, possibly apsidal, predecessor. The porch belongs to the fourteenth century, and the westernmost bay of the nave and the bell turret to the nineteenth century. The south doorway is Norman and of a standard type, with a chevron-moulded arch resting on cushion capitals and angle shafts. The tympanum is plain, but for a sundial or mass clock at its centre scored graffiti-like into the stone. Set into the east wall of the porch is the old piscina, apparently displaced here following the addition of the Thorneton monument to the chancel.

The interior feels unexpectedly roomy, being white-washed, uncluttered, and with a wide chancel arch and a barn-like roof overhead. At the west end of the nave stands the Early English font. This belongs to c.1200 and resembles one at nearby Broadwell to the south-east (though the Broadwell font is less fine, and may be an inferior copy rather than the work of the same mason). The design – of a quatrefoil-shaped bowl, scalloped below and borne on short columns – is extremely effective. Although not the richest medieval font in the county, it is one of the loveliest.

The church contains two other interesting features dating, or apparently dating, from c.1200: the chancel arch and east window. The shafts, capitals and abaci of the chancel arch are Transitional in character. However, the

Norman chancel arch abaci

Westwell: the Early English font

arch itself is thirteenth-century or later. It may represent a widened and re-cut version of the Norman original, perhaps inserted as part of works to enlarge the chancel in the thirteenth century.

The east window also presents problems with dating. Given the other Victorian windows in the church, it might be supposed that this too is Victorian. However, it was here in 1825 (as shown in an engraving by Buckler), several decades before Edward Tarver's restoration of 1869. If the window is medieval, then Transitional (of c.1200) is a possibility. Circular windows are occasionally a feature of late Norman churches (Iffley is a local example). Whatever the date, it is a rare example of the form.

Westwell also boasts two of the more unusual church monuments to be found in Oxfordshire. On the north side of the nave is the enchanting wall monument to Charles Trinder (died 1657) and family. Within a Baroque frame are the kneeling figures of Charles and Jane Trinder, their six sons and eight daughters; the dresses of the female figures looking remarkably like freshly whipped meringue. The monument is topped by a scroll pediment whose formality has been undermined by the playfulness of its carving. Pears cascade from the ears of an angel, a face grimaces between the squeezing scrolls of the pediment, while another glares out from the scroll-top of the crest above.

Trinder wall monument

In the chancel is the second memorable rustic monument. This one is a stone effigy of Richard Thorneton (rector 1599–1614). He lies with his head resting on a Bible, hands clasping a prayer book. Lack of space may account for his compressed form and the partial burying of the chest-tomb on which he lies into the corner of the chancel. The unhappy lion at Richard's feet looks as if he was pinned here, never to escape, when the effigy was shoved into position.

Stone effigy of Richard Thorneton

ALSO OF NOTE

Fragments of stained glass of 1522 in S window of nave; ancient altar slab found under chancel floor in 1933 and restored; fragments of Norman masonry in vestry walls; array of mainly C17 and C18 headstones and tombs in graveyard; colossal base and shaft of preaching cross on green below church.

• • •

WHEATFIELD
ST ANDREW
Striking, unspoilt little Georgian church standing in a field

Wheatfield from the south

Oxfordshire has two fine little Georgian churches: one at Chislehampton, the other at Wheatfield near Thame. While Chislehampton belongs entirely to the eighteenth century, Wheatfield represents the dramatic remodelling of an existing medieval church. The work was carried out in *c.*1730 for the Rudge family, whose nearby mansion, Wheatfield Park, was destroyed by fire in 1814. Widowed now, the church stands adrift in a field, its crenellations recalling the flames.

Close to, the church's underpinnings are betrayed by the blocked fourteenth-century doorways in the north and south walls of the nave, and the later blocked window in the north wall of the chancel. All else testifies to the Georgian rebuild: most conspicuously the pedimented west porch and the round-headed windows (including the Venetian window in the east wall). While crenellated parapets are a common enough feature, they are rarely seen on small, two-cell churches, and almost never deployed on steep gables in quite the way they are here (with each crenel kept plumb as the parapet rises). It makes for a striking silhouette.

The Georgian interior is unspoilt and full of texture, with walls of yellowy-pink limewash, and a well-preserved collection of eighteenth-century furnishings. The only conspicuous remnants of the pre-Georgian building are the re-cut fourteenth-century chancel arch, and possibly the crown-post roof above. The Georgian furnishings include the pews, the hexagonal pulpit (with marquetry underside to its tester) and the reader's desk, all with fielded panels. The manor pew on the south side of the nave has well-carved scrollwork panels, some with the Rudge coat of arms (which also appear in the west window). At the west end of the nave is the Georgian font, a birdbath-like creation with a fluted bowl on a bulbous baluster stem.

Interior looking east

Fittingly, the church contains an impressive collection of eighteenth-century monuments. The most notable of these is the wall monument to John Rudge (died 1739) by

Peter Scheemakers, on the north side of the nave. It has Corinthian columns supporting an open pediment down which two cherubs slide. There are also several attractive monuments in the form of cartouches, including ones to Thomas Isham (died 1670) on the south side of the nave, hung with fruit and flowers; to Sir Thomas Tipping (died 1725) on the north side of the chancel (with what could be a Yale, a medieval heraldic beast with tusks and horns, as its crest); and to another Thomas Tipping (died 1718) on the south side of the chancel, with draperies tied back to reveal its lettering.

Cartouche to Sir Thomas Tipping

The chancel beyond is filled with light from the large, Palladian east window, which is plain-glazed but for the modest depiction of Christ Ascending by Morris & Sons, of 1907. Below the window, until its theft from the church, stood a finely carved altar table of c.1745, possibly by the architect John Vardy.

ALSO OF NOTE

Painted arms of George II over chancel arch, next to painted C18 hatchment apparently to Spencer Churchill and Bernard Morland; remnants of C14 stained glass, including arms of John de Whitfield (whose family held manor between 1194 and 1390) in S window of chancel; C18 memorial slabs with crisp lettering in floor of chancel; numerous other monuments to Tippings family (C17), Rudges (C18) and Spencers (C19).

• • •

WIDFORD
ST OSWALD
Small, atmospheric church adrift in the Windrush valley

St Oswald's is a building in a landscape; a church whose magic is all about place, rather than architecture or fittings. It enjoys one of the loveliest settings of any Oxfordshire church, on a gentle slope of the Windrush valley between Burford and Swinbrook. It was not always so lonely. For much of the Middle Ages it stood among cottages in a village on the fringes of Wychwood forest. Aside from the church, all that remains is the manor house and a couple of cottages. Here and there, a rumpling of the ground is all that tells of the lost village.

Widford from the south

Wheatfield: the church seen from the south-east

Reticulated east window

Blind-traceried pulpit

The church is reached on foot via a dirt track, and is penned within a walled enclosure with a handful of gravestones. Built of local grey limestone and roofed with stone slates, it stands on the site of a Roman villa (a mosaic floor of which survives beneath the current chancel floor). At first glance, it appears to be a single-cell structure, all of one build. However, the gable wall between nave and chancel, and the joints in the flanking walls, confirm a two-unit plan and indicate that the chancel was enlarged at some time. The lancet windows belong to the thirteenth century, the reticulated east window to the fourteenth, and the rest, including the transommed west window, to the sixteenth or seventeenth century (the date of the nearby manor house). The church was restored in 1904, prior to which it was being used as a barn.

The interior is as simple as the exterior, and has little by way of adornment. The nave was fitted out in the eighteenth century with box pews. Behind the door is a plain cylindrical font of the twelfth or thirteenth century. To the left of the chancel arch is a pulpit made up of at least four blind-traceried panels from the wainscot of a c.1500 screen (presumably this church's rood-screen, though it may have come from elsewhere). The panel facing the north wall retains some original colour.

Throughout the church, medieval wall paintings can be discerned. The figures are hard to make out, but on the north wall of the nave is a faded St Christopher, possibly belonging to the fifteenth century, and on the north wall of the chancel there are depictions of the Living and the Dead Kings, possibly of the fourteenth century.

The chancel is only marginally smaller than the nave. It has seventeenth- or eighteenth-century altar rails with cut-out balusters, and a plain altar table beyond. In the south wall is a thirteenth-century piscina, whose trefoil head echoes that of the lancet window next to it. Underfoot, the flagstones are pitted and worn smooth as if by the actions of the nearby Windrush. When visited, especially alone, this is a church that tugs at you not to leave.

• • •

Widford: the interior looking east

Witney from the east

Bale tomb in churchyard

WITNEY
ST MARY
Imposing town church with fine steeple and tracery

Like Chipping Norton to the north, Witney was laid out as a market town in the thirteenth century, becoming an important centre for the wool trade. By the nineteenth century, it was internationally known for its blankets. Unlike Chipping Norton, however, the church of St Mary is by far the most prominent building in the town. It enjoys one of the finest urban settings of any Oxfordshire church, providing a magnificent focal point to views down Church Green; a vista channelled by gentrified housing of the eighteenth and nineteenth centuries. The churchyard behind is more secretive. Here, squirrels flicker among collapsing chest-tombs in the shade of giant cedars.

As befitting the town and its history, Witney church is not only grand, but also complex in both form and evolution. At the core of the present structure, and corresponding with the current nave, is a late eleventh- or early twelfth-century aisle-less church, of nave and apsidal chancel only (though there is some evidence for an early west tower). A north aisle and porch were added in the late twelfth century.

The most obvious remnants from the pre-thirteenth-century church are the north porch and some reused pieces of Norman masonry (including fragments of chevron moulding in the wall of the south transept). The north porch has a Transitional doorway of three orders, with jamb-shafts and stiff-leaf capitals characteristic of *c.*1200. The triple chamfered arch above looks partly rebuilt, and may be later. The original gabled roofline is visible above. The current offset upper storey, with its vaulted niche, was added in the fifteenth century.

In the thirteenth century, the church was remodelled on a grand scale, gaining a south aisle, a pair of aisled transepts (making it cruciform), a rebuilt and greatly enlarged chancel, and a crossing tower. The most conspicuous features from this period are the slender lancets (in the chancel and south transept) and the stately tower and spire. The latter depend for their effectiveness upon a finely judged combination of massiveness and simple detailing.

The spire is closely related in its design to Oxford Cathedral's, the two sharing similar corner pinnacles and gabled lucarnes (topped at Witney with cut-out beasts, possibly lions). Both also belong to the early thirteenth century.

The fourteenth century witnessed further enlargement, with a north-west chapel added to the nave and single-bay extensions to both transepts. While these interventions are modest in footprint, they are characterised by workmanship of the highest quality, including one feature, specifically a window, of spectacular design. The work was almost certainly carried out by the same group of masons responsible for similar work at nearby Cogges and Ducklington. All three churches share glorious and highly distinctive curvilinear window tracery, and Ducklington and Witney share similar diagonal buttresses with canopied niches (though Witney's are the richer of the two).

The north transept's north window is one of the defining features of the church. The rank of stem-like mullions in

North transept window

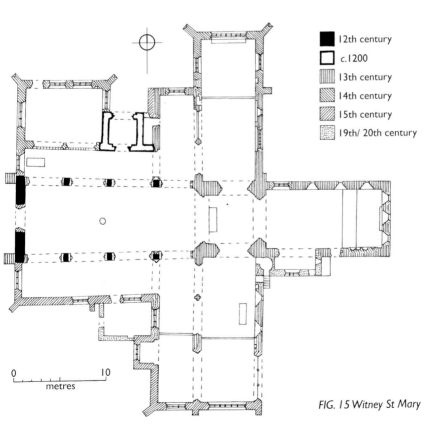

	12th century
	c.1200
	13th century
	14th century
	15th century
	19th/ 20th century

0   10
metres

FIG. 15 Witney St Mary

Doorway to north-west chapel

Carved angel on west window

the lower half of the window blooms into a swirl of petal-like forms in the head of the window. The composition is beautifully resolved. For the masons, the prominence of this gable in views south across Church Green was evidently too good an opportunity to miss. Smaller though equally fine windows survive in the west wall of the north transept and the east and west walls of the north-west chapel. Other notable features of this period include the ogee-topped doorway in the north wall of the north-west chapel, and the cornices of both north transept and north-west chapel (carved with small heads and ballflowers).

In the fifteenth century, the nave was given a large and elaborate Perpendicular west window (with new entrance below) and a clerestory of three-light windows. The south aisle was remodelled and also given a Perpendicular window and clerestory (this one lit by unusual quatrefoil lights). All of the outer walls except those of the chancel were given a plain parapet. The exterior was further enriched with sculpture with the addition of larger gargoyles and grotesques along the parapet cornice (in an echo of the earlier cornice below). The west window of the north aisle is also fifteenth-century. It has three carved angels, each apparently wearing hats and each strangely reminiscent of Mary Poppins.

Although the interior is not without interest, it falls some way short of the rich promise of the exterior. It does so for two main reasons. Firstly, while more daylight was admitted into the nave with the addition of larger windows and a clerestory in the fifteenth century, the chancel kept most of its slender lancets, making it comparatively gloomy (a problem it shares with several other Oxfordshire churches, including Chipping Norton, Bampton and Abingdon). The disparity is further exacerbated by the nave being whitewashed.

Secondly and more damagingly, the interior has had an unhappy recent history of restoration and alteration, with unsympathetic work carried out in the nineteenth century and more recently. A major restoration was carried out by George Street in the 1860s, further to the stated ambitions of the rector of the time to 'gut the church from end to end'. Consequently, the body of the church – the nave and chancel, and how these interrelate – is

Witney: the church seen from Church Green to the north

Nave arcade and tower arches

North aisle parclose screen

spatially unsatisfactory, lacking as it does both any sort of eastward thrust; and, in the case of the nave, the medieval richness of texture so evident outside. The recent appropriation of the north-west chapel and the ends of both transepts has also compromised the interior.

West of the crossing, the most arresting features are the nave arcades and the brass-topped chest-tomb and parclose screen at the west end of the north aisle. The nave arcades are unusual. Rather than having distinct piers, the chamfered mouldings of the arches simply continue unbroken to floor level, the archways reading as holes punched through existing walls. The raising in height of the nave in the fifteenth century, while leaving the earlier arcade intact, has resulted in an oddly proportioned space, with the arcade not as lofty as the roof height would seem to demand. That said, the nave arcades, seen with the impressive crossing and transept arches (all variously chamfered), form one of few architectural pleasures offered by the interior. Over the easternmost bays of the nave arcade are the tops of two twelfth-century window reveals.

The arcade between the north aisle and the north-west chapel beyond has been filled in to create an office, making redundant and incongruous the parclose screen that once formed the sole partition here. The screen is a hefty fifteenth-century piece, largely original, and with the unusual feature of a double middle rail with open-work decoration between (also a feature of the rood-screen at Somerton, this may have been intended to allow those kneeling at the screen to witness Mass in the chapel beyond). As recently as 1910 the screen still formed the sole partition here, and retained some of its original red and green paintwork.

In the aisle outside the chapel is a chest-tomb with brasses to Richard Wenman and his family (who built the adjoining chapel). It was moved from the chapel in 1867. Other brasses and monuments from the chapel were apparently taken by workmen when the chapel was converted into an infants' school in c.1840.

To the east, the nave aisles turn north and south into transept aisles. The arcades here are also double chamfered, only this time the arches rest on clustered piers with moulded bands at capital height. In the east walls of the transepts, a number of thirteenth-century window surrounds with attached shafts survive (this feature can be seen at Adderbury: another thirteenth-century cruciform church that was remodelled in the fourteenth century).

Below the great north window is a pair of beautiful, fourteenth-century tomb recesses. The boldly cusped 'tracery' of each recess springs from the back of a half-figure corbel, and the mouldings are studded with tiny ballflowers. The effigies of an unknown man and woman lie on ledges high above the floor, as if deposited here by receding flood waters; in fact, before its removal in the seventeenth century, there was a crypt here and the floor level was then much higher. In the east wall of the south transept is a blocked pointed arch (also visible outside and with the old roofline above). This once opened into a fourteenth-century chantry chapel, which was as long as the chancel next door. It was demolished in 1821, having been used as a house for the sexton.

South transept Early English lancets

The chancel, whilst still retaining a number of its thirteenth-century lancets, along with its fourteenth-century sedilia and piscina, is essentially a creation of the nineteenth century. Its east window, reredos, roof, tiled floor and stalls are all Victorian.

Happily (and in an echo of the external sculpture) the church remains well populated with old corbels supporting its various roofs. Head-corbels of townsfolk inhabit the south side of the nave; half-figure corbels, including angels, the south side of the south aisle; and wonderful full-figure corbels dressed in long robes, the east side of the north transept.

North transept tomb recess

ALSO OF NOTE

C14 tomb recess with effigy of founder in N wall of NW chapel; Baroque memorial to Sir Francis Wenman (d. 1680) in NW chapel; variety of mainly C18 wall and floor memorials in side aisles (including to Marriott family in S aisle); bright nave W window of 1869 by William Wailes; C19 font with foliage band in centre of nave; small C14 cinquefoil recess with old colour in S wall of nave; marble wall monument of Good Samaritan to Edward Batt (d. 1853) below chancel arch; C13 reredos of four recesses (upper recess with recent sculpture of St George) in E wall of N transept aisle; small C13 chamfered doorway to room over porch in W wall of N transept aisle; C13 reredos of three recesses with band of quatrefoils below in E wall of N transept; late medieval chest in N transept; trefoiled C13 piscina with stiff-leaf label-stops in E wall of N transept; Tudor-arched recess with old colour in E wall of N transept; C13 piscina with roll mouldings in E wall of S transept; two blocked doorways in E wall of S transept (northernmost originally for tower); several aumbries, including in W wall of N transept, N and E walls of S transept; C12 stoup in S doorway of chancel; late C19 stained glass in chancel and transepts by Clayton & Bell (chancel reredos also by Clayton & Bell, but adapted from pre-existing one by Street); damage to church during WWII included most N and some S windows being blown out by bomb which landed on Church Green in 1940, and removal of tip of spire by crash-landing RAF plane in 1942.

• • •

WOODEATON
HOLY ROOD
Small, richly textured church with unspoilt woodwork

Woodeaton from the north-west

Woodeaton lies between Islip and Oxford, a village with scattered houses on one side of the road, a large school on the other. The church stands on a green in the centre of the village, its western gable tight against the churchyard wall and road beyond (possibly explaining why the tower does not stand to the west of the nave, but rises instead from its roof). Adding to the odd proportions is the boxy chancel with its almost-flat roof. This replaced an earlier pitched roof, the line of which can still be seen on the eastern gable wall of the nave.

In terms of date, both nave and chancel belong to the thirteenth century, the tower to the fifteenth century and the south porch to the eighteenth century. The flattening of the chancel roof was also carried out in the eighteenth century, as were a number of internal alterations. Several of the windows, including the plain lancets and the Y-traceried window in the north wall, are thirteenth-century. The narrow priests' door in the south wall of the chancel is also thirteenth-century. The transommed window in the south wall of the nave is Perpendicular, and probably belongs to the fifteenth century.

The inside of the church is a joy. Faded and full of texture, it preserves a happy assortment of rustic carpentry and wall paintings, and is unusually unencumbered by later 'improvements'. The nave is a lofty space, with an open, barn-like roof. At its west end are the massive octagonal piers which support the tower internally.

A considerable amount of original painted decoration survives in the nave. This includes masonry pattern on the walls and window reveals, and scrollwork over the north and south doors. Also over the north door is a large, possibly fourteenth-century St Christopher, bearing the inscription in old French (now barely legible): KI CEST IMAGE VERRA LE IUR DE MALE MORT NE MURRA ('look upon this image and on this day you shall not die an evil death'). Over the chancel arch is an extremely rare painted rood-beam, also bearing an inscription, this time in Latin and roughly translating: 'Come you blessed to my father, go to the eternal fire you accursed'. Given the text, there is a strong possibility that a Doom painting, incorporating a Last Judgement, once existed over the chancel arch.

Alterations carried out during the eighteenth century included the addition of a west gallery, canopied pulpit and reading desk. Fortunately, they did not entail the removal of the medieval benches in the nave or chancel. The nave benches were simply given moulded doors, making them into rustic box pews.

Beneath the chancel arch there is a pleasingly simple and unspoilt fifteenth-century rood-screen, with chamfered framing, a high middle rail, elevation squints cut haphazardly into the wainscot (as they are in the rood-screen at Stanton Harcourt) and shallow, cusped tracery heads. The west side of the screen has linenfold panelling below the middle rail. Two of the panels preserve what may be their original red and green paintwork (a rare feature found also at Church Hanborough and Hornton).

The chancel retains further interesting medieval carpentry, most notably in the poppyheads of the benches. These are finer than those in the nave, and include lively carvings of the Sacrifice of Isaac, Satan being vanquished by St Michael (who holds aloft a fistful of thunderbolts), the Pelican bringing her offspring back to life with blood from her breast, and a kneeling figure (possibly a donor). One of the bench ends is carved with the Instruments of the Passion. The chancel is otherwise plain and relatively unadorned. Its most interesting feature is arguably

Nave looking south-east

Detail of rood-screen and choir stalls

its unusual bench-like sedile. This feature probably dates from the thirteenth century, and is similar to the example at Compton Beauchamp.

ALSO OF NOTE

Plain c.1200 font at W end of nave; small, probably C13 cusped niche in N wall of nave to E of blocked door; C17 carved panel at W end of nave; various floor and wall monuments, several to members of Nourse family, including C18 wall memorial to Anna and John Nourse at W end of nave; several hatchments (cf. Broughton and Great Tew) to Weyland family in nave; plain C13 trefoil-headed piscina in S wall of chancel; partially obscured painted text over S doorway; mass dial on buttress on SE corner of nave; C13 cross base and shaft on green to N of church.

St Michael poppyhead

• • •

YARNTON
ST BARTHOLOMEW
Unassuming church with wonderful stained glass

Yarnton gives few hints that it might conceal a special church in its midst. Its old parts have been overrun by recent housing, and its northern end bisected by a dual carriageway. Even when the church is found, it does little to excite; the eye is more likely to be drawn to the Jacobean manor house beyond. Yet this is a church of surpassing interest, containing the most enjoyable gallery of stained glass in the county.

Yarnton from the south

The church owes much of its richness to Sir Thomas Spencer, builder of the manor house next door. He restored and enlarged the church in c.1611 (so poor was its condition by the end of the sixteenth century that it may owe its very survival to him). The church as found by Sir Thomas was essentially a thirteenth-century revamp of an original twelfth-century structure, consisting of a nave, chancel and south aisle. Externally, the most conspicuous additions of 1611 are the tower (with date stone) and the chapel at the east end of the south aisle. The position of the west tower is misleading, for this does not abut the nave but rather the aisle – the nave and chancel lying to the north.

The church is entered through a south porch added in 1616. The inner walls of the porch are lined with a frieze

Woodeaton: box pews lining the nave

of lions and unicorns, with fleur-de-lis and rampant lion badges beneath. The simple round-headed doorway (presumably reset here when the side aisle was added) is one of a handful of features that survives from the Norman church; inside, the most obvious is the plain tub font now located in the Spencer chapel. Otherwise, the architecture within is largely Early English in character and thirteenth-century in date. The most conspicuous features of this period are the nave arcade and the chancel arch. The latter has attached shafts, with doughnut-like rings to the central shafts. Both arcade and chancel arch have two chamfered orders (hollow-chamfered in the case of the chancel arch).

As well as enlarging and renovating the church, the Spencers also fitted out the interior with a spectacular suite of carved furnishings, including the pulpit, reading desk and screenwork. The choir stalls also incorporate carved work from the same suite, but originally belonging to an elaborate state pew that stood in the south-west corner of the Spencer chapel.

The parclose screen to the Spencer chapel is the most notable of these furnishings, and one of the finest seventeenth-century screens to survive in England. Like other screens of the period (most notably the more elaborate example at Croscombe in Somerset) it employs classical elements – columns, bases, entablatures and so forth – but in a rather haphazard way; its 'architecture' simultaneously enriched yet undermined by the abandon with which its surfaces have been encrusted with carved decoration. As with other screens of the period, the silhouette is enlivened by a crown of strapwork and obelisks. It would benefit from the removal of the glazing over the head-beam, the curtains and other distracting paraphernalia.

Spencer chapel screen

The Spencer chapel itself is a wonderful space, retaining enough of its seventeenth-century fabric – woodwork, armorial glass and monuments – to give a compelling sense of its original appearance. Towering over the space are two gigantic monuments set against the north wall. The easternmost is the earlier of the two, and was erected by Sir Thomas in memory of his father, Sir William (died 1609) and his wife Margaret. At its core, it still comprises recumbent effigies beneath a canopy. However, this is about all it

Armorial glass in Spencer chapel

Yarnton: detail of the chancel north window

Monument to Sir Thomas Spencer

Perpendicular octagonal font

shares with earlier monuments of this type. It is otherwise a dazzling creation, possessing the same busy richness and architectural quirks as the chapel screen.

The monument to the west, to Sir Thomas (died 1684), his wife Jane and their children, makes an interesting comparison. The figures are not bestilled and recumbent, but animated and upright. It is they, rather than any architectural surround, that dominate the composition. Gone is most of the colour, replaced with the stark contrast of white marble against black slate; gone, too, old-school Elizabethan, usurped by flaunting Baroque. Even the use of wife and son to flank the raised figure of Sir Thomas seems consciously to reference the historic use of Mary and John to flank the figure of Christ in Rood-groups.

The chapel, as well as a finely moulded seventeenth-century ceiling (with carved leaves and pendants at the intersections), also retains probably the largest collection of seventeenth-century armorial glass of any Oxfordshire church. This is painted glass, dominated by yellows and oranges, but with some greens, reds and blues. Like all of the glass in the church it rewards close inspection, being of high quality and full of detail.

Spencer was not the church's only benefactor. In the early nineteenth century, further riches were gifted by Alderman William Fletcher. These include the unusual c.1400 font, the superb fifteenth-century alabaster reredos in the chancel, and most of the stained glass. The font (with renewed base) originally stood in Oxford St Michael. Its figurative carvings, which include a swan on the north side, are features rarely found on Perpendicular fonts in this part of the country. Fletcher also funded the paving and repainting of the church in 1793, and oversaw the renewal of its pews in 1802, using a number of fifteenth-century carved bench ends.

Despite all this, it is the stained glass that lingers longest in the memory. Setting aside the armorial glass in the south chapel, just a few pieces of stained glass original to the church survive. These include two fifteenth-century grisaille figures of kneeling monks in the tracery lights of the north-east window of the nave. Everything else was given by Fletcher in c.1812–16. The alien nature of the glass adds much to its enjoyment; for a jigsaw puzzle-like ingenuity resulted in the insertion of fragmentary shards around the edges of some of the lights, like the marginalia of an illuminated manuscript.

The two windows in the south wall to the west of the porch are cases in point. Both are dominated by wonderful depictions of St Michael, all curly tresses and feathers. However, tucked into the base of the left-hand window are snake's head fritillaries, bluebells and parts of a woodpecker-like bird with orange feathers; while in the bottom of the right-hand window, the tiny red face of a cow stares out. Other flora and fauna can be seen on the north side of the church, including, most marvellous of all, the eight birds occupying the north window of the chancel. These belong to a set probably depicting the funeral of Renart the Fox (the speech bubble-like banner above the owl, for example, reads: 'ye schal praye for þe fox').

Fletcher's imported glass belongs mainly to the fifteenth and sixteenth centuries, and comes both from England and the Continent. A number of the windows (for example, in the south wall to the east of the porch) contain Flemish painted glass similar to that found at nearby Cassington and Begbroke. Some of the glass was removed midway through the nineteenth century for depicting subjects deemed 'unsuitable', and the remainder was comprehensively rearranged in 1913.

ALSO OF NOTE

Early C17 studded S door; brass to William Fletcher (d. 1826) in top of chest-tomb at W end of S aisle; remnants of C15 wall painting above chancel arch, with possible depiction of Virgin (in blue); filled mortise holes for rood-screen and rood-loft in chamfers of chancel arch; trace of doorway to rood-loft on S side; monument to Sir William Spencer in Spencer chapel, attributed to Jasper Hollemans (carver of similar monuments to Spencers at Great Brington, Northamptonshire); monument to Sir Thomas Spencer attributed to John Nost, similar to later Nost monument to John Digby, Earl of Bristol, at Sherborne; various other floor and wall memorials in Spencer chapel include monument to Charlotte Spencer Churchill (d. 1850) in SW corner of chapel (addition entailed removal of elaborate C17 state pew from chapel); coffin table in Spencer chapel painted with 'YARNTON OXON' and skull and crossbones; weathered base and shaft of C14 or C15 cross in churchyard outside S porch.

Details of stained glass

• • •

MORE OF OXFORDSHIRE'S BEST CHURCHES

The following is a list containing entries for a further sixty-five Oxfordshire churches. The dates given at the beginning of each entry represent the centuries to which the majority of the fabric belongs, rather than encompassing every change witnessed by the church. Thus, a Norman church almost entirely rebuilt in the thirteenth and fourteenth centuries, with minor additions from the nineteenth and twentieth centuries, might be described as 'C13–C14'; the aim being to indicate the prevailing architectural mood of the church. The entries employ a number of simple abbreviations (*key below*). The italicised abbreviations at the end of each entry aim to summarise the church's chief delights.

Sax.	Saxon	*Arch.*	Architecture
Norm.	Norman	*Font*	Font
Trans.	Transitional	*Gls.*	Stained glass
E.E.	Early English Gothic	*Mon.*	Monuments
Dec.	Decorated Gothic	*Sett.*	Setting
Perp.	Perpendicular Gothic	*Stwk.*	Stonework
		Wdwk.	Woodwork
		Wp.	Wall paintings

ALKERTON ST MICHAEL
C13–C14. Small, on steep hillside. C14 cornice carved with figures and beasts (cf. Bloxham, Adderbury and Hanwell, but heavily weathered). *c.*1200 Trans. nave arcade and attractive C13 E.E. chancel arch of three orders with attached, banded shafts. *Stwk.*

ASTHALL ST NICHOLAS
C13–C15, C19. On bend in lane through village, with memorable N transept forming tall, cross-gabled chapel at E end of N aisle. Lovely interior with rustic *c.*1200 Trans. nave arcade. Cornwell chantry (N transept) with big C14 Dec. canopied recess with weathered effigy of a lady, and beautiful C14 glass. Attractive painted chancel of 1885. Fine bale tomb in churchyard. *Arch. Gls. Mon. Sett.*

BANBURY ST MARY
1797. Close to Banbury Cross, its bulk at first concealed. Colossally massive body of huge, rusticated ironstone blocks. Inventive neoclassical west front with semi-circular Tuscan portico, and lighthouse-like tower above. Hall-like but colourful and theatrical interior. *Arch.*

BARFORD ST MICHAEL ST MICHAEL
C12–C13. Enlarged C12 Norm., of tallish proportions on raised site, with part-stuccoed tower at E end of S aisle. Fine and elaborate C12 Norm. N doorway with two orders of beak-heads, and knotwork tympanum. Interior with well-preserved C15 rood-screen. *Stwk. Wdwk.*

Asthall: fourteenth-century stained glass in the north transept

BECKLEY ASSUMPTION OF THE BLESSED VIRGIN MARY

C14–C15. Rugged and chunky, high above Otmoor. Fine C15 Perp. S doorway with square hood and carved spandrels (door with C15 ironwork). Atmospheric interior with C14 wall paintings over chancel arch and in S aisle. Rare C15 stone book-rest on NW respond of arcade. Good but fragmentary C14 and C15 glass. *Arch. Gls. Sett. Wp.*

BEGBROKE ST MICHAEL

C12, C19. Small Norm., restored C19. Happy sequence of chancel, nave and saddleback tower. Enlarged windows bright with C15–C17 glass (mainly Flemish roundels). *Gls.*

BESSELSLEIGH ST LAWRENCE

C12–C13, C17. Chapel-like beside fast road. Nave and chancel in one. Charming, un-scrubbed interior with C17 and C18 box pews and pulpit. Good C12 Norm. pillar-piscina with apparently unfinished lozenge-cut stem and scalloped top. *Wdwk.*

BICESTER ST EADBURG

C12–C15. Large and much altered (including loss of medieval tracery in C18). Interior with three C12 Norm. arches of original crossing tower and unusual arcades (C13 piers on south side, heavily pared back in C15, now appear too thin for arches above). Eye-catching C19 glass by Morris & Co. Medieval sculpture, including two C14 panels reset over S aisle. Good collection of mainly C17 and C18 monuments. *Gls. Mon. Stwk.*

BLACK BOURTON ST MARY

C12–C13, C15. Self-effacing and atmospheric. Cave-like C12 Norm. chancel with small C12 Norm. S doorway and curious trio of lancets in E wall. Heightened nave with rare C15 Perp. stone pulpit (cf. Combe) and faded C13 wall paintings over c.1190 Trans. arcade (with roundels in spandrels). *Arch. Mon. Wp.*

BLEWBURY ST MICHAEL

C12–C15. Low-bodied and beautifully set among trees. Interior a sequence of rooms cul-minating in lovely, intimate, stone-vaulted C13 E.E. chancel. Excellent C15 Perp. furnishings include bold octagonal font, unusual parclose screen to S chapel, blind-traceried chancel stalls and extremely rare, original, blind-traceried door to rood-loft. Good brasses, including palimpsest. *Arch. Font Gls. Mon. Sett. Stwk. Wdwk.*

BRIGHTWELL BALDWIN ST BARTHOLOMEW

C13–C15. Attractive, largely Dec., overlooking road from sloping churchyard. Good C14 Dec. windows (reticulated in chancel; flowing curvilinear in S aisle E window). Appealing glass (mainly C14) and monuments (including striking C17 memorial to Stone family in N chapel, and important C14 brass). *Arch. Gls. Mon.*

Blewbury: the fifteenth-century door to the rood-loft

BUCKNELL ST PETER

C12–C13, C15. Stately, with part-Norm. crossing tower squeezed between enlarged chancel and nave (cf. Langford). Spare, unspoilt C13 E.E. chancel lit by lancets (those in E wall with waterleaf capitals to shafts). *Arch.*

CHILDREY ST MARY

C12–C16. On edge of village with far-reaching views. Well-preserved C12 Norm. lead font with cartoon-like bishops. Chancel with delightful C15 Perp. Easter Sepulchre carved with oak leaves. Dynamic C14 effigy of knight drawing sword (cf. Dorchester) within cusped ogee recess in N transept. Good collection of monuments, including brasses to Fettiplace family in S transept. *Font. Gls. Mon. Stwk.*

CHINNOR ST ANDREW

C13–C14. Of flint, in shadow of Bledlow Ridge. Consistent C14 Dec. exterior with reticulated tracery. Fine C14 glass and large number of medieval brasses in chancel. Rare C14 Dec. rood-screen, with encircled quatrefoils similar to those in N transept screen at Burford. *Arch. Font Gls. Mon. Wdwk.*

CHOLSEY ST MARY

C12–C13. In flat, open setting to N of village. Impressive and cruciform, with sturdy, part-Sax. (possibly C10) crossing tower, long and low nave, and taller C13 E.E. chancel with geometric traceried E window. Good C12 Norm. S doorway and tower arches (with carved capitals). Agatha Christie buried in graveyard. *Arch. Mon. Sett.*

CLIFTON HAMPDEN ST MARY

C12–C14, C19. Eye-catcher in landscape, on hillside overlooking river Thames. Dramatically remodelled mid-C19 by G. G. Scott, who added octagonal spire and transformed interior into shrine aglitter with brass and mosaics. C12 remains include arcade with waterleaf capitals and reset relief of boar hunt. *Arch. Gls. Mon. Sett. Stwk.*

COGGES ST MARY

C12, C14. Tucked away next to Manor Farm. Little octagonal tower oddly set over W end of N aisle. Fine C14 Dec. N chapel with lovely, curvilinear traceried E window (cf. Ducklington and Witney) and lively carvings of monsters on frieze and corbels inside. Excellent C14 effigy of a lady on chest-tomb with symbols of Evangelists. *Arch. Font Gls. Mon. Stwk.*

CROPREDY ST MARY

C13–C15. Big but tucked away, of golden and rust-coloured ironstone. Good C14 Dec. features include tracery (for example, reticulated E window and curvilinear S aisle windows), cornice carved with ballflower and heads, and rare screen on N side of chancel with dancing mouchettes in tracery. Rare C15 brass eagle lectern. Much-faded C15 wall painting (probably 'Doom') over chancel arch. *Arch. Mon. Stwk. Wdwk. Wp.*

CUDDESDON ALL SAINTS

C12–C13, C15. Magnificent hilltop setting. C12 cruciform with handsome crossing tower, C13 side aisles, C14 west porch and C15 chancel. High quality C12 late Norm./ Trans. work, including splendidly carved W doorway and tower arches. *Arch. Sett. Stwk.*

EAST HAGBOURNE ST ANDREW

C13–C15. In attractive village of half-timber, clay tile and thatch. C14/ C15 W tower with octagonal-topped stair turret and rare pinnacled bellcote for sanctus bell. Inside unspoilt and light-filled (clerestoried throughout and with E window filling E wall). Striking chancel arch corbels (mask-like triple-head on S side). Stiff-leaf capitals to S chapel arcade. Fine Perp. roofs and pulpit (possibly made up from parts of C15 screen). Some colourful C14 glass (including Nativity and Virgin in N aisle). *Arch. Gls. Stwk. Wdwk.*

EAST HENDRED ST AUGUSTINE OF CANTERBURY

C13–C15. Laneside in attractive village. Mainly Perp. character, but nave arcades are C13 E.E. with superb, luxuriant capitals. Unspoilt Eyston chapel to S of chancel is *c.*1500, of flint and ashlar chequerwork (cf. Henley and Ewelme) with distinctive square-headed Perp. windows. Rare medieval lectern with carved dragons, and C16 faceless clock. Some good brasses. *Arch. Mon. Stwk.*

FULBROOK ST JAMES

C12–C13, C15. Mellow and characterful, in sloping churchyard with fine C17 bale tombs. Good C12 Norm. S doorway within C13 porch. *c.*1200 Trans. nave arcade and chancel arch. Lovely, local C17 wall monument to Jordan family. *Mon. Stwk.*

GREAT HASELEY ST PETER

C13–C15. Oddly proportioned with flattened nave and soaring chancel. Lovely reset *c.*1200 W doorway in tower with dogtooth to hood and stiff-leaf capitals to shafts. Magnificent, stately chancel of *c.*1300, with superb E window and richly carved sedilia, piscina and tomb within. Interesting monuments. *Arch. Mon. Stwk.*

GREAT MILTON ST MARY

C13–C15. Handsome C14 Dec. exterior, with memorable two-storey S porch with polygonal stair turret. Large and extremely fine C17 alabaster monument by Southwark School, with three members of Dormer family beneath elaborate canopy, with much relief carving. Beautiful, fragmentary C14 glass in E window. *Arch. Gls. Mon.*

HAMPTON POYLE ST MARY

C13–C14. Down country lane near farm. Pleasing and small, C13 body with bellcote and C14 aisles. Unusual tracery includes fine C13 geometric in chancel E window (with kaleidoscope and trefoil patterns) and mid C14 (almost Perp.) in N aisle. C14 N arcade capital in form of figure with linked arms (cf. Hanwell, Bloxham and Adderbury but less fine: possibly copy rather than by same carver). Good C14 stone effigies of knight and lady, and C15 glass (small quarries of Evangelists). *Gls. Mon. Sett. Stwk.*

HARWELL ST MATTHEW

C13–C14. Cruciform in raised churchyard. Interior with lively stone carving, including chancel arch corbels with figures attacked by dragons, and drinker slumped against top of priest's door. Rare survival of *c.*1300 timber roofs to nave, chancel and S transept; and of rood-screen possibly of similar date (with turned shafts cf. Sparsholt). *Mon. Stwk. Wdwk.*

HENLEY-ON-THAMES ST MARY THE VIRGIN

C13, C15–C16. Sprawling and lively with much flint and stone chequerwork, including to polygonal, turreted buttresses of handsome C16 tower (cf. Dorchester). Spacious interior with enjoyable Victorian work, including fine windows by Hardman in N chapel. *Gls. Sett. Wp.*

HOOK NORTON ST PETER

C12, C14–C15. In heart of rolling ironstone village. Good C14 Dec. tracery (including E window) and C15 Perp. W tower with boldly-hooded doorway. C12 Norm. chancel with original aumbry and sedilia. C15 wall painting and five-light 'Cotswold window' over chancel arch with openwork quatrefoils. Wonderful C12 Norm. tub font with rustic carvings of Adam and Eve, and signs of Zodiac. C18 fire engine. *Arch. Font Wp.*

HORNTON ST JOHN THE BAPTIST

C12, C14. In a sloping rust-coloured village. Textured and unspoilt with wonky clerestory windows. Compelling C14 paintings around chancel arch, including Doom with Crucifixion and Risen emerging from coffins against a black background, and St George on S side. Portion of C15 screen wainscot with rare survival of original colour. *Font Stwk. Wdwk. Wp.*

HORTON-CUM-STUDLEY ST BARNABAS

By William Butterfield (1867). Architecturally modest, but with lovely patterned brickwork throughout in sandy yellows and stronger blues and reds, mellowing to an array of shades. Hall-like interior with inventive font and reredos by Butterfield, and bright glass by F. Preedy. *Font Gls. Stwk.*

IDBURY ST NICHOLAS

C12, C14–C15. Lane-side in isolated hamlet. Mainly C15 Perp. in character, but with fine reset C12 Norm. N doorway with decorated jamb shafts, chevrons and saltire crosses to arch. Peaceful, uncluttered interior with lovely C15 font, rood-screen and bench ends; also, pulpit incorporating interesting C15 work. *Font Stwk. Wdwk.*

IPSDEN ST MARY

C12, C14. Behind isolated houses in sweeping Chilterns landscape of huge fields. Small and unspoilt with blocked C12 priest's door. Shares much with nearby North Stoke, including

Idbury: the fifteenth-century font

Abbey of Bec patronage, survival of C14 roof, and distinctive chancel treatment (including Purbeck shafts with leaf capitals, one with head). *Sett. Stwk.*

KELMSCOTT ST GEORGE

C12–C15. Small and cruciform, textured and engaging. Memorable late C12 Trans. arcade with scalloped and stiff-leaf capitals, C13 quatrefoils with heads in spandrels, and faded C14 leaf scroll in red and orange to arches. C14 wall paintings in N transept (figures beneath trefoil canopies, also in red and orange). William Morris buried in churchyard. *Gls. Sett. Stwk. Wp.*

LEAFIELD ST MICHAEL

1860–74 by G. G. Scott. Imposing and accomplished, reliant on architecture not surface decoration for effect. Careful oblique composition of W front and tower terminating views along main street. Essentially E.E. in style, but never slavishly so (note distinctive gabled aisle windows, and tower with small buttresses against diagonal faces). *Arch.*

LEWKNOR ST MARGARET

C13–C14. Big with ambitiously rebuilt C14 chancel (with roof higher than nave, cf. Great Haseley) containing ostentatious but enjoyable C14 piscina, sedilia, tomb recess and priest's door, all richly carved and with oversized popcorn-like finials. Several interesting monuments (including effigies) and lovely C12 Norm. font covered with interlace of great variety and with small mask-like green man. *Font Mon. Stwk.*

LITTLE FARINGDON ST MARGARET OF ENGLAND

C12, C14–C15. Compact and picturesque, with little C19 bellcote. Surprisingly fine nave arcade for so small a church, with beautiful late C12 Trans. capitals carved with stiff-leaf. Some good scraps of medieval glass. *Stwk.*

LITTLE ROLLRIGHT ST PHILIP

C13, C15, C17. In tiny, isolated hamlet in valley bowl. Simple outline. Fine C15 Perp. E window with panel tracery and image brackets. Unadorned nave with windows in S wall only. Chancel with memorable C17 monuments, including effigy propped on elbow (cf. Fettiplace monuments at Swinbrook). *Mon. Sett.*

LONG WITTENHAM ST MARY

C12–C16. Down track between thatched and half-timbered cottages. Lovely, rustic C15 Perp. timber S porch. C12 Norm. chancel arch with dragon capital. Fine C12 Norm. lead font (cf. Warborough and Dorchester) with wheels in upper half and bishops in arcade around base. Remarkable C13 piscina-monument with angels framing recess and knight effigy piscina bowl. Good *c.*1200 S aisle with fleshy stiff-leaf capitals. C17 stalls with boldly carved poppyheads, and C17 screen to S transept. C16 nave roof. *Font Mon. Sett. Stwk. Wdwk.*

Little Rollright: Jacobean monument to a member of the Dixon family

MAPLEDURHAM ST MARGARET

C13–C15, C19. Memorable setting next to Elizabethan manor house. C14 W tower refaced with brick and flint chequerwork – imaginatively and with trademark boldness – by W. Butterfield in 1863. Over-filled interior with railed-off S aisle. Interesting glass, including medieval fragments and good memorial window of 1879 with white lilies against blue ground. Fine, tall C14 brass, good C17 effigies and painted C12 font. *Arch. Font Gls. Mon. Sett.*

MERTON ST SWITHUN

C14–C15. Even more impressive before loss of N aisle and spire (the latter in 1796). Fine C14 Dec. stonework throughout, including roof corbels, sedilia and piscina in chancel, and E window with curvilinear tracery and flanked by canopied image niches in S aisle. Jacobean stalls, pulpit and font cover. Good C15 roof corbels in nave and C16 wall monument to John Doyley. *Arch. Stwk. Wdwk.*

MINSTER LOVELL ST KENELM

C15. Unforgettable setting beside river Windrush and picturesque ruins. Consistent and accomplished C15 Perp. on earlier foundations. Central crossing tower beautifully expressed inside with freestanding, finely moulded tower piers and vaulted ceiling. Panel-traceried windows with some C15 glass. Fine C15 knight effigy in S transept. *Arch. Font Gls. Mon. Sett. Stwk.*

NORTHMOOR ST DENIS

C14–C15. Remote and unspoilt. Cruciform and part-rendered. Inside, early C14 nave windows have short jamb shafts on head-stops with pre-E.E. foliage-carved capitals. Fine *c.*1200 tub font with Tree of Life in low relief. Faded wall painting related to adjacent C14 tomb recesses with effigies in N transept; canopied C15 niche in S transept. Sumptuously carved C17 communion rail in chancel, and C17 bell ringers' W gallery with inscription. Good, bold C19 glass. *Arch. Font Gls. Mon. Stwk. Wdwk. Wp.*

NORTH MORETON ALL SAINTS

C13–C15. Among big yew trees by village road. Square C15 Perp. W tower with quatrefoil parapet. Fine and unusual tracery, including C13 geometric in chancel E window and early C14 net-like pattern of cusped arches in S chapel E window. Cornice carved with beasts. E window of *c.*1300 S chapel with stunning, early C14 stained glass depicting scenes from lives of Christ, Virgin Mary, and SS Peter, Paul and Nicholas. Also, bright, striking C19 chancel E window by J. F. Bentley. *Arch. Gls. Mon. Stwk.*

NUNEHAM COURTENAY ALL SAINTS

1764. By J. Stuart and first Earl Harcourt. Impressive, neoclassical landscape feature in gardens of big house. Powerful design of simple geometrical forms – rectangle and cylinder – with Ionic portico. Forbidding, mausoleum-like quality heightened by blank arches and doorway, and prison-like Diocletian windows set high up. Interior less powerful but still memorable, with interesting furnishings and monuments. *Arch. Mon. Sett.*

Nuneham Courtenay: the neoclassical chapel

OXFORD ALL SAINTS (*now Lincoln College library*)
1707–08. By H. Aldrich and N. Hawksmoor. Standing imperiously on High Street. Tall, rectangular volume with giant order paired Corinthian pilasters and big round-headed windows, topped by square then round, colonnaded W tower with small steeple. Characterised throughout by exceptional stonework. Beautiful, elegant hall-like interior with extremely fine plasterwork ceiling. *Arch. Mon. Sett.*

OXFORD ST ALOYSIUS (*Roman Catholic*)
By J. A. Hansom in sandy brick (1873–75). Pick-and-mix Gothic with big rose window and floor-to-ceiling attached shafts in dark stone as per French cathedral Gothic. Striking interior with nave, chancel and rounded apse in one, and continuous clerestory. Eastward view culminates in memorable, inverted Colosseum-like reredos of two galleried tiers with statues and busts of angels above (Hansom, 1878): strangely malleable and un-stone-like. Amazing c.1850 font, a softly modelled confection, loosely Dec. in style, with Life of Christ in deep relief. *Arch. Font Stwk.*

OXFORD ST BARNABAS
1868–69 and 1872 (tower). By A. Blomfield. Amid terraces of Jericho, with tall Tuscan Gothic campanile visible from distance. Powerful, pared-back exterior, rendered and with thin strips of red brick loosely deployed for effect. Simple, big windows with brick arched heads. Basilican plan with apses E and W. Incomplete interior, but rich mosaic scheme over N arcade, and Byzantine style apse with much gold, Christ in Majesty and saints below against dark blue ground, and flanked by black-on-gold stencilled design of Evangelists. *Arch.*

OXFORD ST MICHAEL
C11–C15. Iconic rubble-built C11 Sax. W tower standing implacable amid shops and blur of passers-by: plain, but for bell openings with stout barrel balusters. Much-rebuilt body of church has good C15 Perp. nave arcade with image niches. Rich, C15 Perp. font. Pulpit and parclose screen with some C15 work. Notable C13 glass and C17 wall monument to Ann Lloyd. *Arch. Font Gls. Mon. Sett.*

OXFORD ST PETER-IN-THE-EAST (*now library of St Edmund Hall*)
C12–C15. Odd, high-walled exterior with quatrefoil parapet, two fine C14 windows with curvilinear tracery on N side and ornate C12 Norm. S doorway with beakheads. Fascinating c.1130 vaulted crypt with low arcades and capitals with fish-scale, beasts and foliage. Fine C13 E.E. N arcade with stiff-leaf capitals. Rich c.1170 stone-vaulted chancel with cone-topped corner turrets, chevron moulded windows, blind arcading and renewed corbel table. Fragmentary old glass and good collection of monuments. *Arch. Gls. Mon. Stwk.*

PIDDINGTON ST NICHOLAS
C14–C16. In round churchyard encircled by trees. Stubby C16 tower. Unusual E window of three slender candle-like lancets. Inside, beyond plain nave and S aisle, memorable chancel

chockfull of enjoyable E.E. and Dec. stonework, including Easter Sepulchre studded with little angels, steeply-gabled sedilia trimmed with foliage, and unusual rere-arch to E window with trefoiled cusps. Faded C14 St Christopher. *Stwk.*

ROTHERFIELD GREYS ST NICHOLAS

C17, C19. Rebuilt 1865 by W. H. Woodman – except for Jacobean N chapel of 1605. Bare interior relieved by fabulous Knollys tomb, probably by Southwark School, with recumbent effigies beneath canopy, kneeling figures above, children around sides and wealth of carved detail and original colour. Extremely fine C14 brass of Lord Robert de Grey as knight, and low c.1200 E.E. square font with corner shafts and stiff-leaf capitals. *Font Mon.*

SHILTON HOLY ROOD

C12–C13, C15. Humble and unadorned, on slope above village. Restored C12 Norm. nave with arcade of round arches with some old colour, and C13 E.E. chancel arch with roll mouldings. Gorgeous C12 square font, re-cut in C14 with sides carved in high relief with scenes from the Passion; the corners with Evangelists. *Arch. Font Sett.*

SHIPLAKE ST PETER AND ST PAUL

C13–C14, C19. Next to Shiplake College. Largely rebuilt 1868–70 by G. E. Street. Wonderful collection of fine C15 French glass (from Benedictine Abbey of Saint-Bertin at Saint-Omer). Subjects include Coronation of Virgin in chancel E window, and brilliant portrait-like faces of saints in S aisle windows. *Gls.*

SHIPTON-UNDER-WYCHWOOD ST MARY

C13–C15. Happy setting amid trees beyond village green. Handsome exterior with two-storey C14 porch with image niches, and short C13 tower. Attractive spire – like smaller version of Witney's – has lucarnes topped with figures/ animals (with crosses balanced on heads) and corner pinnacles with big ball finials. Light, spacious interior with good C15 Perp. stone pulpit and font. Noteworthy monuments include palimpsest brass in S chapel and superb bale tomb in churchyard. *Arch. Font Mon. Sett. Stwk.*

SHRIVENHAM ST ANDREW

C15, C17. Memorable rarity in both design and date (1638). Mainly Gothic but part-classical. Huge, unusually proportioned rectangular volume with shallow-pitched roof engulfing central C15 Perp. tower. Spacious interior lit by tall, close-set, identical four-light windows. Nave with eccentric Tuscan columns bulging towards bases, and ranks of box pews. Good C17 Jacobean pulpit with tester, and unusual late C12 Purbeck marble octagonal font with blind arcading in low relief. *Arch. Font Gls. Mon. Wdwk.*

SOUTH LEIGH ST JAMES THE GREAT

C15, C19. Handsome C15 Perp. with deeply-set panel-traceried windows and crenellated parapet to nave and tower. C12 chancel rebuilt C19. Unusual, refined C15 N arcade of four-centred arches with reed-like attached shafts. Hugely enjoyable wall paintings at E end of nave and around chancel arch probably more C19 than C15: full-blooded imagery, with Satan emerging from huge, toothy maw on S wall. Other (unrestored) wall paintings at W end of N aisle. C15 screenwork and some C15 glass. *Arch. Gls. Stwk. Wdwk. Wp.*

SPELSBURY ALL SAINTS

C12–C14, C18–C19. Heavily remodelled C18. Likeable, disproportionately big, boxy tower, with short nave and aisles. Otherwise plain interior contains superb, often poignant collection of C17, C18 and C19 monuments to Earls of Lichfield. *Arch. Mon.*

STANTON ST JOHN ST JOHN THE BAPTIST

C12, C14–C15. Happily sited in raised churchyard. C15 Perp. W tower with prominent stair turret. Beautiful, understated *c.*1300 chancel with hooded and deeply-splayed lancets with trefoil heads and highly unusual early Dec. E window with cusped diamond tracery. Much good medieval woodwork, including *c.*1500 chancel bench ends with carved poppyheads in form of addorsed animal and human heads. Fine early glass. *Arch. Gls. Wdwk.*

STONESFIELD ST JAMES

C13–C15, C19. Home of eponymous roofing slate. Oddly proportioned thanks to C19 changes to N aisle. Fabulous C13 E.E. stonework inside, including quatrefoil arcade pier, chancel arch capitals bursting with stiff-leaf, and N chapel lancets with clustered shafts. Chunky and unusual C15 parclose screen and some good medieval glass. *Arch. Gls. Stwk. Wdwk.*

SUNNINGWELL ST LEONARD

C13, C15, C16. Opposite pond and houses on lane through village. Handsome C15 Perp. tower with square-headed windows unusually located in place of N transept. Likeable, offbeat, part-classical, part-Gothic C16 polygonal W porch with Ionic columns and Perp. windows. Inside, view down narrow nave unforgettably channelled by big C16 poppyheads. Colourful E window by J. P. Seddon (1877). *Arch. Gls. Wdwk.*

SUTTON COURTENAY ALL SAINTS

C12–C15. Instructive accretion of medieval styles. Fine C12 Norm. W tower with chevron-moulded windows with attached shafts and corbel table. Memorable C16 two-storey porch in mellow red brick (like gabled bay of small Tudor manor house). Lively interior with part-Norm. chancel arch and E arch of S arcade, and fine C12 Norm. font with blind arcade and fleur-de-lis around base (C19 copy in Abingdon St Helen). Good C14 effigy and C15 screen. Interesting C17 wall paintings and inscriptions. George Orwell (Eric Blair) buried in churchyard. *Arch. Font Gls. Mon. Sett. Stwk. Wdwk. Wp.*

SWYNCOMBE ST BOTOLPH

C12, C19. Romantically alone in rolling Chilterns landscape of big fields and beech woods. Part-flint, small single-cell Norm. with apsidal sanctuary (cf. Checkendon), restored C19.

Interior with C12 Norm. pillar-piscina, renewed wall paintings, and rood-screen and rood-loft of 1914 by W. Tapper (based on C15 screenwork at Partrishow in Breconshire). *Arch. Sett. Wdwk.*

WANTAGE ST PETER AND ST PAUL

C13–C15, C19. Big and sprawling, in churchyard encircled by houses. Sensitively altered and enlarged in C19 by G. E. Street and W. Butterfield. Crisp, uncluttered nave. Impressive chancel beyond flanked by good C15 parclose screens, and with C15 stalls with fine pop-pyheads and some misericords (including pelican and double eagle). Array of Victorian glass by Clayton & Bell, Hardman and others, much of it excellent. Some good monuments. *Gls. Mon. Wdwk.*

WEST HENDRED HOLY TRINITY

C14. Peaceful and picturesque beside stream. Unspoilt late Dec. with timeworn, textured interior. Old trussed-rafter roof and wonderful floor with rare survival of medieval encaustic tiles throughout (*see endpapers*). Good C17 Jacobean furnishings. Some old stained glass. *Sett. Wdwk.*

YELFORD ST NICHOLAS AND ST SWITHUN

Early C16. In a small hamlet. Tiny and chapel-like Perp. of one build, with nave, chancel and S porch. Two-light windows with square heads. Plain interior with box pews, Perp. font and tiny *c.*1500 rood-screen with quatrefoil heads. Charming. *Arch. Font Wdwk.*

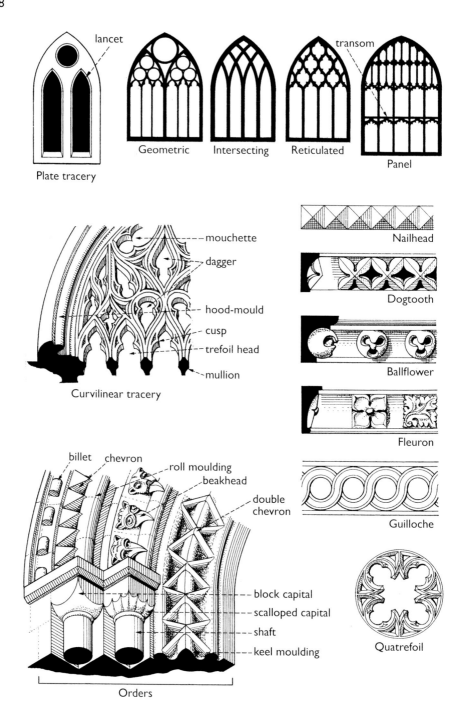

FIG. B **Window tracery, mouldings and ornament**

Images courtesy of Yale University Press
Pevsner's Architectural Glossary

GLOSSARY

ABACUS (pl. **ABACI**) Flat slab forming the top of a *capital*.

ADDORSED Term given to two figures set back-to-back (e.g. carved onto a *font*).

AFFRONTED Term given to two figures set face-to-face.

AISLE Longitudinal space divided from the *nave* by an *arcade*; also called a *side aisle*.

ALTAR Table within a church at which the Mass is celebrated and offerings are made; may be of stone or wood. The *high altar* is the name given to the main *altar* in a church, occupying the *sanctuary* at the east end of the *chancel*.

ALTARPIECE Religious painting or carving generally located on the wall behind an *altar*.

ANGLE BUTTRESS *Buttress* set at 90 degrees to the wall plane at the corner of a rectangular structure (for example, a church tower).

ANGLO-SAXON Architectural style prevalent from the seventh century up to the *Norman* Conquest and the mid eleventh century.

APEX Uppermost point of an *arch*.

APSE Semi-circular, rectangular or occasionally polygonal east end of the *chancel* (see *page 3*).

ARCADE Series of *arches* supported by *piers* or *columns* (can apply to the *lights* of a *rood-screen*).

ARCH Simply or variously curved support spanning a void; may be purely decorative rather than structural.

ARCHED BRACE Curved timber *strut* found at the junction of a *post* and *beam* (sometimes paired to form a supporting *arch* in a roof, for example).

ARCHITRAVE Lowest of the three main parts of the *entablature* in classical architecture (in essence a *lintel*); however, can also refer to the moulded frame of a door or window (described as *shouldered* if the moulded frame has vertical projections at the upper corners, or *lugged* if the projections are horizontal).

ASHLAR Finely dressed rectangular masonry blocks with flat sides, generally bedded together to give a smooth, even wall finish.

ATTACHED COLUMN *Column* that has appearance of being partly set into a wall or *pier*.

AUMBRY Small cupboard or recess for sacred vessels, set into the wall close to the *altar*.

BALE TOMB Stone *chest-tomb* with distinctive rounded top in the form of a bale of wool, and found especially in the Cotswolds.

BALLFLOWER Carved ornament comprising a three-petalled flower enclosing a ball, popular in *Decorated* stonework of the fourteenth century (see *page 248*).

BALUSTER Short, bellied *post* or pillar, typically arranged in a series and supporting a rail (thus 'balustrade').

BAPTISTRY That part of a church divided off to house the *font*.

BARREL VAULT Concave *vault* of continuous semi-circular section.

BAR TRACERY Overarching term for window *tracery* comprising a network of intersecting stone 'bars', popular from the middle of the thirteenth century (see *page 248*).

BASE Lowermost component or foot of a *column*.

BASILICA (Christian) Fundamentally, a church of oblong plan form with *side aisles* and an *apse*, the body of the church separated from the *aisles* by *arcades* or walling (*see page 3*).

BATTLEMENTS See *crenellated*.

BAY Division of an internal or external elevation by means of the *columns* in an *arcade* or windows, for example (therefore, a unit comprising a pair of *columns* and their *arch* would equal one *bay*).

BEAKHEAD *Norman* ornamental motif comprising the stylised beaked head of a bird or beast, typically found on *voussoirs* and together forming a pattern of enrichment most often over doorways (*see page 248*).

BEAM Horizontal support, generally of timber.

BELFRY Bell chamber of a church tower.

BELLCOTE Small roofed or *gabled* frame for church bells (typically found on small churches with no bell tower).

BENCH END The end of a *pew*, often carved and sometimes topped with a *poppyhead*.

BIER A moveable frame, typically wheeled, used to bear a coffin from the church to the grave.

BILLET *Norman* ornamental motif consisting of small raised rectangular or cylindrical forms with spaces in between, often found over doorways (*see page 248*).

BLIND ARCADE *Arcade* of *arches* on *piers* or *columns* applied to the surface of a wall, and thus generally of stone ('blind' because there are no openings in the *arcade*).

BLIND TRACERY Un-pierced, applied *tracery*, of purely decorative rather than structural function, sometimes 'planted' on to a surface (such as to the wall of a church or the *wainscot* of a *rood-screen*).

BOSS Projection, often decorative, located at the intersection of the *ribs* of a *vault*, for example (may be of wood or stone).

BOUTTEL CAP Decorative top to a *bouttel shaft*, from which the *ribs* of the *rood-loft vault* sometimes spring.

BOUTTEL SHAFT Attached *shaft*, usually three-quarters *round* in cross-section, forming a *moulding* on the door-post of a *rood-screen*.

BOX PEW Enclosed wooden *pew*, typically accessed via a closable door, popular in the eighteenth and nineteenth centuries.

BRACE Secondary timber in a roof or frame, generally bracing the primary timbers at 90 degrees to one another, and sometimes treated decoratively (see *wind-braces*).

BRASS Memorial in the form of an engraved sheet of brass set into a floor or wall. The *indent* for a *brass* is referred to as a *matrix*.

BRATTISHING Ornamental crest, typically in the form of miniature *battlements* or *crenellations* and found on the *head-beam* of a *rood-screen*, for example.

BRESSUMER Large horizontal supporting *beam*; however, also refers to the lowermost of the western *beams* of the *rood-loft* (often richly carved).

BROACH SPIRE *Spire* whose square base gives way to an octagonal section further up, through the paring back of its corners to give triangular faces.

BUTTRESS Vertical masonry element projecting from, or built against, a wall to give it extra strength, to counteract the lateral thrusts of a roof, *vault* or *arch*, or to shift the load-bearing burden from the wall to allow for more expansive windows. A *flying buttress* is one in the form of an *arch* or half-arch.

CAMES Lead strips which hold the individual pieces of *stained glass* within a window opening.

CAPITAL Element that caps or crowns a *column* or *pilaster* (see *page 248*).

CARTOUCHE Memorial tablet, generally wall-mounted and roughly oval in shape, with ornate classical frame.

CARVED TRAIL Undulating, naturalistic enrichment sometimes applied to a timber *beam*, for example.

CARYATID Upright support in the form of a carved female figure (one in the form of a male figure is referred to as a *telamon*).

CAVETTO Type of concave *moulding*, *quarter-round* in section.

CELURE Extra-decorated area of roof forming a canopy of honour over the *Rood-figures*.

CHAMFER Flat bevel or slope made by paring away the edge of a right-angle; called a *double chamfer* when applied to both planes of a recessed *arch*.

CHANCEL Eastern part of the church, where the main *altar* is located.

CHANCEL ARCH Archway between the *nave* and the *chancel*.

CHANTRY CHAPEL Chapel endowed for the saying of Masses for the soul(s) of the founder(s) after death.

CHEQUERWORK Chequered pattern of squares of contrasting building material, typically limestone and flint.

CHEST-TOMB Chest-shaped tomb of stone, sometimes surmounted by a recumbent *effigy* when inside a church; also referred to as 'tomb-chest'.

CHEVRON *Norman* V-shaped *moulding*, typically found on *voussoirs* and in series forming an enrichment over *arches* and windows; also called *zigzag* (see *page 248*).

CHOIR Subdivision of the *chancel*, where the divine service is sung.

CHOIR SCREEN Screen, usually of timber, dividing the *choir* and *sanctuary* from the *nave*, typically in a monastic church.

CHOIR STALLS Seating, often compartmentalised, in the *choir*.

CINQUEFOIL See *foil*.

CLASPING BUTTRESS *Buttress*, essentially of square section, but encasing the angle of a rectangular structure (for example, a church tower).

CLERESTORY Window-lit upper storey of the *nave* above the height of the *aisle* roofs.

COLLAR-BEAM Transverse *beam* connecting two *rafters*.

COLONNADE Series of *columns* supporting an *entablature*.

COLUMN Classical upright support of *round* section, strictly comprising a *shaft*, *capital* and *base*.

COMMUNION RAIL/S Low railing enclosing the area around the *altar*.

CONSOLE Bracket of curved or scroll form.

CORBEL Block of stone projecting from a wall, usually to support a *beam*. A 'corbel table' is a series of *corbels* carrying, for example, a *parapet* (in *Norman* architecture such *corbels* are often enriched with carving).

CORNICE Uppermost section of an *entablature*, or a moulded ledge-like feature projecting along the top or *eaves* of a building.

COVE (or **COVING**) Concave underside of a *rood-loft*, for example.

CREDENCE SHELF Shelf beside or within a *piscina* for the sacred vessels.

CRENELLATED In the form of *battlements* (for example, a *crenellated parapet*).

CROCKET Stylised budding or leaf-shaped ornament, often projecting from the angles of a *spire*, *pinnacle*, *canopy* or *gable*, for example.

CROSSING In a *cruciform* church, the space at the intersection of *nave*, *chancel* and *transepts*, generally with a *crossing tower* above.

CRUCIFORM In the form of a Crucifix; used to describe a church plan with *transepts*.

CRYPT Subterranean chamber to house tombs, generally located below the *chancel*.

CURVILINEAR TRACERY Window *tracery* consisting of flowing curves and *ogees*, popular in the fourteenth century (see page 248).

CUSP Projecting points formed by the meeting of two curves; a key motif in *Gothic* architecture, for example, in window *tracery* and *arches* (see page 248).

DAGGER *Tracery* motif characteristic of *Decorated Gothic* architecture, pointed at one end, rounded at the other and *cusped* within (see page 248).

DECALOGUE The Ten Commandments as painted on a wall, or board fixed to a wall.

DECORATED Second phase of English *Gothic* architecture, c.1250–c.1350.

DIAGONAL BUTTRESS *Buttress* projecting diagonally from the corner of a rectangular structure (for example, a church tower).

DOGTOOTH Pyramidal decorative motif comprising a symmetrical arrangement of four lobes or 'teeth' at 90 degrees to one another, popular in the thirteenth century (see page 248).

DOOM Name given to painted depictions of The Last Judgement (often in combination with The Resurrection) found over the *chancel arch*.

DOOR-HEAD Top of the doorway of a *rood-screen*, often containing *tracery*.

DORMER WINDOW Window set vertically on a sloping roof and with a roof of its own; can have gabled or hipped roof.

DOUBLE CHAMFER See *chamfer*.

DRIP-MOULD See *hood-mould*.

DRIP-STONE See *hood-mould*.

DROP-CREST Carved, decorative fringe set along the bottom edge of the *bressumer* of a *rood-screen* for example.

DROP-FINIAL Hanging *finial* (in other words, of pendant form).

DUG-OUT CHEST Church chest formed from a hollowed-out log (popular before c.1300).

EARLY ENGLISH First phase of English *Gothic* architecture, c.1180–c.1250.

EASTER SEPULCHRE Ceremonial *chest-tomb* located against, or set into, the north wall of the *chancel*.

EAVES Lowermost edge of a roof, where it meets with, or overhangs, an outer wall.

EFFIGY Monument in the form of a sculptural representation of the deceased; usually of stone but occasionally of wood or metal, the figure recumbent and set upon a *chest-tomb*.

ENCAUSTIC TILE Red earthenware tile with pattern stamped in, often with contrasting use of white clay and yellow glaze, popular in the fourteenth and fifteenth centuries, and again in the nineteenth century.

ENGAGED COLUMN See *attached column*.

ENTABLATURE Strictly, the collective name for the three horizontal elements (*architrave*, *frieze* and *cornice*) carried by a *column* or wall.

FAN-VAULT *Vault* in the form of a concave masonry cone with *ribs* 'fanning' out from a common *springing* point, and decorated with *blind tracery*.

FILLET *Moulding* in the form of a narrow, raised band with a flat top.

FINIAL Ornamental feature in the form of a ball, spike or other form commonly topping a *canopy*, *gable*, *pinnacle* or *spire*.

FLÈCHE Small decorative *spire* set on the *ridge* of a roof.

FLEURON Decorative motif in the form of a four-leafed square (*see page 248*).

FLOWING TRACERY See *curvilinear tracery* (*see page 248*).

FLUTINGS *Mouldings* in the form of shallow, parallel concave grooves.

FLYING BUTTRESS See *buttress*.

FOIL Lobed shape formed by *cusping* the inside of a circle or other shape: *trefoil* for a three-lobed form, *quatrefoil* for a four-lobed form and *cinquefoil* for a five-lobed form (*see page 248*).

FOLIATED Decorated with leaf ornament.

FONT Baptismal vessel, usually made of stone but occasionally of lead (or, rarely, wood).

FOUR-CENTRED ARCH Form of late medieval flattened *arch* whose arcs are drawn from four centres.

FRETWORK See *openwork*.

FRIEZE Strictly, the middle division of an *entablature*; however, more generally used to refer to a horizontal band of decoration.

GABLE Triangular upper portion of a wall at the end of a pitched roof.

GABLET A small *gable*.

GARGOYLE Projecting drainage spout, designed to throw rain water clear of the walls below, generally of stone and often carved in the form of a human or beast. A 'gargoyle' which is purely decorative and does not act as a water spout is usually termed a *grotesque*.

GEOMETRIC TRACERY Early form of *bar tracery*, of the second half of the thirteenth century in particular, characterised by compositions employing simple geometric forms, especially circles (*see page 248*).

GOTHIC Dominant style of European architecture c.1200–c.1500 (and beyond), traditionally characterised in religious architecture by pointed *arches* and *rib vaults*, and in England subdivided into *Early English*, *Decorated* and *Perpendicular* phases.

GOTHIC LIGHT See *loop light*.

GOTHIC REVIVAL Appropriation, often scholarly, of the language (and spirit) of medieval *Gothic* architecture during the seventeenth–nineteenth centuries, but especially during the nineteenth century.

GREEN MAN Human mask, generally carved, and typically with foliage issuing from the mouth (if the foliage is a vine, the figure may be emblematic of Christ).

GROIN VAULT *Vault* created by the intersection at right angles of two *barrel vaults*.

GROTESQUE See *gargoyle*.

GUILLOCHE Classical ornamental pattern of undulating bands overlapping to give a series of circles (*see page 248*).

HAGIOSCOPE Opening cut through a wall (typically the *chancel* wall) or the *wainscot* of a *rood-screen* to allow a view of the main *altar*; also known as a *squint*.

HALF-ROUND See *round*.

HAMMERBEAM Braced, horizontal bracket forming a cut-off *beam* at the level of the *wall-plate*, the end carrying a *hammerpost*, which in turn supports a *purlin* above.

HAMMERPOST See *hammerbeam*.

HATCHMENT Lozenge-shaped timber panel painted with a coat of arms and generally mounted on the wall of a church (typically in the *nave* or a *side aisle*).

HEAD-BEAM Uppermost western *beam* of a *rood-screen*.

HEAD-STOP Terminal to a *hood-* or *drip-mould* in the form of a human head.

HIGH ALTAR See *altar*.

HOLLOW Concave *moulding*.

HOLLOW CHAMFER *Moulding* formed by the concave paring away of a right-angle.

HOOD-MOULD Moulded stone hood over an *arch* or *lintel* (*see page 248*).

IMPOST Horizontal moulded *base* set into the wall, often slightly projecting, from which an *arch* springs.

INDENT The shaped depression in a stone slab to house a *brass*.

INTERLACE Relief decoration in the form of interwoven stems or strands, popular in the twelfth century around the rims of *Norman fonts*; and in the later Middle Ages as *carved trails* along the *beams* of *rood-screens* and *rood-lofts*, for example.

INTERSECTING TRACERY Like *Y-tracery*, an early form of *bar tracery* comprising a pattern of interlocking curves of the same radius, developed at the beginning of the fourteenth century (*see page 248*).

INTRADOS Underside or inner curve of an *arch*.

IONIC One of the orders of classical architecture, characterised by *columns* with *volutes*.

JACOBEAN Style of the era of James I (1603–1625) and beyond, characterised by the distinctive use of classical ornament in carved decoration (especially woodwork).

JAMB Vertical side of a window or door.

JOISTS Horizontal timbers supporting a floor.

KEYSTONE Primarily the central, uppermost stone in an *arch* or *vault*, but occasionally used in raised form as a decorative feature in a *lintel* for example. See *voussoir*.

KING-POST Upright *post* rising from the centre of a *tie-beam* to the *ridge-beam* above (sometimes referred to as a *king-strut*).

KING-STRUT See *king-post*.

LABEL-MOULD Horizontal stone hood over a window *lintel*, for example. See *hood-mould*.

LABEL-STOP Projecting feature terminating a *label-mould*.

LADY CHAPEL Chapel dedicated to the Virgin Mary.

LANCET Tall, narrow, pointed arched window characteristic of *Early English Gothic* architecture (*see page 248*).

LANTERN Windowed stage of a dome or tower.

LEDGER Stone slab, usually letter-cut, set into a church floor to mark a tomb or grave.

LESENE A narrow, low-relief vertical masonry strip, like a *pilaster* but generally without a *base* or *capital*; a characteristic form of wall decoration in *Saxon* architecture (especially in towers).

LIERNE VAULT *Vault* with purely decorative *ribs* that do not spring either from one of the main *springers* or the central *boss* (a *lierne* being a short decorative *rib*).

LIGHT Vertical division of a window (or a *bay* in a *rood-screen*, for example) as defined by the *mullions* to either side.

LIMEWASH Breathable lime-based surface coat, generally white or cream, applied to either internal or external wall surfaces.

LINENFOLD Decorative carved treatment, generally in wood, resembling vertical parallel folds of linen, popular in the sixteenth century.

LINTEL Horizontal *beam* spanning the void between uprights.

LOOP LIGHT *Tracery* form characteristic of *Perpendicular Gothic* architecture, consisting of a thin, vertical *light*, *cusped* at the top to give a motif akin to a burning candle.

LUCARNE Small, generally window-like opening in a *spire*.

LUGGED See *architrave*.

LYCHGATE Covered gateway into a churchyard.

MASS CLOCK Sundial for the indication of Mass, fixed to the wall of a church.

MATRIX See *brass*.

MIDDLE RAIL Horizontal *beam* framing the top of the *wainscot* of a *rood-screen*.

MISERICORD Shelf, often carved, on a bracket fixed to the underside of a hinged *choir stall* seat to provide support when standing during services.

MORTISE AND TENON Joint formed by the fitting into a socket (*mortise*) of a projecting element (*tenon*); commonly used to secure together a timber *post* and *beam*.

MOUCHETTE *Tracery* motif characteristic of *Decorated Gothic* architecture, similar to a *dagger* but curved (see page 248).

MOULDING Decorative contours given to the face or edge of stonework or woodwork (for example, to a stone *arch* or wooden *post*).

MULLION Vertical *post* dividing a window into two or more *lights* (see page 248).

MUNTIN Vertical upright dividing the *wainscot* of a *rood-screen* into separate panels, for example.

NAILHEAD Carved ornament in the form of a regular series of small pyramids, a characteristic feature of *Early English Gothic* stonework (see page 248).

NAVE The western body of the church, for the laity.

NICHE Vertical recess set into a wall, *buttress* or *pier*, often arched and intended for a statue.

NORMAN Pre-*Gothic* architectural style of the period 1066–c.1180, characterised by massive forms and rounded *arches*.

OFFSET That part of a *post* exposed horizontally when the portion above is reduced in thickness (often sloping).

OGEE Double curve comprising concave followed by convex elements. The *ogee arch*, pointed at the top, is especially characteristic of *Decorated Gothic* architecture.

OGIVAL Oval compartment with pointed opposite ends of *ogee* form, found in *reticulated* window *tracery* for example.

OPENWORK Carved work that is cut through rather than *blind*, such as the *tracery* of a *rood-screen*.

ORGAN LOFT Gallery housing the organ.

ORIEL Bay window supported on brackets or *corbels*, generally at first floor height.

OSSUARY Place where bones are kept; a *crypt*.

OVOLO Convex *moulding*, *quarter-round* in section.

PALIMPSEST Meaning literally 'scraped again' and used to describe a surface or object that has been reused or appropriated at a later date for a different purpose (for example, a re-cut *brass* or an over-painted wall painting).

PALLADIAN WINDOW Window with semi-circular arched central *light* flanked by a pair of rectangular *lights* whose tops are level with the *springing* of the *arch* of the central *light*.

PALMETTE Ornament in the form of a stylised palm leaf.

PANEL TRACERY Grid-like *rectilinear bar tracery* comprising vertical *mullions* and horizontal *transoms*, characteristic of *Perpendicular Gothic* architecture (see page 248).

PARAPET The heightened portion of outer wall above *wall-plate* height, often treated decoratively on churches (with *blind* or *openwork* decoration, or *crenellated*), but also used to conceal shallow-pitched roofs behind or to give a more imposing silhouette. *Parapet* is also used to describe the gallery front or back of a *rood-loft*.

PARCLOSE SCREEN Screen, usually of timber, separating a chapel from the body of the church (the chapel is sometimes called 'a parclose').

PATERA Carved shallow relief ornament of round or oval form.

PEDIMENT Classical ornamental *gable*, typically of shallow triangular or *segmental* form, and found over a window or doorway.

PERPENDICULAR Third phase of English *Gothic* architecture, c.1350–c.1540.

PERPENDICULAR LIGHT See *loop light*.

PEW *Nave* seating, generally a form of bench (though *pew* strictly refers to an enclosed seat).

PIER Large upright support, generally of stone, for an *arch*.

PILASTER Flattened version of a classical *column* set against a wall.

PILLAR PISCINA A *piscina* of sometimes birdbath-like appearance; generally freestanding, but sometimes set against a wall.

PINNACLE Small pyramidal or conical crowning element often ornamented with *crockets*.

PISCINA Basin, usually of stone, with a drain for the washing of the sacred vessels, generally located in a wall adjacent to an *altar*.

PLATE TRACERY The precursor to *bar tracery*, developed at the end of the twelfth century, in which forms such as circles are cut through solid masonry (see page 248).

POINTING Visible mortar jointing between courses of stone or brickwork.

POPPYHEAD Carved *finial* found on a *bench end*.

POST Vertical support, generally of timber.

PRESBYTERY That part of a monastic church to the east of the *choir*.

PRINCIPAL Major *rafter* dividing roof into sections or *bays*; also known as a '*principal rafter*'.

PULPIT Raised platform from which the sermon is preached (may be of stone or wood).

PULPITUM Stone screen in a major church separating the *choir* from the *nave*.

PURLIN Horizontal, longitudinal timber running between the *principal rafters*.

PUTTO (pl. **PUTTI**) Small boy or cherub figure.

QUARRY Small square- or diamond-shaped pane of glass (typically, stained glass) supported within a window opening by lead *cames*.

QUARTER-ROUND See *round*.

QUATREFOIL Ornament, typically circular, divided by *cusps* into four lobes (see *page 248*).

QUEEN-POSTS Pair of upright timbers set symmetrically on a *tie-* or *collar-beam* supporting the *purlins* above; sometimes referred to as *queen-struts*.

QUEEN-STRUTS See *queen-posts*.

QUOINS Cornerstones at the angle of a building, differentiated in some way from the primary walling material (for example, by being of *ashlar* or projecting slightly from the established wall plane).

RAFTER Inclined, lateral timbers sloping from the *wall-plate* up to the *ridge*.

RAINWATER-HEAD Containing feature at the junction of a gutter and downpipe, generally at *eaves* height and often made of lead.

REBATE Groove or channel, generally rectangular, cut along the face of a piece of timber or stone to receive the tongue or edge of another piece.

RECTILINEAR Name sometimes given to *tracery* consisting of straight lines intersecting at right angles; also known as *panel tracery* (see *page 248*).

REEDING *Mouldings* in the form of shallow, parallel convex ridges.

RELIQUARY Container or place of safekeeping for religious relics.

RENDER Plaster or concrete facing of an outer or inner wall (see *stucco*).

RERE-ARCH *Arch*, often primarily decorative, set back from the arched head of a window and flush with the inner wall plane.

REREDOS Ornamental screen found above the *altar*, set against the east wall of the *chancel*.

RESPOND Half-*pier* carrying one end of an *arch* and bonded into a wall.

RETICULATED TRACERY Name given to *tracery* comprising a net of interlocking *ogivals*, a characteristic feature of *Decorated Gothic* architecture (see *page 248*).

RETURN Continuation of, for example, a wall or *moulding* in a new direction, typically at a right-angle.

REVEAL The exposed face of a *jamb* between the wall plane and the frame of a window.

RIB Projecting band or *arch* on a ceiling or *vault* (can be structural or purely decorative).

RIB VAULT Masonry *vault* comprising framework of intersecting *arches* or *ribs*.

RIDGE The uppermost horizontal, longitudinal element in a pitched roof, supporting the top ends of the *rafters*.

RIDGE-BEAM Longitudinal *beam* forming the *ridge* of the roof; sometimes referred to as the *ridge-piece*.

RIDGE-PIECE See *ridge-beam*.

ROLL MOULDING Rounded *moulding* generally in stone, at least semi-circular in section and found in *Norman* door surrounds, for example (see *page 248*).

ROMANESQUE Dominant European architectural style of the eleventh and twelfth centuries, characterised by round *arches* and massive forms (called *Norman* in England, and supplanted by *Gothic* in c.1200).

ROOD Carved figure of Christ upon the Cross, generally located high up at the east end of the *nave* prior to the Reformation (also called the 'Great Rood' when located here).

ROOD-BEAM *Beam* to support the *Rood*; may be free-spanning above the *rood-screen*, or the *top-beam* (either western or eastern) of the *rood-loft*.

ROOD-FIGURE Christ or the attendant figures of the Virgin Mary or St John.

ROOD-LOFT Galleried platform surmounting the *rood-screen*.

ROOD-SCREEN Name given to the screen dividing the *nave* from the *chancel* (deriving from its location beneath the *Rood*), usually made of wood (oak), but sometimes stone. After the Reformation, with most *Roods* taken down, sometimes referred to as the *chancel* screen.

ROOD-STAIRS Access to the *rood-loft*, often built into the wall at the east end of the *nave*.

ROOD-TYMPANUM Hoarding, of either timber boards or plaster over wattle and lath, used to fill in the *chancel* archway above the height of the *rood-screen* and *rood-loft*; often originally painted with the *Doom* or Christ in Majesty.

ROSETTE Flower-shaped ornament.

ROUND Semi-circular *moulding*, at least 180 degrees of a circle in section; a *half-round* is strictly 180 degrees of a circle in section; a *quarter-round* is 90 degrees of a circle in section.

ROYAL ARMS Coat of arms of a king or queen, painted on (or carved from) wood, and often set up in place of the *Rood* over the *chancel arch* after the Reformation.

RUSTICATION Classical treatment of masonry to suggest strength or evoke antiquity, typically involving the use of large blocks with *chamfered* edges and recessed joints.

SADDLEBACK Tower roof of pitched form (*gabled* to either side).

SALTIRE CROSS Cross with four arms of equal length set diagonally.

SANCTUARY Space occupied by the *high altar* at the eastern extremity of the *chancel*.

SCALLOPED CAPITAL *Capital* whose concave lower face is carved with wide *flutings* (see page 248).

SEDILIA (sing. **SEDILE**) Seats for priests, generally three in number (thus 'triple *sedilia*') and set into the south wall of the *chancel*.

SEGMENTAL Curved in the form of a portion of a circle; often used in conjunction with an *arch* or *pediment*.

SENTENCE Short religious text painted onto the wall of a church.

SEXFOIL See *foil*.

SHAFT Upright, typically of stone or wood and of *round* section (see page 248).

SHOULDERED See *architrave*.

SIDE AISLE See *aisle* (see page 3).

SILL Lowermost (floor-level) *beam* of a *rood-screen*.

SOFFIT Underside of a *rood-loft*, *lintel*, *arch* or canopy.

SOUNDING-BOARD Flat timber canopy over a *pulpit*; sometimes called a *tester*.

SPANDREL Triangular space between the side of an *arch*, the horizontal drawn from the level of its *apex*, and the vertical of its *springing*.

SPIRE Pointed upper portion of a *steeple*, generally octagonal or circular in section.

SPRINGER Lowermost stone of an *arch* or *vault rib*.

SPRINGING Point at which an *arch* or *vault* rises from its uprights.

SPUR Diagonal projection at the *base* of a *column*.

SQUINT See *hagioscope*.

STAINED GLASS Coloured or painted glass.

STALL Bench seat in the *choir* or *chancel* for choristers or the clergy.

STEEPLE Name given to the combination of a tower and *spire*.

STIFF-LEAF Stylised ornament in the form of an unfurling leaf, characteristic of *Transitional* architectural stonework (especially *capitals*) of c.1200.

STOP Terminal of a *moulding* or *chamfer* (for example a *label-stop* or *head-stop*).

STOUP A basin for holy water.

STRAPWORK Ornament consisting of interlacing bands with the appearance of cut leather, popular in the sixteenth and seventeenth centuries.

STRING COURSE Projecting *moulding* running horizontally along a wall.

STRUT Vertical or angled timber supporting a *truss*, for example.

STUCCO A hard-wearing form of lime plaster, generally used as a protective external coating to a building (see *render*).

SWAG Ornament in the form of fabric slung between, and partly overhanging, two supports.

TABERNACLE WORK Ornamentation in the form of applied canopies yielding small *niches*.

TELAMON See *caryatid*.

TESTER See *sounding-board*.

TIE-BEAM *Beam* spanning the void between the *bases* of a pair of *principal rafters*.

TIERCERON VAULT *Rib vault* with secondary (decorative) *ribs springing* either from one of the main *springers* or the central *boss*.

TOP-BEAM Uppermost *beam* – either eastern or western – of a *rood-loft*.

TOP-CREST Carved ornamental fringe running along the uppermost edge of a *bressumer*, *head-beam*, *top-beam* or *rood-beam* of a *rood-screen* or *rood-loft*.

TORCHÈRE Tall stand for a candle.

TRACERY Openwork lattice of stone or timber found in an opening, such as a window (see *page 248*).

TRANSEPT Transverse portion of a *cruciform* church, aligned north–south (see *page 3*).

TRANSEPTAL CHAPEL Chapel in the position of, or opening off, a *transept*.

TRANSITIONAL Applying to any period of transition between the defined phases of architectural style; however, most commonly used for the transition from *Norman* to *Early English Gothic* in the last quarter of the twelfth century.

TRANSOM Horizontal dividing bar in a window (see *page 248*).

TREFOIL Ornament divided by *cusps* into three lobes (see *foil*).

TRIFORIUM Middle storey of a church interior, between the main *arcade* and the *clerestory*, sometimes treated as a *blind arcade* or with a wall passage with an open *arcade*.

TRUMPET CAPITAL See *scalloped capital* (see *page 248*).

TRUSS Braced framework of timbers together spanning a void.

TUDOR ARCH Type of late medieval flattened, pointed *arch* (similar to a *four-centred arch*, but with straight edges between the corners and *apex*).

TUDOR ROSE Distinctive, stylised five-petalled rose form.

TUNNEL VAULT See *barrel vault*.

TYMPANUM Infilling between a *lintel* and the *arch* above (of stone and often carved in the case of a *Norman* doorway *tympanum*; or of timber or plastered panelling over a *rood-loft*).

VAULT Arched stone roof.

VAULTING SHAFT *Shaft* from which a *vault springs*.

VOLUTE Spiral scroll ornament.

VOUSSOIR Wedge-shaped stone used in the formation of an *arch* (the *keystone* is the *apex voussoir*).

WAGON ROOF Roof with close-set *rafters* or *braces* (may be plastered or panelled).

WAINSCOT Solid, panelled lower portion of a *rood-screen*; that part below the *middle rail*.

WALL ARCADE See *blind arcade*.

WALL-PLATE Timber set longitudinally along the top of a wall, onto which *rafters* are set.

WALL-POST Vertical supporting *post* set against the wall.

WATERLEAF Broad, stylised leaf shape, of tapering form and turning over at the top; characteristic of *Norman–Early English Transitional capitals*.

WEST GALLERY Raised singing gallery at the west end of the *nave*.

WIND-BRACE Curved *brace* connecting *purlins* with *ridge-beam* or *principals*.

WINDING SHEET Burial shroud in the form of a tightly-wound sheet of cloth.

WYVERN A dragon with the legs and wings of a bird and with a serpent for a tail, common in Wales and the Welsh Marches.

Y-TRACERY *Tracery* of the same basic pattern and date as *intersecting tracery*, but giving a two-*light* window with a single, central *mullion* splitting to form a 'Y' shape in the head of the window (see page 248).

ZIGZAG See *chevron*.

FURTHER READING

OXFORDSHIRE

Arkell, W. J. *Oxford Stone*, Faber and Faber, 1946.

Brabant, F. G. *Oxfordshire*, Methuen, 1906.

Catchpole, A. et al, *Burford: Buildings and People in a Cotswold Town*, Phillimore & Co. Ltd., 2008.

Davies, R. H. C. *Mason's Marks in Oxfordshire and the Cotswolds*, Oxford Archaeological Society, 1938–9.

Hobart Bird, W. *Old Oxfordshire Churches*, Ed. J. Burrow & Co. Ltd., 1932.

Howard, F. E. *Screens and Rood-Lofts in the Parish Churches of Oxfordshire*, Hunt, Barnard, 1910.

Lethbridge, R. *Oxfordshire Churches*, The Stonesfield Press, 2000.

Newton, P. & Kerr, J. *The County of Oxford: A Corpus of Medieval Stained Glass*, OUP, 1979.

Parker, J. H. *Guide to Architectural Antiquities in the Neighbourhood of Oxford*, Oxford Society for Promoting the Study of Gothic Architecture, 1842.

Piper, J. *Shell Guide to Oxfordshire*, Faber and Faber, 1953.

RCHM, *The City of Oxford*, HMSO, 1939.

Sherwood, J. *A Guide to the Churches of Oxfordshire*, Robert Dugdale, 1989.

Sherwood, J. & Pevsner, N. *The Buildings of England, Oxfordshire*, Penguin, 1974.

Tyack, G. *Oxford: An Architectural Guide*, Oxford Paperbacks, 1998.

Tyack, G., Bradley, S. & Pevsner, N. *The Buildings of England, Berkshire*, Yale, 2010.

Victoria County Histories of Oxfordshire and Berkshire.

GENERAL

Addison, W. *Local Styles of the English Parish Church*, Batsford, 1982.

Batsford, H. & Fry, C. *The Greater English Church in the Middle Ages*, Batsford, 1943.

Betjeman, J. (ed.) *Collins Guide to English Parish Churches*, Collins, 1958.

Binney, M. & Burman, P. *Change and Decay – The Future of Our Churches*, Studio Vista, 1977.

Blair, J. *The Church in Anglo-Saxon Society*, OUP, 2006.

Bond, F. *Gothic Architecture in England*, Batsford, 1906.

Bond, F. *Screens and Galleries in English Churches*, Henry Frowde/ OUP, 1908.

Bond, F. B. & Camm, Rev. Dom Bede. *Roodscreens and Roodlofts* (2 Vols.), Sir Isaac Pitman, 1909.

Bony, J. *The English Decorated Style*, Phaidon, 1979.

Braun, H. *An Introduction to English Medieval Architecture*, Faber and Faber, 1951.

Brown, R. J. *The English Village Church*, Robert Hale, 1998.

Bury, T. T. *Remains of Ecclesiastical Woodwork*, John Weale, 1847.

Clapham, A. W. *English Romanesque Architecture after the Conquest*, OUP, 1934.

Clapham, A. W. *English Romanesque Architecture before the Conquest*, OUP, 1930.

Clarke, B. *Church Builders of the Nineteenth Century*, SPCK, 1938.

Clifton-Taylor, A. *English Parish Churches as Works of Art*, OUP, 1989.

Clifton-Taylor, A. *The Cathedrals of England*, Thames and Hudson, 2000.

Clifton-Taylor, A. *The Pattern of English Building*, Batsford, 1962.

Cox, J. C. & Harvey, A. *English Church Furniture*, Methuen, 1907.

Cox, J. C. *English Church Furniture and Accessories*, Batsford, 1923.

Cox, J. C. *The Parish Churches of England*, Batsford, 1937.

Crossley, F. H. *The English Abbey – Its Life and Work in the Middle Ages*, Batsford, 1942.

Crossley, F. H. *English Church Craftsmanship*, Batsford, 1941.

Crossley, F. H. *English Church Design, 1040–1540* A.D., Batsford, 1945.

Crossley, F. H. *Timber Building in England*, Batsford, 1951.

Dirsztay, P. *Church Furnishings*, Routledge & Kegan Paul, 1978.

Duffy, E. *The Stripping of the Altars*, Yale, 1992.

Esdaile, K. *English Church Monuments 1510–1840*, Batsford, 1946.

Friar, S. *A Companion to the English Parish Church*, Sutton, 1996.

Hall, J. *Hall's Illustrated Dictionary of Symbols in Eastern and Western Art*, John Murray, 1994.

Hart, S. *Medieval Church Window Tracery in England*, Boydell, 2012.

Harvey, J. *English Mediaeval Architects*, Batsford, 1954.

Harvey, J. *The Perpendicular Style*, Batsford, 1978.

Hewett, C. A. *English Historic Carpentry*, Phillimore & Co. Ltd., 1980.

Hoskins, W. G. *The Making of the English Landscape*, Leicester, 1955.

Howard, F. E. *Fan-Vaults*, Hunt, Barnard & Co. Ltd., 1911.

Howard, F. E. *Mediaeval Styles of the English Parish Church*, Batsford, 1936.

Howard, F. E. *On the Construction of Mediaeval Roofs*, Hunt, Barnard & Co. Ltd., 1913.

Howard, F. E. & Biver, P. *Chantry Chapels in England*, Hunt, Barnard & Co. Ltd., 1909.

Howard, F. E. & Crossley, F. H. *English Church Woodwork*, Batsford, 1927.

Howell, P. & Sutton, I. *The Faber Guide to Victorian Churches*, Faber and Faber, 1989.

Hutton, G. & Smith E. *English Parish Churches*, Thames and Hudson, 1957.

Jenkins, S. *England's Thousand Best Churches*, Allen Lane, 1999.

Jones, L. E. *The Beauty of English Churches*, Constable, 1978.

Kemp, B. *English Church Monuments*, Batsford, 1980.

Laing, L. & J. *Art of the Celts*, Thames and Hudson, 2000.

MacCulloch, D. *Reformation – Europe's House Divided 1490–1700*, Penguin, 2003.

Macklin, H. W. *Monumental Brasses*, George Allen & Unwin Ltd., 1953.

Mâle, É. *The Gothic Image*, J.M. Dent & Sons, 1913.

Morris, R. *Churches in the Landscape*, Dent, 1989.

Murray, P. & L. *The Oxford Companion to Christian Art and Architecture*, OUP, 1998.

Parker, J. H. *ABC of Gothic Architecture*, Parker, 1888.

Pevsner, N. *Pevsner's Architectural Glossary*, Yale, 2010.

Pounds, N. J. P. *A History of the English Parish*, CUP, 2000.

Pugin, A. W. *A Treatise on Chancel Screens*, Charles Dolman, 1851.

Robinson, J. M. *Treasures of the English Churches*, Sinclair-Stevenson, 1995.

Rosewall, R. *Medieval Wall Paintings*, Boydell, 2008.

Scarisbrick, J. J. *The Reformation and the English People*, Blackwell, 1984.

Short, E. H. *A History of Religious Architecture*, Philip Allan, 1936.

Tisdall, M. W. *God's Beasts*, Charlesfort Press, 1989.

Vallance, A. *English Church Screens*, Batsford, 1936.

Vallance, A. *Greater English Church Screens*, Batsford, 1947.

Vallance, A. *Old Crosses and Lychgates*, Batsford, 1920.

Williamson, P. (ed.) *The Medieval Treasury*, V&A Publications, 2002.

Zarnecki, G. *et al. English Romanesque Art 1066–1200*, Arts Council of Great Britain, Weidenfeld and Nicolson, 1984.

LIST OF CHURCHES

INDEX OF PLACES

INDEX OF PEOPLE